COGNITIVE DEVELOPMENT TODAY

Peter Sutherland taught for ten years in a variety of schools, both primary and secondary, and has since been a lecturer in education, specializing in psychological topics. He worked at two colleges of education before moving to the University of Stirling in Scotland. There he teaches student teachers and teachers on in-service MEd and BEd courses.

His major interests lie in the cognitive development of children and in adolescence. He studied for his PhD with Professor E. A. Peel on stage development across the school age-range. After his PhD he undertook research on the formation of values in adolescents. More recently, he has researched into primary children who have learning difficulties in maths.

His qualifications include a BEd, an MA (Ed) from London University and a PhD from Birmingham University. He is a chartered psychologist and a committee member of the Education Section of the British Psychological Society.

COGNITIVE DEVELOPMENT TODAY:
Piaget and his Critics

PETER SUTHERLAND

P·C·P
Paul Chapman
Publishing Ltd

Copyright © 1992 Peter Sutherland

Paul Chapman Publishing Ltd
144 Liverpool Road
London
N1 1LA

British Library Cataloguing-in-Publication Data.
A catalogue record for this book is available from the British Library.

ISBN 1−85396−133 7

Typeset by Setrite Typesetters, Hong Kong
Printed and bound in Great Britain by
Athenaeum Press Ltd, Newcastle upon Tyne

CONTENTS

This book is dedicated to Duncan and Malcolm.
Just as Piaget was spurred to study child
development by his children, so have I been by
mine

PREFACE

This book is intended to provide a basic introduction to the main present-day ideas and theories about cognitive development. It is about practice as well as theory, and so the implications of the ideas are worked through for school teaching situations, from the nursery class to the sixth form.

It is hoped that student teachers of all types of schools as well as serving teachers (particularly those taking in-service courses on children's understanding of curriculum material) will find the book of value. It is also hoped that undergraduate and A-level students of psychology (taking cognitive development courses) will find it useful. Most chapters, therefore, have a further-reading section that suggests texts that are relatively easy to follow and that may be consulted after the initial introduction provided here. For further in-depth reading, the reader is recommended to consult the appropriate references in the Bibliography.

A summary at the end of each chapter gives a quick overview of the issues discussed. Also at the end of each chapter, a series of questions is provided that may be used by teachers for discussion during a seminar or class, or students may like to use these as a starting-point for their own informal discussions (those who are not in a group can always debate these issues with themselves).

In writing the book, various conventions have been adopted. The child is referred to as 'he' while the teacher, psychologist or other adult is referred to as 'she'. No sexist connotations are intended; a decision had to be made for clarity — since the majority of primary-school teachers are female, it seemed logical to use 'she', leaving 'he' for the child.

I am grateful to Rudolf Schaffer, Margaret Sutherland, Helen Haste, Chris Kyriacou, Nicholas Hawkes, Chris Holligan, Ros Sutherland, John Wilson and David Carr for their comments on whole chapters, and to Richard Skemp, David Galloway, Norman Graves, Colin Peacock, Sally Brown, Morag Donaldson, Lynn Michell, David McNab, Paul Rideout, Jim McNally, Alan Weeks, Lyn Moore, John Elliott, Bryan Ward and Derek Indoe for their comments on sections from chapters. Most of all, I am grateful to my editor, Marianne Lagrange, for her advice.

I have been fascinated by Piaget's ideas and their relevance to teaching since my first year of teaching 26 years ago, and I was introduced to Piaget's ideas by Professor W. H. O. Schmidt while studying for an in-service degree; I hope I have succeeded in passing on some of that enthusiasm (if modified by critical awareness) to the reader.

Peter Sutherland
Stirling, 1991

1
INTRODUCTION

How do children and adolescents learn? Does learning differ at various phases of children's and adolescents' lives and, if so, how? Of what relevance is our knowledge of their learning to teaching? These are the key questions this book aims to answer. At present, however, psychology has no universally agreed perspective from which to answer such questions as these. Rather, they are answered from various, often conflicting, perspectives. One perspective that had an enormous influence on developmental psychology and on the teaching of young children in the 1960s and 1970s was that of the Swiss epistemologist, Jean Piaget. It is now some ten years since Piaget died, and much has happened in the field of understanding children's thinking in both the decade before Piaget's death and in the decade after. Do his theories of cognitive development still have relevance or have his ideas been convincingly refuted by the revolution in cognitive theory of the last twenty years?

In this book we examine Piaget's original theories and their relevance to teachers and psychology today as well as examining other, competing, ideas about cognitive development. Jargon is used as little as possible, but there is a minimum of technical terminology that cannot be avoided. This terminology applies particularly to Piaget himself, because he evolved his own terms for most of his key concepts. For example, he labelled the ability to think in an abstract way 'formal operations'. Such terms as these have to be used to get to grips with Piaget's ideas and with the other theorists discussed in this book, as well as to work out the implications of these ideas for teachers and psychologists. (A glossary of terms is provided at the end of the book.)

An outline of Piaget's stage theory of thinking is given in Chapter 2. Each stage is summarized, including substages where they exist, as well as the details as outlined by Piaget himself. The emphasis is always on those aspects most relevant to teachers. Stage theory is based on the idea that children's intellectual development progresses through various levels of thinking. At each stage the child thinks in a different way from that of the previous stage — for example, in terms of words rather than physical actions. This concept of children's intellectual development is still very controversial, and some of the criticisms of it and alternative viewpoints are outlined in Chapter 9. Piaget's less controversial notion of epistemology is summarized in Chapter 2. The gist of this notion is that knowledge evolves through a biological process of adaptation to the environment (termed 'equilibration') that involves two opposing mechanisms — accommodation and assimilation.

Language in general (and reading in particular) is the focus of major interest in education at the present. Piaget's ideas here are less revolutionary compared to his ideas on stage development but, nevertheless, his contribution to the debate on the relative importance of language and nonverbal thought to cognitive behaviour is significant (this is summarized in Chapter 3). This discussion is followed by a review of the different concepts of the acquisition of the home language by toddlers. The two main psychological theories on the teaching of reading are also outlined.

Piaget's first major critic (as well as his chief opponent in the language-and-thinking debate discussed in Chapter 3) was Vygotsky. Vygotsky's views on education and psychology are outlined in Chapter 4. Piaget's theory was a reaction to the views of the behaviourists, the leading exponent being, in recent times, Skinner, whose influence was at its peak during the 1960s. Skinner's ideas are outlined in Chapter 5. Bruner (Chapter 6) started with Piaget's ideas but found them too passive and deterministic for teaching purposes. Bruner stresses the need for teachers to intervene actively in the process of cognitive development. Bruner is a major figure in his own right and was one of the first to challenge some of Piaget's ideas in the English-speaking world. His critique, however, is not as radical as others.

Some of the criticism of the 1970s and 1980s is presented in Chapter 7. In Britain, this challenge to Piagetian orthodoxy has included the work of Peter Bryant at Oxford and Margaret Donaldson at Edinburgh. In 1971 Bryant published his seminal criticism and revision of Piaget's work on the concept of number (1952). Piaget had indicated that 5-year-old children could not grasp the conservation of number — for example, a number is still the same if the two groups of objects (of the same quantity) to be counted are laid out differently, as illustrated in Figure 7.1. Bryant showed that, if children are given the appropriate help from teachers, they can understand 1:1 correspondence. Children are then well on their way to grasping the conservation of number. This trend-setting and subsequent work by Bryant and his colleagues are discussed (with illustrations) in Chapter 7, along with the critiques of Cowan.

In 1978 Donaldson published *Children's Minds*, which, to an even greater extent than Bryant's work, has reshaped our understanding of what children can do. What children can do depends, according to Donaldson, on how the learning situation is perceived by the children and whether they are given optimal help by teachers in understanding what is expected of them. Language has emerged as the major factor in helping children to understand and do what Piaget had said they could not. (This is also discussed in Chapter 7.)

The alternative or constructivist movement developed from Piaget's ideas. Fundamentally, this movement's supporters believe children construct their own knowledge from their own experiences, independently of adults to a much greater extent than Piaget indicated. Constructivists reject Piaget's concept of stage theory but accept his concept of the acquisition of knowledge. As most movements, the constructivist movement has two elements: the radical element (represented in the UK by Maureen Pope, for example) claims to have replaced Piaget's ideas, while the moderate element (represented in the UK, for example, by Ros Driver) regards its ideas as evolving out of Piaget's. The Bryant and Donaldson viewpoints emphasize the teacher's direct role; however, the constructivists see the teacher playing more of an enabling role. A broad outline of their ideas is given in Chapter 8. The implications of constructivist ideas are examined for primary teachers generally (and primary science particularly) in Chapter 14, and for maths teachers (both primary and secondary) in Chapter 15.

Today there are several alternative points of view to Piaget's theories of cognitive development, and these views are sources of current empirical work and influence. In the main American in origin, these theories are summarized in Chapter 9. One such movement is information processing (IP), which has arisen from the evolution of the computer and uses this as a tool to model how the brain functions.

A major criticism has been mounted on a central Piagetian idea from within the developmental tradition: this criticism denies that the evidence of children's performance in different domains supports Piaget's concept of stages. The alternative view is the domain-specific one, analysed in Chapter 9. A similar position is taken by the structuralists, who look for quantitative development in children within a developmental framework but who do not see any evidence of stages.

The metacognitive movement (Chapter 9) is very influential in British as well as American theories of cognitive development at present. This movement focuses on children's awareness and understanding of their own learning, particularly on an awareness of learning their home language. This seems to imply that teachers must try to make their pupils more consciously aware of their own learning. The nativist movement is perhaps even more 'biological' than the Piagetian one. Nativists propose that children have an innate ability to learn various things and that they need only to be exposed to the appropriate environment to learn. These ideas are also outlined in Chapter 9.

Some cognitive developmentalists, however, still hold largely to a Piagetian position. A few of these are fundamentalists but others (such as the author of this book) take into account most of the valid criticisms (neo- and post-Piagetian stances are discussed in Chapter 10). One modification arises from British research carried out separately but simultaneously in the 1970s by Shayer, Kuchemann and Wylan (1976) and Shayer and Wylan (1978), and by Sutherland (1982, 1983). This research found Piaget to have been over-optimistic about what pupils are capable of understanding. This is contrary to the findings of the Bryant and Donaldson schools, and applies only to science. Nevertheless, it is part of the overall picture of pupils' capabilities. The implications of this evidence are of considerable importance to secondary teachers and are outlined in Chapter 16. During the 1960s, Smedslund replicated a number of Piaget's studies and pointed out flaws in them. Smedslund also offers a modified version of Piaget's work, which is summarized in Chapter 10. The current state of affairs in psychological theory is summarized in Chapter 11; this is followed by a consideration of some of the outstanding issues to be resolved.

The remainder of the book turns from psychological theory to educational practice. Some implications of the theories for teaching are discussed, something few introductory psychological texts attempt to do. Chapter 12 gives an overview of the current situation in the application of cognitive development to education. It is argued that the Piagetian and constructivist positions are not necessarily mutually exclusive – both have important messages for teachers. At present, Feuerstein (Chapter 13) is a controversial figure in this field. He has absorbed other influences besides Piaget and has synthesized the whole into his teaching technique, 'instrumental enrichment'. He claims this helps to bring children who are behind at school back to the normal range of attainment for their age.

The mixed-ability class has been a major concern for comprehensive teachers in British schools over the past decade or so but has been the norm for primary teachers since the early 1970s when the 11-plus examination was phased out. Mixed-ability classes have been the most common way of grouping pupils in the first three years of secondary school since the early 1980s. The evidence summarized and re-presented in this book has important implications, first, for the way in which a year group is allocated into classes and, second (if the decision is made to favour mixed-ability groups) for the way the teachers subdivide a class — even if this is only in their own minds. This and other issues are discussed in Chapter 14. The relevance of cognitive developmental findings to the National Curriculum and to national testing is also investigated in Chapter 14. The focus of Chapter 14 then switches to the teaching of different age-groups: secondary, junior, and infant and preschool. Pupils with special educational needs have been given careful attention in recent times, particularly since the Warnock Report (1978). In this book the focus is on intellectual handicap. The implications for children with a less-than-adequate ability to utilize any of the alternative ways of learning are hence discussed in Chapter 14. Science is now a core subject in the National Curriculum for all pupils from 5 upwards. For this reason a special section in Chapter 14 has been included on the teaching of primary science.

Mathematics is also a core subject in the National Curriculum. Cognitive development in general, and Piaget's theory in particular, has more relevance to this subject than to any other in the school curriculum. For this reason a special chapter (15) is included to outline some of the findings and to work out possible implications for the teaching of maths, particularly for the primary teacher.

In Chapter 16 we look at the work of a secondary teacher. The ideas of Peel and his students are analysed, with sections on the teaching of English, science, history, geography and religious studies. Where they are relevant, the impact on and implications for teaching of some of the newer ideas (such as IP and metacognition) are worked out.

Piaget's original research into children's moral thinking prompted psychologists such as Kohlberg to dedicate their working lives to further explorations in this field. This is explored in Chapter 17.

Summary

Piaget's ideas have provoked criticism from several significant sources during the past two decades: in Britain from the Bryant and Donaldson schools, on the one hand, and from the constructivists on the other. In America, the IP school is the major alternative, together with the domain-specific concept. In both countries at present the metacognitive movement is very influential. Vygotsky, Smedslund and Feuerstein have been among the critics. Are the positions of Piaget and his critics incompatible with one another so that professionals have to base their work on the one or the other, or is a compromise possible? The implications of these views (both separately and in a compromise form) are worked through in subsequent chapters.

Questions for discussion

1. Discuss the merits and demerits of mixed-ability classes.
2. How important is the learning children acquire *outside* school?
3. Do teachers have a responsibility to find ways of helping children to understand problems (such as 1:1 correspondence) most would not have understood on their own?

2
THE PIAGETIAN LEGACY

Piaget's work has been heavily criticized in the decade or so since his death. This criticism is discussed in Chapters 4–9. However, before looking at the criticisms, what Piaget had to say should be considered first.

Background

Jean Piaget was born in 1896 in French-speaking Switzerland, where he was to spend all his life except for a few years at the Sorbonne in Paris. His background was academic (his father was a professor) and so it is not surprising that high-level cognitive activity dominated his childhood. During his adolescence he developed a strong interest in biology, and his ontological studies of various creatures had a lasting influence on his thinking. He married one of his research students and, following the birth of his three children in his twenties, his focus of study switched to the problem of epistemology: how do we acquire knowledge? His ideas came from case studies of his own children. This research led to a succession of brilliant (but difficult to read) books on different aspects of knowledge and how they are acquired by young children – e.g. number, physical causality and objects themselves.

For the English-speaking world, however, the Piagetian revolution began only in the 1960s following the translation into English of many of his works. These include (with Szeminska) *The Child's Conception of Number* (1952), *The Origins of Intelligence in Children* (1953), *The Child's Construction of Reality* (1954) and (with Inhelder) *The Growth of Logical Thought* (1958). The overwhelming impact of his findings for primary and preschool education finally became clear.

Until then Piaget himself had not been interested in educational matters but, during the last two decades of his long career, he responded to many prominent educationists (such as Bruner) who had been stimulated by his work and himself wrote on education (1970). His later life hence revolved around working out various aspects of his ideas at his Institute for Epistemological Studies in Geneva right up until his death in 1980 at the age of 84.

The stages of development

What Piaget became most famous for was his claim that children passed through a series of stages of thinking that were qualitatively different from each other. In the first quarter of this century the prevailing view of children's cognitive activity was that it was the same as adult's cognitive activity, only less efficient. Just as a child's body was similar to an adult's only smaller, so was his mind. Since a baby could not speak, he could not possibly think.

Piaget's notion that a baby thought and learnt in a radically different way from an adult was a revolutionary one. Likewise, Piaget proposed that a toddler — despite speaking a simplified version of the adult language — thinks and learns in a totally different way from an (educated) adult. This too was considered astounding at the time. Many of his contemporaries did not accept his concept of different ways of thinking. They maintained that, as a child grows to adulthood, there is only quantitative and not qualitative progress. Many cognitive developmentalists (such as the domain-specific school) have returned to this view, arguing that there is insufficient evidence to justify the idea of stages that operate in different domains. Growth in thinking, learning and development with age is purely quantitative.

The controversy over whether stages in fact exist is discussed frequently in subsequent chapters. The remainder of this chapter outlines Piaget's stages and theory of knowledge.

Period of Sensorimotor Activity

This period particularly covers the early months of a baby's life, before the first word is learnt. In most cases this will start to change to the next period at some time during the second year. Although Piaget's (1953, 1954) ideas were a major influence at the time, research on babies has since undergone a revolution. However, there are still many points of interest for psychologists and teachers of young children.

The dominant activity was considered to be perception, and this is still accepted in principle by such authorities as Butterworth (1981). Perception is oriented towards *action*. The baby's mental world is geared towards doing (rather than symbolic activity, such as language). The period of sensorimotor thinking consists of six stages.

(i) Stage of reflexes (0–1 m.)

Piaget regarded this as a stage of mere mechanical response to outside stimuli, such as blinking at a bright light. But this, more than any of his other stages, has been shown to be wrong. Many psychologists over the past twenty years have concentrated on unravelling babies' capabilities. Tom Bower (1977) is one, with his work on babies' early perception of shapes suspended above their heads. Uzgiris and Hunt (1970) are others; they found that babies from 3 months onwards look for a longer time at novel rather than familiar objects. Babies are also inclined to imitate adults' vocal sounds and hand and facial gestures, provided these have a novelty value for them. As a result of this and other research, the onset of intelligent behaviour has been successively moved back to perhaps a few hours after birth.

(ii) Stage of primary circular reactions (1–4 m.)

The baby can now carry out some primitive (hence primary) forms of intelligent activity. He responds to toys presented to him, possibly by grabbing them. Piaget used the term *circular* for these reactions because of the repetitive nature of the play involved. The term 'circular reactions' comes from Baldwin (1925), who described them as partially formed, overt concepts linked to sensory input. The baby repeats an action for its own sake. Circular reactions involve the repetition of an action that produces pleasant stimulation. Overproduction of actions occurs and this creates a pool of actions to be used in the process of accommodation (see p. 25). Unlike a reflex, a circular reaction enables the baby to reproduce a result himself, which was originally produced by the environment. He does this by going back to the beginning, e.g. putting his fingers in his mouth deliberately. This marks the beginning of intent in the baby's behaviour, since he has decided the thumb is worth sucking but other objects are not.

Assimilation (see p. 25) is the dominant mechanism at this stage. In other words, objects are made to fit the baby's preconception of them. Circular reactions are an example of assimilation. These activities can be seen as autism: they are carried out for the pleasure they give independent of any communication with others.

The ability to repeat an act (which was not possible at the reflex stage) represents the dawning of memory.

(iii)   Stage of secondary circular reactions (4−8 m.)

The baby now takes the initiative in grabbing a toy of his choice. He shows a greater degree of intent than in the stage of primary circular reactions. Because of the enjoyment he receives from playing with it, he continues to do so. Whereas in primary circular reactions the baby repeated an action for its own sake, an action is now repeated to achieve a goal in the environment around him. He grabs a rattle and brings it to his mouth. The baby is aware of the result of his own activity and he deliberately repeats this. A secondary circular reaction represents a modification of a circular reaction in order to obtain a desired effect. The co-ordination of hand and eye, which develops at about this time, considerably extends the baby's range of possible actions.

The cognitive units of this stage are forerunners of what Piaget called *classes* or *concepts* in children of 2 and over (since classifying is involved). The technical term he used is a *scheme*. This is a broader term than a *schema*. A single scheme encapsulates a number of schemata. The age of 4−8 months is very early for such an advanced concept to occur in babies. Later, once language has been acquired, schemes become much more common (i.e. in pre-operational and operational thinking). However, a baby may have a scheme for 'objects to shake', which includes the schemas of 'rattles' and 'bells'.

Recognitory assimilation, in the form of repeatedly playing with an object, shows a baby is aware that the object exists. This awareness is a forerunner of the object constancy of stage v. It is also a preliminary to the naming of objects in the (verbal) operational period, which follows shortly after that. It is as though he is giving a nonverbal name to the object by playing with it in a certain way.

(iv)   Stage of the co-ordination of secondary circular reactions (8−12 m.)

The baby can now combine two activities simultaneously. He can play with a rattle in one hand and knock a hanging bell with the other. The onset of this stage usually more or less coincides with the baby's ability to crawl. As a result of the combination of the two abilities, he is no longer limited to the objects he can reach from the seated position. The complexity of the subsequent play is enriched. However, he is *not* yet capable of searching out and finding an object hidden in front of him. This is illustrated in Figure 2.1, where a baby can no longer find a cup after it has been hidden behind a screen. The baby now makes what Butterworth (1981) calls the A−B error: continuing to search in spot A when an object has been moved to spot B.

One scheme can serve as the means for the realization of another: a

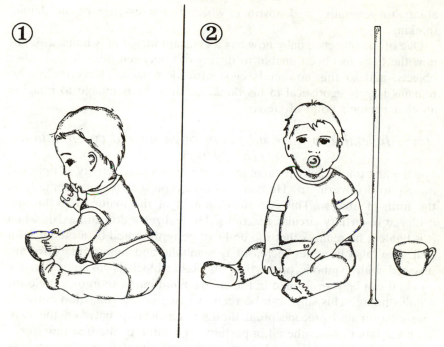

Figure 2.1   A baby who has not yet attained tertiary circular reactions

baby pushes away his father's hand in order to grasp a match-box. A baby can now achieve new goals and does not simply repeat goals previously achieved.

(v)   Stage of tertiary circular reactions (12−18 m.)

In one of Piaget's most famous experiments, the baby now seeks out and finds a favourite toy when it is hidden behind a screen by an adult with whom he is familiar. He can now do what he could not in Figure 2.1. This is an enormous breakthrough in cognitive development as it means the baby can remember that an object exists. He now has what Piaget calls a *schema*.

This is the beginning of *mental representation*, a key idea in the Piagetian theory. It is also termed the achievement of *object constancy*. The baby now knows an object still exists even when he cannot actually see it. Tertiary circular reactions allow the constructive deduction of an abstract 'object concept' that is not tied to any particular sensory experience. In other words, the child is able to build up a mental picture of an object as it appears in a number of different contexts. This is the beginning of the ability to generalize and abstract, which is the essence of 'academic' thinking.

One of the objects a baby now has a constant image of is himself. Until now the baby has been unable to distinguish between himself and other objects, and so this now ends egocentric dominance. Nevertheless he remains largely egotistical in his thinking, since he is unable to imagine another person's point of view.

(vi)   *Invention of new means through mental combinations (18–24 m.)*

For the first time a baby is capable of inventing a play activity as opposed merely to discovering it. He can also now represent objects mentally in the form of images. This is a development of the major breakthrough achieved in tertiary circular reactions. He realizes a doll still exists when it is hidden; he realizes that the doll can be represented by a picture of a doll. Play also becomes increasingly symbolic and important. Toys are invested with symbolic properties. A plastic block is no longer just a block; it can be transformed in the child's mind into a train or a table for a doll's house. This stage can be seen as essentially a transition between sensorimotor and preconceptual thought, an overlap between the two. With the latter comes the all-important acquisition of the first few words of language. Cognition is no longer purely sensorimotor and the toddler's cognitive activity is transformed. Piagetians refer to this as the development of *post-sensorimotor representational intelligence*. In other words, toddlers are constructing and recording their experiences in terms of language instead of terms of actions. This is analogous to Bruner's spiral curriculum (illustrated in Figure 6.1 and discussed in Chapter 6). By the end of the sensorimotor period, the toddler realizes that an object retains its identity in space and time.

The toddler is now capable of negation: of having in mind a possibility and deciding not to do it. This is a very primitive form of the hypothesis – testing of the formal – operational period.

Assessing Piaget's six stages, nearly forty years after their first publication in English, there is a case for combining at least the first two stages (reflexes and primary circular reactions), bearing in mind the critiques of reflexes made above.

Period of Operational Thought

Stage of pre-operational thought

The first word has been learnt; symbolic representation has begun.

Substage of preconcepts (1 y. 6 m. to 4 y.) According to Piaget, sensorimotor activity is dominated by action, as the name denotes. So in the first substage that follows, action is still dominant but it is now *internalized*. The toddler knows how to use a spoon once he has had experience of one.

Piaget characterized this in terms of transductive logic. One man is called Daddy, so all men are called Daddy. A 3-year-old (as reported by a mature student at the author's university) saw a pregnant woman. The reason for the fatness was explained to her. When she later saw a fat man, she exclaimed: 'I know. He has a baby!' There is no clear separation of cause and effect. However, Piaget does *not* regard toddlers at this substage as capable of grasping concepts. The same thing applies to the toddler recognizing people under confusing conditions. Piaget claimed a child could not recognize his sister when she was dressed up as someone else. The same phenomenon of confusion is found in number. Boyle (1969) found that 3-year-olds would say that one pile of beads had more in it than another because the first pile was green. This is the type of muddled categorization Piaget had pointed to.

At the substage of preconcepts children cannot discriminate classes hierarchically. This means they cannot understand that oranges and apples are both fruit. From biology this is known as the genus/species classification. Piaget's son says he cannot be in Geneva and Switzerland at the same time. Nevertheless, toddlers learning to speak hunger to classify every object encountered at a species level. Parents are constantly asked 'What's that, Daddy?'

Another fundamental Piagetian process is *internalization*. A child's experiences are internalized. He makes them intellectually part of himself. During babyhood, everything has to be acted out physically. A physical action, such as shaking, becomes internalized: the baby can do it automatically, he has it in his repertoire. A year or two later, when the child has access to language, he can use a word or words to encapsulate his experience (or schema) and store it in his memory in verbal form.

A different aspect of preconceptual thought is the overall way toddlers judge what they see. The toddler's world view is an absolute rather than a relative one, as exemplified by the rules of marbles discussed in Chapter 17. Any breaking of the rules is seen as worthy of punishment, regardless of possible exonerating circumstances.

Piaget argued that toddlers are egocentric in their thinking. They are not capable of realizing that another person could see a scene differently from the way they do. One of the examples given by Piaget and Inhelder (1956) was the mountains problem, as illustrated in Figure 2.2. The child is faced with three mountains, distinguished from each other in various

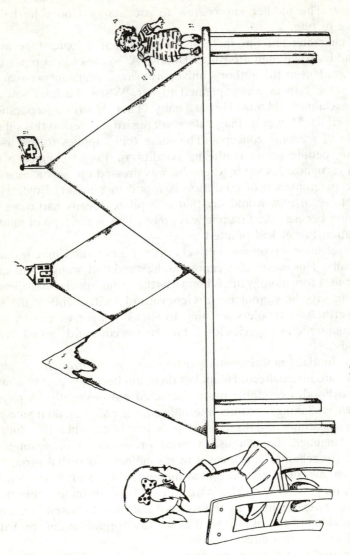

Figure 2.2 The mountains problem

ways: one has a flag on the top, another a house and the third snow. A doll is placed at various positions around the mountains. The child has to say what the doll would see. As this is difficult to do verbally, the child is given a set of ten pictures. He has to pick the one that represents the doll's view. Alternatively he is given a model of the three mountains and asked to arrange it to represent what the doll would see. Piaget found that preconceptual children could not do this.

However, Piaget's allegation of egocentric thought dominating this age-group has been one of the most strongly criticized of any he made. The original opponent was Vygotsky (1986), to be followed by Donaldson (1978) and others (see Chapters 3, 4 and 7). Overall, however, this is the substage on which the least empirical work has been done, whether by Piaget or subsequent researchers. There are methodological reasons for this in terms of the difficulties of researching reliably on 2- and 3-year-olds. First, it is hard to establish they have understood the requirements of the task situation. Second, it is not easy for the researcher (or even a parent) to understand what the toddlers say when they still speak either in two-word sentences or in an abbreviated form of the adult language. Even if the task is entirely nonverbal, the problem of understanding the task remains. The clinical method (which Piaget pioneered) can be used: one adult interacts with one child and this is video- or audio-recorded.

Because of the problems of conducting research, this substage must be regarded as having the lowest validity within the Piagetian canon.

Substage of intuitive thinking (4−7 or 8 y.)   This substage is only a slight advance on preconceptual thinking. Immediate perceptions still dominate and the child is still easily tricked by an apparent change in appearance. Butterworth (1981) regards perception as the dominant mechanism in the sensorimotor period. As perception is still dominant until the end of the pre-operational stage, the whole phase from the outset of the sensorimotor period to the end of the intuitive substage could be seen as one of perceptual dominance.

The ability to *decentre* (in Piaget's terminology) is beginning to develop. In other words, children are getting better at seeing the *whole* of any scene, rather than just concentrating exclusively on one aspect of it, as centring implies. Their logic is still transductive, but they now give reasons for their actions and beliefs. They cannot yet compensate mentally. They cannot yet see that if John is Susan's brother then she must be his sister.

Intuitive thinkers' fundamental cognitive activity becomes less action based and more verbally based. They reason more in verbal terms alone. They now give more reasons. Their favourite question is 'Why?' rather than 'What?' In Piagetian terms, the action-laden *preconcepts* decline and give way to *pseudo-concepts*. These have the trappings of adult concepts but have flaws. Where true concepts (ones acceptable scientifically) are used, they are used without understanding of their meaning. This is the 'intuitive' nature of this substage. For once in Piaget's terminology, the term means what it says and requires no definition. Hence, in Piagetian terminology, *accommodation* becomes the dominant mechanism.

Piaget argued that animism is common. This means children endow inanimate objects with human qualities, but neither Beard (1969) nor Sutherland (1980) found evidence for this among British first-year infant pupils. The child is still not capable of classifying in the hierarchical sense. He cannot yet group 'horses' and 'cows' under 'animals'. In fact the end of the intuitive thinking substage is defined mainly in terms of what the children *cannot* do as opposed to what children who are operational *can* do.

Stage of concrete operations (7—11 y. in Piaget's view; 5—12 y. in Sutherland's)

Operational thinking is one of the key Piagetian concepts and perhaps the area in which most replication and development of Piaget's work has taken place. It is also the concept that has the greatest application to primary teaching, particularly of maths and science. With primary science now a core subject in the National Curriculum, this application is of added interest to primary teachers.

What does operational thinking mean? First and most crucially, it is the ability to hold an idea in one's head while one is dealing with a problem. The ideas cannot yet be manipulated purely mentally, as they can be in formal operations. The elements have to be present physically; hence *concrete* operations. It is a major advance over pre-operational thinking because the child is no longer a victim of apparent change. The ability to abstract an aspect of the situation mentally is a great help. Second, it means the ability to think reversibly: for instance, to understand that the volume of air a person breathes in is approximately the same as that which he or she breathes out.

One of the classic Piagetian experiments is the conservation of quantity (Figure 2.3). A tall jar is three quarters filled while the child watches. The water is then poured into a wide jar. The child is asked whether the tall or the wide jar has more water in it. The child is not given the option of the correct answer to choose from. The pre-operational child says the tall jar. This has been interpreted as being because the water 'seems' more in the tall jar. The concrete operational thinker can compensate mentally: the second jar is not so tall; on the other hand, it is wider.

The actual wording of the questions Piaget asked is, of course, very

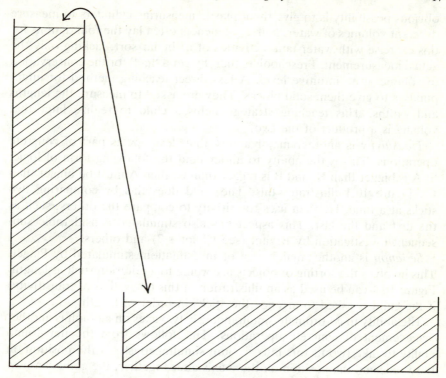

Figure 2.3 The conservation of quantity

important. There has been much criticism of this aspect of Piaget's work (outlined in Chapter 7). However, there remains a problem for English speakers of getting the precise nuances from their translations from French.

A second example of the conservation-of-quantity task is to show a child two lumps of Plasticene of equal volume in the shape of a ball. One of the balls is then rolled out into the shape of a sausage in front of the child. The adult then asks the child, 'Do both of these (the ball shaped and the sausage shaped) possess the same amount of Plasticene?' The non-operational child says the *apparently* larger sausage-shaped one is bigger.

These experiments have frequently been replicated with varying results, mainly due to the differences in the materials used, the questions asked, the methods of assessment and the final interpretations. It could be argued that one way to help children grasp the conservation of quantity more quickly is to give them plenty of practice in measuring volume. An obvious possibility is to give them plastic measuring cylinders to measure different volumes of water. Nursery teachers often lay the foundations for this exercise with water-tank activities of a similar sort, lacking only the actual measurement. Preschoolers thereby get a 'feel' for the conservation of volume at an intuitive level. A less direct teaching method for infant pupils is to give them solid blocks. They are asked to measure the lengths and widths. This teaching strategy helps a child to realize later that volume is a product of the two.

Transitivity is another major ability that develops as part of concrete operations. This is the ability to understand the following form of logic: 'if A is bigger than B, and B is bigger than C, then A must be bigger than C'. Figure 10.1 illustrates this. The child does this by comparing two sticks at a time. He then uses transitivity to compare the others, such as the first and the last. This aspect has also stimulated considerable subsequent investigation by Bryant (see Chapter 7) and others.

Seriation is another major area of investigation, stimulated by Piaget. This involves the sorting of objects according to a criterion such as length. Figure 10.1 can be used as an illustration of this (as well as of transitivity) if the child is asked to arrange the sticks in order of length.

The ability to co-ordinate simultaneously two axes on a graph is another achievement of concrete operations. This follows from the new-found ability to take two factors into account simultaneously. If the position on the x axis and the position on the y axis alter together, the child can now remember the position of x while he alters the position of y.

The conservation of number is a crucial concept for primary teachers. When do children realize that two groups (or sets) of objects represent the same number, even though their appearance is different (see Figure 7.1)? Five Smarties in a pile represent the same number as five toffees spread out in a line. Or six beads spread out is the same number as six beads closer together. Piaget's pioneering studies have generated much subsequent work (see Bryant and Cowan in Chapter 7). This is actually one of the easier conservations to achieve. Even Piaget found it to be achieved by about 7 years. It is not surprising therefore that the average age of attainment is lower than for mass, volume or density. In fact, in order to grasp the conservation of density, the conservations of mass and volume are prior requirements, so the conservation of density is only achieved at an average age of about 13.

It follows from this that a child cannot be said to be concrete operational on all tasks simultaneously at a single moment. Instead, according to Piaget, he becomes operational on different tasks at different ages. He termed this horizontal *décalage* (or 'lag' in English).

Period of Formal Operations

The fundamentals of this period were outlined by Inhelder and Piaget in their important work, *The Growth of Logical Thinking* (1958). The name of the book implies an emphasis on the capacity of the adolescent to reason in a logically consistent way, *without* the help of any concrete props. This feature distinguishes it from the preceding concrete operational stage.

A stress on the abstract mode of thinking is implied. The formal operational adolescent thinks most effectively in *symbolic* terms. This has implications for teachers of a wide range of subjects. In physics, formulae are easily understood and used; in religious studies, difficult concepts, such as the Holy Trinity, can be grappled with; in literature, allegories and similar literary forms can be understood; and in history the concept of historic time can be understood.

Although Piaget's concept of formal operational thought has been very useful in both psychology and education, the details of what it involves are rather arcane. It is derived empirically from situations in logic and physics unfamiliar to most teachers and psychologists. Peel (1971) has really given us a much more understandable and useful version of this type of thinking with his *explainer* thinking, outlined in Chapter 10.

Piaget's formal operational thinking is hypothetico-deductive. The adolescent can conceive of a new idea, try it out in his head and then test it, either in reality in the case of practical subjects such as science or on paper in the case of writing a story. Deduction is now used. The adolescent can now deduce an implication from a general principle. In maths a follow-up proposition can be deduced by a pupil from a general proposition given to him. This supplants the inductive reasoning of the concrete operational phase.

As Inhelder and Piaget (1958) said:

> The great novelty of this stage is that by means of a differentiation of form and content the subject (i.e. the adolescent) becomes capable of reasoning correctly about propositions he does not believe, or at least, not yet: that is propositions that he considers pure hypotheses. He becomes capable of drawing the necessary conclusions from truths which are merely possible.

Thinking is no longer limited to reality or personal experience. For instance, in mathematics infinity can now be conjured up and understood. Bet (11 y. 7 m.), when asked by Inhelder and Piaget the question, 'How many points could I put on this line?' answers: 'One cannot say. They are innumerable. One could always make some smaller points.'

The adult follows up: 'About how many are there roughly?'
The child replies: 'It is impossible to say.'
The adult perseveres: 'But approximately ten thousand, one hundred thousand, a million?'
The child reiterates: 'It is impossible to say. One cannot say how many there are.'
The adult changes tack: 'Make me the shortest line it is possible to make.'
The child responds: 'No, one cannot, because it is always possible to make a still shorter one.'

Perhaps Flavell's (1963) interpretation of Piaget's general message is more revealing than anything Piaget himself said. Formal thought is not so much this or that specific behaviour as a generalized orientation towards problem-solving. For instance, the adolescent can now make such qualifications as 'all other things being equal'. In this and other ways a formal operational thinker is much better at organizing and structuring the elements of a problem than a concrete operational thinker. It is a *systematic* way of thinking.

To be able to think formal-operationally is useful for the problem-solving demanded by GCSE. For example, a history pupil may be given the problem of finding the causes of the French Revolution. Provided he is a formal operational thinker, he will be able to sift through his material, analyse the causes and structure the resultant material into a coherent answer.

The adolescent's intelligence can now reflect on itself. This enables the adolescent to be much more aware of himself as a person. A range of literary possibilities are opened up by this. Novels such as *The Go-Between* (Hartley, 1958) become relevant to the adolescent's ability to examine himself and his relationships with adults. The metacognitivists believe a child can be aware of his own learning from the earliest possible age, as is elaborated in Chapter 9. In this small way Piaget was a pioneer metacognitivist.

At the concrete operational stage the child became able to classify. The genus/species distinction was learnt, i.e. that apples and oranges are both fruit. Now the ability to use this classification improves qualitatively. The intelligent adolescent is very good at classifying hierarchically and takes great delight in doing so. He may have hobbies that make use of this new-found classifying ability, such as collecting stamps and filing them under their countries of origin.

Inhelder and Piaget put a great deal of emphasis on the ability to perform operations on operations. Algebra is an example of this. The more abstract system of xs and ys is superimposed on the number system of 1s and 2s, but hierarchically above it. However, the formal operational system is combinatorial and not merely hierarchical as are concrete operations. In formal operations the elements interact with each other. The element x can be multiplied by y to give xy or added to y to give $x + y$, whereas in concrete operations only the latter is possible.

The examples the Genevans themselves gave were usually from the fields of propositional logic, maths or physics. An illuminating example is the pendulum. Each factor involved can be varied to give a different result, e.g. the length can be shortened or lengthened, or the distance the pendulum is raised from the vertical can be varied. Alternatively, the combination of the different factors can be calculated. Logical propositions too can be tested, e.g. if the length of the pendulum is doubled, how will this affect the time of the swing?

Another example is the hydraulic press, as illustrated in Figure 2.4. The intuitive thinker knows the left-hand side will go down under the weight and the right side will go up. The concrete operational thinker adds the compensatory element: the left side is wider than the right, so the left will sink less than the right will rise. However, the formal operational thinker can actually calculate the distances the liquid will move up or down the cylinder. He can use the appropriate formula: $v = rh$, where v is the volume, r is the radius and h the height.

Another example that illustrates formal operations is the amount identical bars made of different metals will bend under different weights.

Much of Inhelder and Piaget's original empirical work on formal operations was done on the understanding of propositional logic and the 'INCR' transformations, which consist of four groups: I, which stands for identity, e.g. a rotation of 360 degrees returns a point to its original position; N, which stands for negation − the opposite of any element; R, which stands for reciprocal; and C, which stands for correlative.

The hydraulic press (Figure 2.4) illustrates the four transformations. The left-hand side represents action forces, whether adding or subtracting. The right-hand side represents reaction forces, i.e. the element of negation. Removing weights from the left side is the negation (or inverse) of adding them. The effect produced by the liquid displaced on the right, due to its height and density, is the reciprocal of adding the weight to the left-hand side.

Inhelder and Piaget did an interesting study on correlation. To young adolescents of 12−14 years they presented cards, each of which had a different combination of hair and eye colour. Those youngsters who had the ability to correlate (i.e. formal operational thinkers) could see a relationship between the two: that brown hair was more likely to go with brown eyes and fair hair with blue eyes.

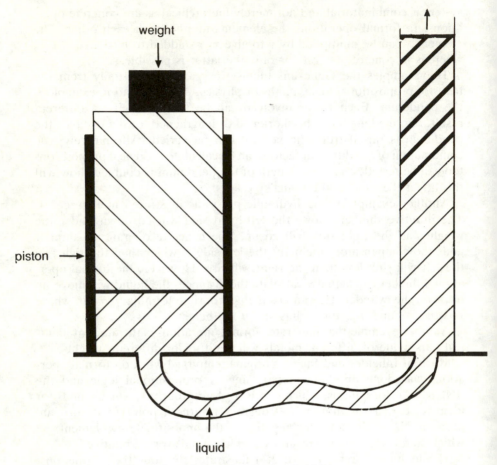

Figure 2.4 An illustration of formal operational thinking

These four elements (or transformations) were derived within a context of propositional logic and can only be really understood within this context. They are inherently obscure to the mind not trained in this discipline and − interpreted in a strictly technical sense − their relevance to cognitive activity in more general contexts, such as education, is dubious.

Piaget's second-order classes (as opposed to the first-order classes of the concrete operational stage) may also seem somewhat obscure. These are more abstract concepts, such as theorems. In fact some may wonder whether these aspects of Piaget's work have any relevance beyond such subjects as maths and philosophy. However, interpreted more liberally, formal operational thinking underlies incisive thinking about English literature, analysing historical episodes and reasoning about geographical events, etc. The ability to handle classes and relations simultaneously instead of separately also develops in formal operations. For example, different amounts (relations) of different coins (classes) are compared at the same time.

By the end of the process of becoming a mature, formal operational thinker, an adolescent can analyse accurately, combine propositions according to the laws of logic, deduce proofs and conjure up hypotheses of which he has had no experience, as outlined by Smith (1986). As a result of the development of these various new abilities, the formal operational thinker has a more stable intellectual view than the concrete operational one.

The social context necessary for formal operations to develop is of considerable interest to both psychologists and teachers. Co-operation with peers and teachers is essential. Hence discussion is a vital method of teaching. This gives pupils plenty of practice in translating from one form of representation to another, e.g. written to spoken. In order for formal operations to develop, the teacher has to try to help adolescents see new relationships between elements and to make connections they would not otherwise have made. In English this might be done by getting pupils to link such words as 'mystery' and 'carnival' in a story or poem. In history the teacher might suggest a new reason for Scotland's defeat of England at Bannockburn, apart from those mentioned in the textbook.

There is disagreement among Piagetians whether the ability to think in the formal operational mode necessarily applies to all situations and all academic subjects. A person might be a formal operational thinker in maths but not in literature or vice versa, as C. P. Snow's classic science or arts specialist. It is only really in someone's areas of highest intellectual performance that he is formal operational. This implies that people will regress to an intellectually lower stage of thinking in those areas where they are getting little or no stimulation in the higher stage. Hence Snow's classic English high-school pupil who specialized in science from the age of 14 may well remain at a concrete operational level in literature or even regress to the intuitive substage. Likewise, the pupil who concentrated on the arts for A-levels and gave up the serious study of science at 14 might remain at the concrete operational stage in this domain. It is hoped that the broadening effect of the National Curriculum may help more youngsters to attain formal operations in more subject areas.

However, the alternative view is that formal operational thinking applies to all subjects and topics. Once an adolescent has reached formal operations he will apply this manner of thinking to all intellectual challenges. The discrepancy between the two views is one of the Piagetian problems that remains to be solved. Piaget seems to have lost interest in cognitive development at adolescence. Adult thinking, however, has been investigated by Entwistle (1985) and many others.

Some General Points about Piaget's Stage Theory

For the individual child there will probably be a great deal of *lag* (or *décalage* as Piaget termed it) between his stage of development in some subjects compared with others. The rate of progress will also be uneven over the whole process of the acquisition of new knowledge. Horizontal lag is within a stage of development. For instance, in attaining concrete operations, most children acquire the conservation of number some years before acquiring the conservation of volume.

Vertical lag is between stages. For example, a baby/toddler at the end of the sensorimotor period can find his way around the rooms of a house, but he will only be able to imagine his experiences in his brain in visual terms *as a map* when he reaches the operational period. He will then be able to represent those sensorimotor experiences figuratively in his brain as an image or diagram.

A child has to progress systematically through the stages and periods. He cannot skip one. A child will normally be operating at the highest stage he has achieved, say formal operations for a secondary pupil. However, if he is not getting any stimulation in a particular area, he may regress back to a lower stage. This is a well-known phenomenon to adults who acquired a high grade of proficiency on a musical instrument in their youth but, through lack of practice, now operate at a far lower level of proficiency should they try out their old instrument again. This point shows the importance of the environment in Piaget's stages of development. It is the environment that provides the stimulation for the development of the mind and for sustaining that development.

According to Piagetians who have replicated the studies around the world, Piaget's stages are universal in all cultures tested. Formal operations, however, does not appear to exist in some non-Western cultures that do not include abstract thinking. However, the rate at which children move through the stages varies in different cultures, according to the quality of environmental stimulation. In Martinique, where French is spoken and the culture is Francophone, there was a four-year delay in the acquisition of operational thought compared to French-speaking Switzerland. In Teheran, the stages were achieved at the same average age as in Switzerland, but in the villages of Iran there was a two-year delay.

These findings are based on the premiss that cognitive development depends on two factors: internal maturation of the child and external stimulation by the environment. External stimulation was not originally conceived as including specific teaching, although Piaget did acknowledge this in his later years. This has led to a later model of the Piagetian teacher as one who sets up an appropriate learning environment for the pupils to learn but who also does some direct teaching when that is appropriate.

The theory of learning

We learn by a process of adjustment to the environment. Piaget's model is a highly biological one. He was influenced by Darwin's notion of the survival of the fittest. As Piaget himself wrote (1952):

> Intelligence is an adaptation. In order to grasp its relation to life in general it is therefore necessary to state precisely the relations that exist between the organism and the environment. Life is a continuous creation of increasingly complex forms and a progressive balancing of these forms with the environment. To say that intelligence is a particular instance of biological adaptation is thus to suppose that it is essentially an organization and that its function is to structure the universe just as the organism structures its immediate environment.

There are two basic alternative mechanisms to the process: *accommodation* and *assimilation*, which are balanced by the process of *equilibration*. Accommodation is the child's ability to adapt to the environment. The environment makes demands on the child. He must change himself to cope with them. If there is an object in the way of a toy railway line, the child finds a solution that enables him to remove it.

Assimilation is the child's ability to change the environment to suit his imagination. The child has an idea of what he wants and modifies the environment to achieve this. The child may do this mentally, e.g. Duncan (4 y. 1 m.) pretends a straw is a magic wand. Or it may be the child actually changing the environment physically, e.g. by digging up the garden in order to make a castle. In non-jargon this is called play. Assimilation and play are closely related concepts. Toddlers love to play and assimilation is a psychological mechanism for explaining this. In imaginative play the child transforms objects to fit his own imagination. Duncan (4 y. 7 m.) builds a lovely castle out of sand in the sandpit.

Assimilation involves transforming experience within the mind, whereas accommodation involves adjusting the mind to new experience. At any one stage, such as the preconceptual, accommodation or assimilation dominates for a while and is then supplanted by the other. Eventually an *equilibrium* is reached for that stage by the process of *equilibration*. The child is operating at full efficiency for that stage.

An equilibrium can be visual or intellectual. An equilibrium has the characteristics of being mobile and stable, both in space and time. For example, equilibria for classification ranged from a baby looking for toys in his cot to an adolescent classifying animals. The classes of animals (such as mammals, birds, etc.) help to bring intellectual stability to the adolescent's mind. Equilibration is the ability of the child to organize and regulate. This very important function of self-regulating on the part of the child allows him to compensate actively in response to external stimuli. The adjustment is either retroactive (a loop system or feedback) or anticipatory (a set of compensations).

All commentators agree there are three fundamental aspects to Piaget's theory: internal maturation, responses to the environment and logico-mathematical thought. According to Phillips (1981), equilibration integrates logico-mathematical experiences with the other two. For these reasons, Ginsburg and Opper (1969) see equilibration as the backbone of mental growth. It should be stressed that Piaget's theory regards learning as the exact opposite of a sponge soaking up water. It is more like eating food: absorbing the nutritious part and making this part of itself. This process of learning is the same, whatever stage the child is at and whatever the content of the lesson. Equilibration can be seen in information-processing (IP) terms (see Chapter 9): providing a useful strategy for maximizing the gains of information and minimizing the losses.

In preconceptual thinking, it is assimilation that dominates as the toddler uses his rich imagination on his environment. Most objects are endowed with magical qualities. A rod becomes a witch's broomstick. However, at the same time he also needs to come to terms with the actual physical world around him. So accommodation takes over as the dominant mechanism. The rod is seen as a stick to use in the garden. Thus an equilibrium is reached for the pre-operational stage, which gives the child a working grasp of the world around him without depriving him of imaginative play. Thinking at this substage is now at its most effective.

This equilibrium does not last long. In the unstable process of cognitive growth to maturity, it is soon upset by some new event. A good example of this comes one substage later when the intuitive thinker realizes that apparent changes are not always real changes. The child escapes from dominance of perception. Cutting up a piece of material in order to sew it does not change it irreversibly. The pieces can be joined up again to make the initial piece. The child understands that changes are reversible. This signals the start of concrete operational thinking.

In the example of the attainment of conservation of quantity, Piaget rolled out a lump of Plasticene into a sausage in front of a child. The child accommodates to the changing shape of the Plasticene. It is accommodation that dominates the process of equilibration in concrete operational thinking. The process of assimilation, accommodation and equilibration is repeated successively at each higher stage of learning, until mature adult thought is achieved.

The trigger for the moving out of the equilibrium of the previous stage and the beginning of the new one may be an internal event, such as the onset of puberty, or an external event such as his first word. An alternative process Piaget proposed was one of an action and counteraction. He saw the process as follows:

1. A disturbance to the previous equilibrium, which motivates the child towards new actions.
2. Regulation − the modification of a particular bit of behaviour.
3. Compensation − whereby the child performs an opposite action to cancel out the effect of the first one.
4. Equilibration − whereby the conflict between (2) and (3) is resolved and thinking again reaches a stable state.

Another Piagetian concept of central importance is that of a *schema*. This means a concept but it also has a unique meaning, closely bound up with the theory of learning outlined above. For each schema the same pattern follows: assimilation followed by accommodation (or vice versa), leading to an equilibrium for that schema at that stage. Then a new experience (or internal awakening) upsets the equilibrium and the schema must adjust all over again. However, as a result of being thrust into a new stage, the schema becomes more mature, more useful and better adjusted to the environment the child is living in.

For example, a baby accommodates to the shape of a rattle and assimilates by trying to impose his wishes on it. He may want to rattle it against the bars of his cot. He reaches an equilibrium for the sensorimotor period when he is using the rattle successfully (accommodation) in a way that is stimulating to him (assimilation). The assimilation appeals to his sense of play and fun.

However, once he is capable of learning language, the process of learning starts all over again at the pre-operational stage. He has to accommodate to the word 'rattle'. He may use assimilation to shake the rattle as a musical instrument together with other toddlers in an improvised band. By these two means he achieves a new equilibrium for this schema at the higher stage. In the case of a rattle, the process may end there. But with more abstract schemas, the process will continue through the higher stages up to formal operations.

Of course, a child does not have just one schema but sets of schemas (schemata is the alternative plural) termed *schemes*. He needs one for every notion he needs to adjust to or he has thought of himself. These schemes cover a whole broad area, such as making music, ranges of sounds or ranges of timbres.

A child's schemas are constantly helping him to adjust to his environment by changing it. A toddler does not like the potty in his room, so he uses assimilation to imagine it as a pool. When schemas have to be modified, accommodation is used. This may take the form of trying out possibilities, asking questions or trying new combinations. A child of 6 at the intuitive substage, according to Sutherland (1980), describes clouds as 'fluffy'. But when he is rained on this schema has to be modified to include the notion of dampness in it.

The processes outlined here are an indication of Piaget's lifelong interest in the problem of epistemology: the study of how knowledge is acquired. This underlies his whole contribution to cognitive development.

Summary

The stage theory of cognitive development consists of three periods: sensorimotor activity, pre-operational thinking and operational thinking. Within the latter is an important distinction between concrete and formal (abstract) operations. A child has to follow the stages and periods in sequence without skipping any one. The theory of learning involves two complementary mechanisms of accommodation and acceleration. Each dominates alternately until an equilibrium is reached for that stage. Schemas are Piaget's term for concepts. A schema evolves along the same lines as above. A child will at any age have a set of schemas that help him to cope adequately with his environment.

Questions for discussion

1. What sensorimotor activities can the schoolteacher (primary or secondary) encourage her pupils to use?
2. What is the relevance of concrete operational thinking in her pupils to:

(a) the primary teacher;
(b) the secondary teacher?

3. How can a secondary teacher adequately teach a class of mixed stages, i.e. intuitive, concrete operational and formal operational?
4. How does Piaget's stage-development theory fit in the field of psychology?
5. Does Piaget's theory of learning apply to your subject? If so, how?
6. How does Piaget's theory compare to others in the field of learning psychology?

Further reading

For a straightforward outline, see Beard, R. (1969) *Piaget's Stages of Development*, Routledge & Kegan Paul, London, or Elkind, D. (1976) *Child Development and Education: A Piagetian Perspective*, Oxford University Press. For a substantial heavy-weight outline, see Flavell, J. H. (1963) *The Developmental Psychology of Jean Piaget*, Van Nostrand Reinhold, New York, NY.

3
THE ROLE OF LANGUAGE

Language is probably the most vital aspect of cognitive development. It is the basis for most communication between a child and the important adults in his life, and with other children. It is the chief means of education during the school years.

The relationship between language and thought

The relationship between language and thought is indeed a fascinating one. Does thinking determine language possibilities or does language determine thought? Or is there a more interactive relationship between the two? Here a spectrum of viewpoints will be outlined, starting with the primacy of language and moving across to the opposite pole, the primacy of thought.

The Primacy of Language

Benjamin Whorf (1956) is one of the best-known exponents of the linguistic relativity view. At its strongest, this view argues that the language a person hears at home decides what thoughts are possible to that person. The person cannot escape from it into any other way of perceiving the world. The weaker view of linguistic relativity argues that the language(s) influence the thoughts of that person.

Whorf's fieldwork was done on such groups as Inuits (Eskimos) and North American Indians (mainly Hopi). For Inuits, the varieties of snow are of great importance for hunting and survival, etc. They have many more words for types of snow than English and therefore a much finer classification. They can hence think 'thoughts' English speakers cannot. Their language adapted itself to this by 'creating' the appropriate words.

Local dialects may have unique words that give speakers access to thoughts others do not have. The Scots have the word 'dreich' to cover the cold, drizzly, depressing weather so common in Scotland. Likewise, children may have words in their peer-group language that give them thoughts private to themselves and inaccessible to adults, unless the adults make a study of this language – an excellent idea for teachers.

Although in many ways very different from the American anthropologist Whorf, the Austrian philosopher Wittgenstein (1961) argued a similar case: that the limits of one's language are the limits of one's world. In this version, a person's world view is determined by the language he or she has access to.

Language Predominates over Thinking

Luria, a Russian psychologist, also believed in the supremacy of language, although he had less extreme views than Whorf. In a famous study with Yudovich (1971), a pair of identical twin boys was referred to him. They were 5 years old but were found to be incapable of coping with their first year of schooling. They had been left on their own for most of the preceding years. No adult or other child had interacted with them, although their mother could give a seemingly accurate account of their development. She seems, however, to have cared for them physically quite adequately. The twins' language had been behind from the age of 2, when other toddlers start making good progress. They had built up a language of their own, a restricted version of Russian, which was adequate for their needs. Since they were in each other's company so much, each could interpret the other's nonverbal communication – often without the need to verbalize. Even then a short utterance such as 'ball' would be sufficient for the other twin to interpret it as 'let's play football'. They had also developed a nonverbal language of gestures and expressions that aided their successful communication with each other. Their play was at as low a level as their speech. There was no evidence of any imagination being used. Little wooden bricks were never used for construction. Games consisted solely of the monotonous repetition of activities.

Luria devised a remedial programme whereby the less backward twin, Liosha, was put in an ordinary first-year class, but away from his brother. This forced him to make his meaning explicit, as neither the teacher nor his classmates understood the private language he and his brother had evolved. The more backward twin, Yura, was given a carefully devised remedial programme aimed at improving his grammar and forcing him to make his meaning public and thereby explicit.

After six months of this programme, the first twin, Liosha, had improved in his language use almost to the average level expected of the class. The second twin, Yura, had made even more spectacular progress and was now ahead of his brother. Both were then capable of thinking more efficiently, as was illustrated in their performance on nonverbal intelligence tests. Naturally, there are important messages for teachers from this classic study. The need to encourage children to make their meaning explicit is one.

The early work of Basil Bernstein (1959) pointed towards children who are linguistically deprived being given access to the 'acceptable' language of that society. In the UK this is standard English. He termed 'acceptable' language the *elaborated* code and the local dialect as the *restricted* code.

To implement this policy of giving such children the opportunity to learn standard English, we may look more to the health visitor or social worker rather than to the teacher. They have access to the home and can try to influence parents to provide standard English in some form even if this is in addition to the local dialect. In other societies, such as Germany, children learn both the local dialect and the formal code (high German). The dialect is used for everyday conversation and the formal code on such occasions as school lessons.

Language and Thought Aid each other's Development

In his important book, *Thought and Language* (1986), Vygotsky analysed the relationship between language and cognition ontogenetically: he considered the development of a baby from birth through the early years of childhood. As can be seen from Figure 3.1, he looked at babies during their first 18 months and distinguished noncognitive language in the form of cooing and crying. This served an emotional and social function in building bonds between the parents and the baby. Simultaneously there is nonlinguistic thought of the type Piaget outlined in his sensorimotor activity (see Chapter 2), such as using a rake to reach another toy. When these two developmental patterns coincide on the acquisition of the first word, there is an explosion of progress. For each new word a child hears, he wants to know the meaning of it. For each new experience (perhaps going to the zoo) or object encountered (for example, a star), the toddler wants to know the naming word: 'What's this called, Daddy?' Each strand helps the other.

Language acts as the so-called *second signalling system*. Pavlov regarded conditioning as the first signalling system. However, language is so much more powerful than conditioning in the way in which it shapes thinking.

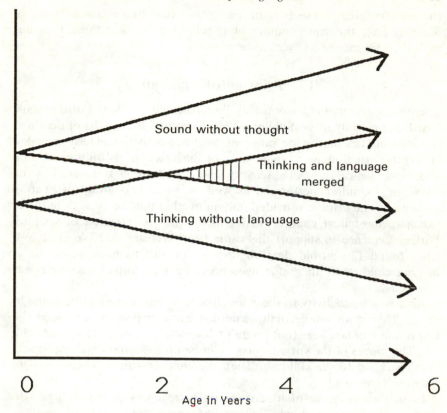

Figure 3.1   Vygotsky's model of the fusion of language and thought

By implication, the culture in which the language is saturated will shape the thinking.

The Development of Thought Predominates over that of Language

Piaget (1953) himself made the initial contribution to this as with so many other topics. In his early work (coming from his biological background), he argued that it is in thinking that children progress. Language follows behind, providing a means of encapsulating the 'pure' thought in symbolic form. Just as a child's body's growth determines what size and shape of clothes he needs, so a child's thinking determines the language he needs. For instance, a child makes the breakthrough into operational thinking in the conservation of number: he can grasp that two different piles of Smarties have the same number of sweets in them. The thought comes first, then the necessary word, 'same'.

The Primacy of Thought

The primacy of thought was forcefully advocated by Hans Furth (1966), based on his study of deaf children. He compared the results of deaf and hearing children on a wide range of cognitive activities. These included symmetry, visual memory span, tests of Piaget's conservation of volume and mass, logical symbol discovery and classification transfer. On the whole deaf children performed as well as a matched group of hearing children on these tests, provided only nonverbal thinking was tested. For example, most deaf children had grasped the conservation of volume. Further evidence to support this came from Webster and Wood (1989). They found 12-year-old deaf children to be just as good at maths as hearing children of the same age, provided no complex language was involved.

An analogous activity to the nonverbal tests Furth used is the game of chess. This is an intellectually complex game that does not need the involvement of language (not even sign language) − except to say 'Check', etc. The moves of the various pieces can be taught separately by physical demonstration to the children. Then the children can be encouraged to play the game itself.

From this spectrum of ideas it is up to teachers or psychologists to make up their own minds which viewpoint they accept. This is a potentially rich area for discussion, and some questions are offered at the end of the chapter. The decision for a primary teacher has important implications. If she supports the primacy of language, or that language predominates over thinking, she will be giving a great deal of emphasis to language as such. New words will be introduced to try to improve children's vocabulary. If she supports the concept that the development of thought predominates over that of language, or the primacy of thought, she will be putting the emphasis on physical activities to stimulate nonverbal thinking. LOGO programs might be devised, following the ideas of Papert (1980) (as discussed in Chapter 9). If she supports the idea that language and thought aid each other's development, she will compromise between the two extremes. Language will be used to stimulate nonverbal activities. A few key words may cue new thinking. In teaching science, advice on how to use a microscope may increase the pupil's manipulatory skill. Likewise, physical activities will prompt language development. A trip along a nature trail may elicit a number of new names of plants and animals. The expression of these experiences in either oral or written form increases language capacity.

The acquisition of the home language

Another major language topic of interest to teachers and psychologists is how language is first learnt by a young child. A massive amount of research has been done in this field over the past three decades. An attempt will be made to summarize some of it here.

A number of theories have been put forward. The American behaviourist Skinner (1957) was one of the pioneers. His theory is based on the mechanism of operant conditioning. This involves the baby being conditioned by the parent. The baby operates on the environment around him. The parent has to wait for the baby to make a sound that, to her ears, vaguely approximates to a word in her language. For instance, the baby may be near a ball and purely accidentally make a sound 'baw'. The parent immediately rewards this response strongly with praise and smiles. The baby is then more likely to reproduce that sound (or preword) again. The parent should now only reward a response that is near to the goal word. Finally, only the correct word, 'ball', is rewarded. The baby's utterances have been shaped by a programme of discriminatory rewarding (or 'reinforcement', in the jargon of psychology).

A number of important points need to be made about Skinner's account. First, it depends totally on the external rewarder in the environment, i.e. motivation is extrinsic. Second, it depends on the baby's arbitrary production of a sound suitable to be shaped. There is nothing the parent can do to get the baby to produce the initial sound. She just has to wait for it to occur and then make the most of the opportunity by maximizing the rewarding process. Third, the actual process of shaping for any one word may be long drawn out.

Noam Chomsky (1959) mounted a critique of Skinner's account in much more fundamental terms. Chomsky pointed out that Skinner was at best only explaining the acquisition of the first few words (largely nouns), but not how they are combined together. It is the learning of the rules of grammar that is the really incredible feat for a child of about 2 years. As any adult who has tried to learn a foreign language knows, the intellectual demands of learning the rules of grammar are immense. These demands are certainly far greater than 2-year-olds are capable of in other areas. Chomsky offered a nativist explanation for this in terms of the language acquisition device (LAD). According to this, a child has an innate ability to learn the rules of grammar informally, provided he is exposed to an oral language environment. He will learn that particular language, even if he is genetically of another racial stock. For instance, a Tibetan baby adopted at birth by British parents will learn English and not Tibetan. This process occurs unconsciously and (in stark contrast to Skinner's account) no deliberate teaching by the parent is necessary. (There is a more general discussion of the nativist position in Chapter 9.) The child has only to be present physically in a language environment, such as parents chatting at the tea table or the sound from a TV programme.

If Chomsky's account is accepted, a number of implications for society arise. What happens if this process of exposure to a language environment does *not* occur? It needs to happen at the critical period from around 2 years. In most families the child hears the language of adults and siblings. In many families the child probably hears more language on television than in real life. However, there are many one-parent families with just one child, and there is then no conversation to overhear (except when other family or friends visit). These cases of language deprivation need to be diagnosed by social workers and remedial programmes of some kind offered. Otherwise primary teachers may have to deal with the sort of language problems Luria and Yudovich (1971) drew attention to. Chomsky's interpretation has been challenged from a metacognitive perspective by Karmiloff-Smith (1986) (as outlined in Chapter 9).

Chomsky's account has in its turn been followed by research into the precursors of oral language. Schaffer's (1971) work on the relationship between mother and baby underpinned many of the subsequent language studies. He pointed out that from a very early age, baby and mother establish a means of communication that does not depend on oral language. He stressed it is the baby who takes the initiative. The baby draws the mother's attention to something and the mother then responds to him. Butterworth (personal communication) denies this is always so: the baby sometimes follows the mother's gaze.

Schaffer (1989) stressed it is the quality and not the quantity of the interaction that is important. It is not the time the mother and baby spend together that aids language development. The important point is that the baby should have the opportunity to initiate at least some of their joint activities. The baby must have the opportunity to take the leader role in the dyad (two-person group). The mother should be sensitive to what the baby is trying to communicate. A mother who is insensitive to the baby's needs, and always wishes to initiate the activity herself, may end up with an insecure baby. In any event, such a mother-initiated pattern leads to low-quality language development.

Bruner (1986) is one of the many psychologists who have pursued this line. As he is also an educationist, we shall concentrate on his account. Bruner diagnosed further the actual mechanisms by which the process of nonverbal communication works. Pointing is one of the baby's main means of catching the parent's attention. Typically he may point to a video he wants to see. The parent enters into a 'dialogue' with him and probably shows it to him. Eye gaze is a more subtle means of communication. The baby looks at a toy he desires; the parent tries to follow his line of regard. The two of them then develop a joint focus on the toy. A sensitive mother who realizes what the baby wants will then give the toy to him. Not all the interactions need to have the baby in such a selfish role. Activity may revolve around having fun, smiling at each other or such reciprocal games as peekaboo. Through all these means the baby is learning how to communicate reciprocally with an adult before the first word is learnt. Later oral communication is then built up on a strong foundation of taking turns. (A more general discussion of Bruner's views is given in Chapter 6.) If the baby does not experience this pattern of warm interaction with his mother, there may be disastrous consequences for the baby's later language performance. This was shown by Bowlby (1953), although his work has been much criticized and modified.

Even if only some of these various powerful approaches are accepted, it is clear that very important experiences for the child take place before he starts formal schooling. Some children start with superior experiences because of the superior quality of their mothering. By implication those children whose maternal interactions have been of low quality will be problems to their teachers and schools. Considerable resources are devoted to learning-support teachers, to try to raise these children to average competency in their home language.

Besides the various theories that have attempted to explain the acquisition of language, factual empirical data have accumulated. These point to a consensually agreed pattern of stages for the development of oral speech. This starts with Skinner's first word and finishes with 'correct' speech. During the *one-word-sentence* phase the baby can use a word to convey a multitude of different meanings. 'Ball' can mean 'Give me that ball' or 'Let's play ball' or 'I'm looking at the ball'. During the *two-word-sentence* phase there is a simple grammar. The first word is the pivot and the second the open. The pivot can be coupled with a large number of opens to give the sentence different meanings, e.g. 'Allgone sweeties', 'Allgone drinkies' or 'Allgone cream' (meaning ice-cream).

The two-word sentence gives way by a process of expansion to *telegramese*. Children now use an abbreviated form of English grammar, eliminating articles and other lesser features. Malcolm (2 y. 6 m.) says 'Me go shop'. Parents and preschool teachers may respond to the child's sentence with a full English sentence: 'I want to go to the shop.' This acts as a model for the child. He may then try to improve his effort to a sentence closer to that of the adult.

By the time he starts school the 'normal' child will have mastered the hearing and speaking of the home language in a simple version of the adult form. This is an amazing intellectual achievement.

Reading

Once a child starts formal schooling, reading becomes the most important cognitive challenge. Wells (1987) has indicated the importance of parents reading to children at home as a vital preparation to this. This is most effective when the parent does three things: elaborates on the text; refers to the child's own experiences; and interrupts the reading to ask questions. Television might be seen by some as a substitute in view of its considerable story-telling ability, but Wells points to the lack of just these three qualities.

The experience of being entranced by a story can act as a bridge to the decontextualization needed by reading. In other words, the child so wants to follow the printed story he has a strong motivation to overcome the problems of the abstract nature of the letters. They are just arbitrary shapes. Each letter, such as 'a', is encountered by the child in a wide variety of circumstances: on the American TV programme, *Sesame Street*, on a corn-flakes packet or in *Topsy and Tim Go to the Park*. He has to abstract that shape from the various surroundings and to realize it is the same letter. Margaret Donaldson (Chapter 7) calls this *disembedding*. When the child has done this with all 26 letters (and learnt how to utter them phonically), he can decode words into stories.

Since the teaching of reading is a major issue in the UK at the moment, the psychological input is now of renewed importance. Two of the main alternative methods of teaching reading, *look-and-say* and *phonics*, have been supported by different groups of psychologists.

In look-and-say the child starts by reading whole words. He then reads sentences, gaining insight into the meaning from the context, pictures, etc. In other words, the semantic element is emphasized. Children learn the meaning first. This approach finds theoretical psychological support from Goodman and Goodman (1979). They argue for a top-down approach. Children start with the meaning of a sentence such as 'The cat sat on the mat'. Only when this process has been fairly successfully achieved does the teacher try to help children recognize the actual letters that make up the words of the sentence, such as 'c', 'a' and 't' for 'cat'.

On the other hand, Bryant and Bradley (1985) stress the need for phonological skills to be developed. They do not, however, support the old-fashioned phonic-drill approach. Rather they advise exposing children to rhyming and to common spelling patterns. On the basis of his empirical work done with Bradley (1985) and Goswami (1990), Bryant regards these rhymes and patterns as of considerable help in the development of young children's reading. Their bottom-up approach means that children are taught to translate the individual letters of the alphabet into sounds (the grapheme—phoneme correspondence). They then have the bricks (i.e. the skill of recognizing letters) with which to construct the buildings (i.e. the words).

Bryant and Goswami (1990) argue that attempting to match groups of poor and good readers on a basis of either age or reading level is not a scientifically successful strategy. This is because the direction of causality cannot be worked out from the results. Does being at a low reading level cause the child to be a poor reader or does being a poor reader cause the child's reading level to be low? In their review of the state of research, they suggest that researchers should concentrate instead on longitudinal studies of the same children's patterns of progress (or failure to progress) in reading. This is the most hopeful methodology for scientifically valid research for the future. However, it would be some time before any useful results were obtained. At present Bryant and his colleagues are concentrating their research efforts on the skills children bring to school at the age of 4 or 5. These are regarded as being very important precursors of reading skill. When these have been worked out in detail, it will presumably be up to nursery school teachers, playgroup leaders, health visitors and parents to encourage the development of these skills. (There is a more general discussion of Bryant's views in Chapter 7.)

Besides the two methods of teaching reading already mentioned, there is also the *real-books* method advocated by Frank Smith (1978). He argues that a young child reads best in the same way as a literate adult: in the first place he wants to choose a book that interests him. Then he will pick up the meaning of the words he doesn't know from the context and the pictures. The child is learning whole words. Hence the real-books method does utilize look-and-say, but the child rather than the teacher decides which words to learn. The metacognitive movement believes it is productive to make children aware of their own learning while they are learning to read (this point is discussed further in Chapter 9).

The field of cognitive developmental investigation of reading is a specialist one only touched on in this book. There is concern at present about the apparently alarming proportion of 7-year-olds who haven't yet learnt to read. National testing figures on less able 16-year-old school-leavers may reveal even more distressing figures on their inability to read, if informal reports from employers are any guide. What can be done to help the poor reader? First, he (and it is more likely to be a he rather than a she) needs to be identified (or screened) as early as possible. Second, the nature of his learning difficulties needs to be diagnosed. Third, such children need to be brought under the provision of special educational needs as soon as possible. Ideally they should then be given extensive and high-quality teaching. How this is to be resourced is a critical political issue. Free resources by way of adults (mainly mothers) helping to hear children read are available. However, such children really need expert learning-support teachers.

For problem readers, the extralinguistic factors become even more important than they are for good readers. Thus children should be allowed to feel the shapes of letters. Colour should be used as much as possible: different colours for different shapes. An even higher proportion of coloured pictures should be included on reading pages to motivate children to follow stories.

All this implies extra resources. These could take the form of new course material such as videotapes. These have already been used in Western Australia without any formal evaluation as yet, according to Grieve (personal communication). Margaret Donaldson's insights into the difficulties of reading are included under Chapter 7.

Other aspects of language

There are many other aspects of language that relate to cognitive development. One is gender differences. Developmentalists have long noted that, in general, girls are superior to boys at any age. Developmentalists hold that two different modes of using language exist: a more aggressive male and a more refined female mode, and that girls and boys should be exposed to both. This is discussed by Frazier and Sadker (1973).

In this chapter we have had to limit coverage to the preschool and early primary years. Whichever of the theoretical viewpoints the reader supports, the quality of a child's preschool language environment seems to emerge as vital. So too does the quality of the teaching of reading in the early years at school. (There is, however, a separate discussion of the role of the secondary-school English teacher in Chapter 16.)

Summary

Which dominates cognitive development, language or thinking? A spectrum of viewpoints is offered. When language is studied by itself, a number of theoretical views are offered to the question, How do children acquire language? Some children fail to do this adequately and we suggest some implications for teachers. How does a child learn his home language? Is it by operant conditioning, LAD or adequate prelanguage interaction with a parent?

There are two main ways of teaching reading: look-and-say and phonics, each supported by a psychological theory. As a preliminary to this, stimulating story sessions from a parent seem vital.

Questions for discussion

1. Which of the five views on the relationship between language and thought do you agree with? Why?
2. What are the implications of each for teachers?
3. What can society do to help children from backgrounds where the quality of the mother—baby interaction was low to learn to speak their home language sufficiently well to cope with the first year of primary school?
4. What can schools do to help such children if they are seriously behind the remainder of the class in language?
5. Is TV a benefit or a hindrance to children's language development?
6. How important is preschooling for language development?
7. Which is the best way to teach reading?

Further reading

Bruner, J. (1986) *Actual Minds, Possible Worlds*, Harvard University Press, Cambridge, Mass. (Chap. 5).

Fletcher, P. and Gorman, M. (1986) *Language Acquisition*, Cambridge University Press.

Greene, J. (1975) *Language: A Cognitive Approach*, Open University Press, Milton Keynes.

Smith, F. (1978) *Reading*, Plenum Press, New York, NY.

4
VYGOTSKY AND THE VYGOTSKYANS

Vygotsky himself

Vygotsky (1986) was one of the first major figures to respond critically to Piaget's ideas. During the decade 1924–34 he outlined what some consider to be the most powerful alternative to Piaget's ideas. His ideas were only published after Stalin's death in the Soviet Union, and some time later in the English-speaking world. At that time, during the 1950s and 1960s, he was a powerful influence, not least on Bruner. His star waned relatively during the 1970s and early 1980s. However, his ideas are now once again a major force in cognitive development. They provide a significant theoretical input into the influential social-interactive perspective, which argues that a child's intellectual development cannot be considered in a social vacuum.

Mugny, De Paolis and Carugati (1984) have done much research from this perspective. The child's classmates, friends and parents must be taken into account if a realistic picture is to be painted. Cognitive development takes place as a result of mutual interaction between the child and those people with whom he has regular social contact.

In addition, both the information-processing (IP) and metacognition movements (outlined in Chapter 9) might consider Vygotsky their founding father. IP is concerned with the factors involved in learning and how performance in these can be maximized. One such factor is memory, which Vygotsky saw as equivalent to tying knots in hankies or building monuments to a revered figure. Metacognition is concerned with the child's conscious control of his learning, which Vygotsky regarded as a desirable goal. However, Vygotsky held that unconscious learning precedes conscious control, for example, in the development of linguistic skills in a 2-year-old.

However, during his short career, Vygotsky put his energies into analysing the overall process of education rather than concentrating on empirical studies. Unlike Piaget, he did not himself manage to follow up the empirical implications of his own ideas. Instead Vygotsky attempted to synthesize all the factors affecting the transmission of knowledge. Yet despite this very theoretical approach his work has great import for teachers. (He worked for a while at a teacher-education college, although he never taught in a school.)

In contrast with the current (Piaget-influenced) ideology that advocates an enabling role for teachers, Vygotsky sees teachers occupying a didactic role. This is shown by his definition of intelligence as the capacity to learn *from instruction*. This implies a teacher should guide her pupils in paying attention, concentrating and learning effectively. A teacher will hereby scaffold a pupil to competence in any skill. Whereas Piaget focused on the child, Vygotsky focused on the teacher. In many ways the original debate in the 1930s between these two giants of educational cognitive development encapsulates the main alternative views psychologists offer teachers today: the progressive and the traditional. Until the 1960s the teacher-centred view prevailed in British education. Then the Piagetian revolution led to a switch to child-centredness for the education of younger children.

With the introduction of the National Curriculum and national testing, the government has put the emphasis back on the teacher. Vygotsky does *not*, however, advocate mechanical formal teaching where children go through the motions of sitting at desks and passing exams that are meaningless to them. This is what some educators have termed 'disaster studies'. On the contrary, Vygotsky stressed intellectual development rather than procedural learning.

Unlike the behaviourists (outlined in Chapter 5), he did not believe in the teacher operating a rigid control over exactly what the child learns. Like Piaget and most of the progressive theorists considered in this book, however, Vygotsky saw *activity* by the children as central to education, and the teacher as having much more control over this activity. He advocated pupils learning directly from the teacher. His alternative is worth bearing in mind at a time when resource-based learning has become the norm in most secondary subjects.

Compared to both the Piagetians and the constructivists, Vygotsky was far more of an interventionist in his view of the teacher's role. The teacher should extend and challenge the child to go beyond where he would otherwise have been. This is encapsulated in one of Vygotsky's key phrases: *the zone of proximal development*. As illustrated in Figure 4.1, a child, Mary, is at present at level x. However, she has the potential (innately/environmentally derived) to reach level $x + 1$. The area in

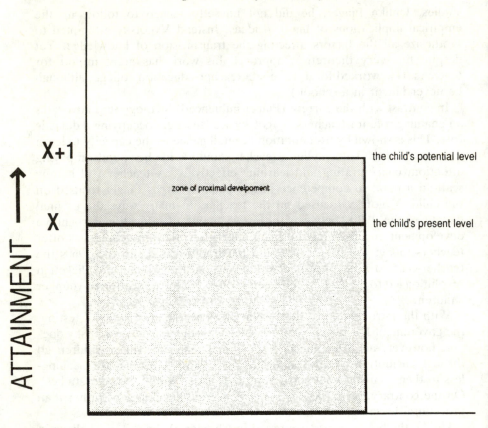

Figure 4.1   Vygotsky's zone of proximal development

between is the zone of proximal development. It is the teacher's duty to try to achieve $x + 1$ for each pupil in her class. Perhaps she can give a pupil just the cue he needs. It may be just one particular step that gives a particular child the breakthrough he needs, or the teacher may take the class through a series of steps, which help them to solve the problem. On this point Vygotsky was a powerful influence on Bruner.

✳ Children of approximately the same ability may differ in the areas (or sizes) of their zones of proximal development. A child with a large zone will have a much greater capacity to be helped by teachers than a child with a narrow zone. However, the teacher still has a duty to help the latter child.

It was the work with twins conducted by Luria and Yudovich (1971) (outlined briefly in Chapter 3) that led Vygotsky to the conclusion that different children have varying capacities for development of their potentials. However, they need teachers in order to do so. The school years are the optimum ones for instruction, which requires awareness and deliberate control on the part of the pupil. The school has a special value in offering disciplined thinking. Hence Vygotsky believed grammar should be taught at school. This conflicts with the progressive, Piaget-influenced ideology of the past two decades in Britain. During this time the formal study of grammar has been largely dropped. However, this is under review in the aftermath of the Kingman Report (1986).

Vygotsky believed the relationship between instruction and internal learning to be exceedingly complex. This contrasts with the simplistic model of the behaviourists, the other main psychological school supporting a more formal, teacher-centred approach. The co-operative relationship between the teacher and the child is all important. It is up to the teacher who accepts the Vygotskyan view to build up her professional relationship with her pupils as an intelligent instructor of their learning.

The relationships of a child with others in the class are also important. This is something that has been largely ignored by Piaget and most of the other views considered in this book (with the exception of the constructivists). Vygotsky advocated using a more advanced child to help a less advanced child. For a long time this was used as a basis of egalitarian Marxist education in the Soviet Union. The socialist rationale was one of all children working for the general good rather than the capitalist one of each child trying to get out of school as much benefit as he can without putting anything back into it. The brighter child is helping society by helping the less able one, since the latter will (it is hoped) be more of an asset to society as a literate than as an illiterate adult. Vygotsky argued that this act is not necessarily one of self-sacrifice on the part of the more advanced child. By explaining to and helping the other child, he may well gain a greater explicit understanding of his own learning, on metacognitive lines (Chapter 9). And, by teaching a topic, he consolidates his own learning.

Constructivists such as Skemp (1976) and Denvir (1985) also advocate the use of the peer group for teaching. Secondary teachers could consider using this strategy at a time when they are having to learn to cope with mixed-ability teaching. The class can be broken into small groups of mixed ability, with the more able pupils in a substitute teacher role.

Vygotsky also focused on the individual child and how he learns to think. This is done by a process of *internalizing* external and social activities and making them part of his own mental structures. This happens in three stages:

1. Assistance is provided by more capable others, e.g. teacher, more able peer.
2. Assistance is provided by the child himself by talking aloud in order to solve problems.
3. Internalization of the concept.

Thus either a teacher or a peer is required. A process of inner dialogue takes place to accompany the internalization: a child talks silently to himself as he works something out. In a similar manner to current meta-cognitive ideas, the child hereby learns about the task and about his own learning. Vygotsky's concept of internalization is a similar one to Piaget's but with an added sociocultural dimension. This follows from the broad context in which Vygotsky saw learning taking place: the culture is transmitted from one generation to the next by means of the education of children. This means that, at an individual level, a child becomes himself through others.

Vygotsky also made an enormous contribution to our understanding of language development (his ideas on its relationship to thinking are summarized in Chapter 3). Here again he was a pioneer metacognitivist, advocating that by talking to others a child develops awareness of the communicative functions of language. Language plays a vital role in the evolution of concepts. Mature concepts only evolve after a child goes through three preliminary stages:

1. The *vague syncretic* stage, when the child depends mainly on trial-and-error actions.
2. The *complexes* stage, when the child uses a variety of more or less appropriate strategies, but fails to identify the required attributes.
3. The *potential concept* stage when the child can deal with one aspect of an object at a time but cannot cope with more than one aspect simultaneously.

These stages arose out of one of Vygotsky's rare empirical studies where he showed blocks of varying height and shape to young children. On the underside of each block was a nonsense syllable, which the child could use to help him categorize it, e.g. 'zat' could stand for 'tall and square'. At a primitive level, this showed how concepts can be mediated by verbal means. As with Piaget's stages, a child has to pass through Vygotsky's stages systematically, without missing one out. Like Piaget (but unlike the IP and domain-specific viewpoints), Vygotsky believed that qualitative changes do occur.

In many ways Vygotsky was some decades before his time. Perhaps this is the reason for the current revival of interest in his ideas. One of these ways was in distinguishing scientific from spontaneous concepts. Spontaneous concepts are those that arise from a child's own observations — generally at home or at least outside school. Scientific concepts are those that arise from formal teaching. It is just these scientific concepts adolescents are expected to use in GCSE, A-level and other formal examinations. His distinction between the two types of concepts is very similar to that made nowadays by the constructivists (Chapter 8). They see informal concepts and strategies coming from the home, while 'academic' concepts and formal strategies are encountered (mainly) at school. The two meet each other in the classroom: the rich but disorganized spontaneous concepts of the child meet the systematic and logical approach of the adult (teacher).

This phenomenon can also be conceptualized in terms of the zone of proximal development (Figure 4.1). The child's existing concepts are at level x; the required formal understanding is at level $x + 1$. It is the teacher's job to try to move the child's understanding from x to $x + 1$. This phenomenon can also be personalized: the child's mind meeting the teacher's mind. The teacher sets up the adult pattern of thinking the child has to try to aspire to. Ideally, a fruitful interaction and dialogue is set up that ultimately leads to the adult conceptualization being internalized by the child.

Vygotsky was also before his time in the attention he gave to semiotics: the signalling function of language. He argued that gestures have an important role in development. This has been revived by psycholinguists unravelling the origins of the development of language in a child. As outlined in Chapter 3, such workers as Bruner saw gesture language as having an enormous impact on the later development of sound language.

Hickman (1985) evolved an interesting application of Vygotsky's ideas for primary teachers. This involves showing a child a short film or video and then asking him to tell an adult about it. Alternatively a child can be presented with a sequence of pictures (like a cartoon strip) and asked to tell an adult the story. (If their school is lacking in audio-visual facilities, pictures may be easier for most primary teachers to organize.) Hickman argues that this exercise helps a child to develop his own language by describing the story to an adult. According to the Vygotskyan paradigm, learning how to read involves the child interacting with the text. He must not simply read mechanically but try to interpret the text. As with other intellectual skills, the child gradually internalizes the process. Skilled self-regulation plays an important role in achieving this.

Although both Vygotsky and Piaget were both developmentalists (unlike the information processers and many other current approaches), they differed profoundly in their conceptions of that development. Although both were fundamentally interested in the whole sweep of mental growth from babyhood to adulthood, Piaget's biological concept of development as a matter of maturation and unfolding was an anathema to Vygotsky. Vygotsky regarded a child's adaptation as much more active and much less deterministic. Vygotsky put much less emphasis on biological inheritance and much more on culture, as did Bruner (Chapter 6). A particular culture consists of its oral language, books, pictures, tools, etc. Since Vygotsky's day many of these elements have been combined simultaneously in the form of TV. Surely he would have considered TV to be an immensely powerful educational medium, if used constructively?

In the process of becoming socialized into their culture, children learn to understand things that are common features of their social experience, for example, the myths, fairy tales, songs and history. Tools are an extremely important part of a culture. A child needs to gain an understanding of such vital tools of our culture as pencils, rubbers and books.

The importance of context is another key Vygotskyan notion that has been revived recently. (This has had a great influence on Donaldson in particular – see Chapter 7.) The context in which it takes place must be taken into account in order to understand a specific example of a particular child's behaviour. For instance, if the child is interpreting pictures in a book at home we need to look at the whole context of the reading situation. Is a parent helping? Is the TV a distraction? Are books common in the home? This specific context then needs to be seen within the overall culture. For most children this is one dominated by TV. Here Vygotsky has a powerful message for the information processers in particular: the total context in which information is exchanged and understood needs to be taken into account.

In view of all these brilliant different insights, it is not difficult to see why there is a considerable revival of Vygotskyan influence at the present time.

Present-day Vygotskyans

Should we therefore return to Vygotsky as our guru? Rudolph Schaffer (1971) is one who supports this proposition. In the present era the ideas of Vygotsky have been developed by Doise and Palmonari (1984). A child learns by collective construction, imitation of others, resolving opposites or the acquisition of a social heritage. This stress on the social heritage is part of the Vygotskyan influence. However, his is synthesized with several other influences: constructivist, metacognitive and sociological.

Some of these authors may consider themselves neo-Vygotskyans rather than unreconstructed Vygotskyans.

Intelligence is defined in terms of a child being able to adjust judgements to a social situation (as opposed to Piaget's definition: adjustment is purely to a physical situation). Intelligence develops by a child co-ordinating his own actions and judgements with those of others in situations characterized by sociocognitive conflict. In other words, there is a conflict between his own perspective and that he hears presented within the group. The child then needs to resolve this conflict.

Doise has been influenced by Bourdieu's (1980) genetic sociology with its emphasis on the internalization of society's structures. The individual absorbs the dominant concepts of his or her society. For instance, in Western society abstract thinking is highly admired, as Piaget illustrated in making it the pinnacle of his stages of thinking.

As socioconstructivists, Doise and Palmonari (1984) aim to co-ordinate various perspectives: Piaget's equilibration, Bourdieu's interiorization and Trevarthen's (1982) co-operative understanding (whereby a mother helps her baby to perceive objects). Doise and Palmonari have a spiral concept of development, analogous to Bruner's (Figure 6.1). Initially a child is at a particular state: *In*. He then interacts with other people in his social environment: *Sn* + 1. This results in a new individual state for the child: *In* + 1. By means of successive social interactions, cognitive development continues to proceed up the spiral. Doise and Palmonari try to maximize the interaction between the individual and the group. The individual takes part in various social conventions, such as discussions. He is influenced by these structures of society but in turn tries to modify them.

Mugny, De Paolis and Carugati (1984) changed Piaget's methodology from an experimental situation to a group one. The idea was to introduce a child to another's perspective. Is the child's own perspective then altered by this experience? If so, how? Mugny, De Paolis and Carugati found that the child may not always recognize the clash of perspectives. He may just recite both mechanically. When these authors focused on the nature of the social situations, there were some interesting findings. If the other person is an adult rather than another child, the child is even more likely to be influenced. However, when adults give (deliberately) incorrect solutions, it was found that children who defy adults are more likely to progress in post-tests than children who do not. The authors then applied the Vygotskyan message of the importance of context: they shifted the testing situation to the familiar context of school. This helped children to defy adults who gave incorrect answers. If the other people in a group are children, a child is more likely to be influenced by two others than by one other. So it seems that Asch's (1956) social-conformity effect is operating here.

If a particular child's concepts are poorly developed, he has a greater need to absorb the concepts presented in a social situation than a child with well-developed concepts. Those who have not built up adequate concepts at home will need the strongest direction from the teacher. If the social situation is a classroom, the teacher therefore needs to know what concepts the child has at the start of the lesson. This message is very similar to that of the constructivists (discussed in Chapter 8), but in an explicitly social setting.

Another finding of Doise and Palmonari (1984) is important for both teachers and psychologists: children demonstrate their cognitive attainments in some social situations, but not in others. A pupil might demonstrate what he knows to one teacher but not to another. A child might demonstrate his understanding in one situation but not in another — even with the same teacher.

As a result of meaning being shared, Schaffer (1989) saw *shared* understanding developing between a child and an adult. This process leads to the origins of intentionality (a child is able to decide to do something for himself) and self-consciousness.

Summary

Vygotsky advocated the value of direct teaching but with the child as an active learner. He recommended using the more advanced children in a class to help teach the less advanced ones. To help the individual child develop his own thinking, Vygotsky advised getting him to have inner dialogues with himself. A child evolves his own spontaneous concepts that later meet scientific concepts at school. This creates a zone of proximal development between his present level of understanding and his potential level. Vygotsky also analysed, on a broad intellectual front, the factors that led to successful learning. He deduced culture to be a crucial factor. This led him to focus on language. By talking to others, a child develops awareness of his own language.

Present-day neo-Vygotskyans, such as Doise, Mugny and Schaffer, tend to blend Vygotsky's stress on the social situation with other current influences, such as the child constructing his own concepts.

Questions for discussion

1. How can a teacher best exploit pupils' zones of proximal development?
2. Alternatively, how can a teacher fruitfully use the clash between a child's spontaneous concepts and the scientific concepts he is meant to learn at school?
3. Which concept of development do you agree with: Piaget's biological or Vygotsky's cultural one?
4. How can a child's oral language development best be stimulated?
5. Is Vygotsky's idea of peer teaching a valid method of solving the problems raised by mixed-ability teaching?
6. To what extent should teachers use his idea of direct instruction of the pupils?
7. From a Vygotskyan perspective is TV an admirable medium for teaching?

Further reading

Bruner, J. (1986) *Actual Minds, Possible Worlds*, Harvard University Press, Cambridge, Mass. (Chap. 5).
Moll, L. C. (ed.) *Vygotsky and Education*, Cambridge University Press.

5
THE BEHAVIOURIST REACTION

Piaget reacted against behaviourism so that, strictly speaking, it is inaccurate to include this prominent group as critics of Piaget. However, during the decades of Piaget's greatest prominence — during the 1960s and early 1970s — it was the behaviourists who disputed this prominence most powerfully. This battle raged particularly fiercely in the USA, where the behaviourists were the dominant force both within psychology and within education at the time when Piaget's influence started to be felt there.

How do children learn? Is the pattern linear, cumulative and additive (as the behaviourists argue) or are there qualitative breakthroughs (as the Piagetians allege)? By comparison with behaviourists, Piagetians are a progressive force. In other words they are child centred, emphasizing a child's own personal learning in terms of building up a rich store of concepts in all fields relevant to him, e.g. the animals around him, the physical causation of objects moving and the mathematical representation of these experiences by way of numbers. It did not matter whether his answers to a test were right or wrong as long as he was building up his understanding of the world around him.

In contrast, according to the behaviourists, children learn most efficiently when they are subjected to a linear programme of material devised by expert teachers and curriculum planners. A pupil is presented with a course to work through sequentially. Initially this consists of an easy point to learn. He is then asked a question to test whether he has mastered it or not. He has to give the correct answer from a multiple choice of possible answers. Only if the pupil does so may he move on to point two. If he chooses a wrong answer, he will be presented with a remedial lesson, then asked question one again. Step by step the pupil works through from the easy to the difficult concepts, proceeding individually at his own pace.

The behaviourist approach to curriculum design is particularly suited to sequential subjects such as maths and foreign languages.

There is a crucial disagreement between behaviourists and Piagetians as to the type of motivation involved in learning. Why do children learn (if they do in fact learn)? According to some behaviourists, children will only learn if they are rewarded extrinsically for doing so (although according to Cullen (personal communication), Skinner believed pupils had to want to learn). According to Piagetians children do not need extrinsic rewards from the teacher or psychologist as they find learning so intrinsically exciting. They will learn anyway.

Some might argue that the behaviourists are not really developmentalists. They belong in the cognitive-science branch of psychology rather than in the cognitive-development branch. This may seem to the lay person a pedantic distinction but, for the topic of this book, it is a vital one since cognitive scientists are not concerned primarily with how an individual develops but with the process of learning generally.

Others might argue that behaviourists see development in a different light from Piagetians, i.e. development is viewed as the end-point of sections of learning. Once a particular course of study or section of work has been thoroughly learnt and over-learnt, development can be said to have taken place. Learning is therefore cumulative and additive, whereas Piaget regarded development of cognitive structures as the key element, with learning taking place at the child's stage level. The behaviourists' antistructural view is supported by some other schools at the present time, such as the information processors, as discussed in Chapter 9. Piaget, on the other hand, saw the development of cognitive structures as paramount. Learning takes place at the stage level of the child.

The behaviourists' interest lies in the act of learning at a particular moment in time, whereas the Piagetians' interest lies in the ongoing sweep of cognitive development from birth to adulthood. The behaviourists are interested solely in the external factors that cause learning to occur, such as stimulation, motivation, etc. Unlike the information processors, however, they are not interested in any factors inside the child's mind, such as the abilities to scan visually or to reason inductively. Skinner went so far as to argue against the existence of a 'mind', but he did have a Darwinian concept of inherited intelligence.

On some points the behaviourists' ideas resemble those of the traditional movement in education. Both are teacher centred, believing that the teacher should control learning. Children should only learn those items of knowledge teachers believe they should learn. It is therefore an authoritarian model. However, its supporters argue that teachers have had vastly superior experiences to children, both of education generally and of specific subjects. Teachers are mature whereas children are not. Teachers have overall plans of where the learning of children is leading. This gives teachers the right and the duty to decide what is to be learnt.

However, in the mode of presentation of the material to the child lies a vital distinction between the behaviourists and the traditional teachers: behaviourists believe in individualized learning. Each child must learn at his own pace. So the material is generally presented in the form of sequences of work-cards, sections in books or computer programs. Behaviourists do not believe a class of children of mixed ability can be taught formally at the same time by a teacher. Here the behaviourists part company with traditional, formal teachers. The similarity between the two lies in assessment rather than in presentation.

The behaviourist model (although not known as such) has been popular in parts of British education for some time, particularly secondary schools. Teachers find it helpful for those adolescents who have little intrinsic desire to learn. Their teachers need to offer them rewards, either short-term class points that accumulate towards a desirable outing or long-term school-leaving certificates that will, it is hoped, provide entry to jobs. Such teachers are accused of 'bribing' children. However, most adult paid work is done in order to obtain money rather than for the intrinsic pleasure of the job.

Behaviourism has made a major contribution to the science of rewarding (or *reinforcement*, as it is known in psychological jargon). Skinner in particular noted the usefulness of *continuous reinforcement* (every time a pupil makes the desired response) in order to establish a desirable pattern of behaviour. However, this technique loses its effectiveness over time. In the longer term, *fixed-time* or *fixed-ratio* reinforcement is a more effective motivator. The fixed time could range from a half-hour lesson to a week (for calculating accumulated class points) to a school year (for prizes, certificates, etc.). The fixed ratio could similarly vary from every second to every hundredth desired response being rewarded. In either case it must be a pattern that is credible to the particular pupils being rewarded. Younger, less able pupils will need to be rewarded more often. Older, more mature pupils can work for longer-term goals.

Behaviourism has also established a niche for itself in parts of special education. For instance, similar regimes to the above have been set up successfully for maladjusted youngsters. The same principles have been used in a very different way to help slow-learning children. Computer programs have been set up that build in a great deal of repetitive exercises together with a maximum of rewarding. This comes from the machine by way of feedback for having obtained the right answer.

Teaching is defined by behaviourists as training rather than education. Kendler and Kendler (1962) taught children of 5 and 8 two components of a problem separately. The children were then tested to see if they could combine the two. Each child had to press a button in order to produce a charm and then put marbles into holes to obtain the charm. However, they were largely unable to do so. The 5-year-olds could not cope at all, while the 8-year-olds were not much better. The Kendlers' explanation was that each experience had been learnt separately, and that children of such a young age are not capable of linking the two. College students, however, could do so. For once behaviourists were in agreement with Piagetians: 8-year-olds are not capable of making deductive inferences.

From the mid-1940s, B. F. Skinner was the dominant force within the behaviourist movement in education. In many ways his model (1969) is an exact antithesis of Piaget's. The teacher's role is one of total dominance; she decides exactly what is to be learnt. In Skinner's system, the individual teacher teaches only what she is instructed to do by higher authority. Liberal educators have been aghast at the vision of total adult authority proposed in Skinner's *Walden II* (1976). Since this authoritarian model has been the pattern of education in the Soviet Union, Skinner's ideas have not found favour with conservatives either.

Skinner also introduced a specific mechanism of learning he called *operant conditioning*. The child operates on the environment but is only rewarded by the adult if he makes the response the adult desires. The child then goes on to step two and 'passes' this only when he has given 'the right answer'. This process goes on until the child has achieved the final goal the teacher/psychologist has decided in advance. This constitutes a linear programme for learning Skinner called programmed learning. Skinner applied operant conditioning to the acquisition of the home language, as summarized in Chapter 3. He also advocated its use in state schools, as part of his notion of total control of society. Beside rejecting Skinner's totalitarian philosophy, humanist critics have pointed to the lack of scope for individual initiative or for emotional response. Defenders of Skinner (such as Cullen) deny these points.

Although I share other liberals' horror of Skinner's system, I do not entirely reject his ideas. They can be very useful for teaching children with learning difficulties who need a highly structured step-by-step programme. Many behaviour-modification programmes (as they are called) have been derived for use in special education. On them children may learn efficiently on a Skinnerian model where otherwise they would be frightened rather than stimulated by being offered a choice. Such children also thrive on the high degree of reward at each step.

Other learners may find such a structured approach helpful if they know exactly what it is they wish to learn, for instance, how to operate a new piece of machinery. Skinner's ideas are most suitable for linear subjects, such as computing, where tackling one topic depends on the successful achievement of the previous one. It is a tribute to the enduring power of his notions that the principles behind his programmed instruction (fashionable during the 1960s) have been reborn as computer-assisted learning.

Behaviourist ideas remain influential in the method of assessment called multiple-choice testing, so popular in America. For each question the learner is presented with a number of alternative answers to choose from. He is only rewarded with a mark if he marks the 'correct' answer.

Behaviourism has long been a highly controversial school, in both psychology and education. A hard core of adherents in Britain has defended it devoutly: Cullen in special education and Kevin Wheldall and his colleagues at Birmingham and Reading Universities. However, it has aroused the antagonism of humanists, Piagetians and many others who value the individual. Within psychology it has a recognized position, stressing rigorous experimentation. Within education I am putting forward a compromise position: rejecting it as a general theory for all teaching situations yet regarding it as being highly effective in certain very particular situations.

Summary

In the behaviourist explanation the educational authority or the teacher decides in advance exactly what they want children to learn. This is achieved in Skinner's version by a process of operant conditioning. Much stress is placed on the role of reward in learning.

Questions for discussion

1. What are the merits and demerits of behaviourism?
2. According to the behaviourist view, what is the role of the teacher?
3. Is a computer really the best teacher?
4. Who should decide what children should learn at school: the teachers (implementing the instructions of government authorities) or the pupils?
5. Can extrinsic motivation be used effectively in your psychological or teaching situation?
6. If so, what form can it take?
7. Discuss multiple-choice testing.

Further reading

Fontana, D. (1981) *Psychology for Teachers*, Macmillan, London (Chap. 15, 'Class control and management').

Skinner, B. F. (1972) *Beyond Freedom and Dignity*, Penguin Books, Harmondsworth.

Wheldall, K. (ed.) (1987) *The Behaviourist in the Classroom*, Allen & Unwin, London.

Vargas, J. (Skinner's daughter) (1977) *Behavioral Psychology for Teachers*, Harper & Row, New York, NY.

6
AN INTERVENTIONIST: BRUNER

Jerome Bruner was one of the early critics of Piaget's work in the English-speaking world. In a number of highly influential books during the 1960s he suggested teachers should search for pedagogic means of prodding slower developers, stimulating lazy kids and boosting those from deprived backgrounds, such as the inner cities. It would be helpful (if it were possible) to accelerate such children's development in order to solve this problem. Bruner urged teachers to try to get pupils through the successive stages as quickly as possible. Subsequent critics have denied this is actually possible. However, successful acceleration studies have been carried out, e.g. that of Adey, Shayer and Yates (1989), reported in Chapter 10.

Bruner's case for acceleration seems worth examining, particularly at a time when there is a special concern for below-average pupils. One reason for the introduction of the National Curriculum is to improve standards of attainment among the bottom 40 per cent of the school population. How can teachers reach the targets set by the government without some form of acceleration of the slow learner? Are the most able pupils being fully stretched in comprehensive schools, particularly in mixed-ability classes? Should they be accelerated on to the next stage?

Bruner argues that language is one of the main weapons for acceleration (as discussed further in Chapter 7). Lessons must be presented in such a way as to stimulate pupils' interest. Piaget emphasized the environmental factor, the need for the physical environment to be as stimulating as possible, so that the child wants to learn from it. The teacher needs to prepare material that will grab pupils' attention and interest. However, Bruner criticized Piaget's failure to take account of the child's previous experiences and insightful teaching.

In his earlier work, Piaget regarded the child's cognitive development as stemming from an innate potential that may or may not be realized in a particular environment. Bruner added the dimension of teaching. If the teacher intervenes in the child's environment to ensure he does have the appropriate experiences, this optimizes the chances of the child's full potential being realized. Material should be presented to a pupil before he is at, for instance, the concrete operational stage. This might challenge the pupil to reach concrete operations. This is similar to McVicar Hunt's notion of a deliberate mismatch, designed by the teacher.

At the same time the language used by the teacher must help pupils to perceive the situation as helpfully as possible, as both Bryant and Donaldson argued. The language should be simple enough for the child to understand, yet be challenging intellectually. Bruner regards the development of language as vital for a child's overall cognitive development right from birth. Language includes the use of gestures, such as pointing, as is discussed in Chapter 3.

The spiral curriculum is another Brunerian concept relevant to teachers. This is illustrated in Figure 6.1. A particular topic, e.g. volume, can be introduced to babies at a sensorimotor level: they can play with water in buckets on the beach. The same topic can be reintroduced to the same child when he becomes a preschooler (then at Piaget's pre-operational substage) by giving him buckets of water to play with. However, language is now associated with the experience. Words such as 'bucket' and 'more' are introduced. Simultaneously intuitive concepts are encouraged, such as 'more water' (when water is poured into the bucket) and 'less water' (when water is poured out). So, with the help of his teacher or playgroup leader, parents and peer group, a child develops preconcepts and later intuitive concepts.

In the junior school the same pupil may be re-exposed to the phenomenon of volume in a variety of settings. The teacher will now, it is hoped, use the word 'volume'. As a result of the child's spontaneous activity and activities planned by the teacher, he should achieve conservation of volume (see Chapter 2) and understand the concept at a concrete operational level. He returns to the concept when he reaches secondary school, but now at Piaget's formal operational level. The teaching is now in abstract, symbolic terms. He needs to learn the formulae for calculating volume without needing any practical props.

Bruner's spiral curriculum could equally be applied to Peel's describer and explainer notions. A primary teacher first introduces a pupil to a concept in the describer mode, for example, having an election for class captain. A secondary teacher (of history) later returns to the notion but now at the explainer level, for example, a detailed historical analysis of the concept of democracy, including hypothesizing new possibilities.

Cognitive Development Today

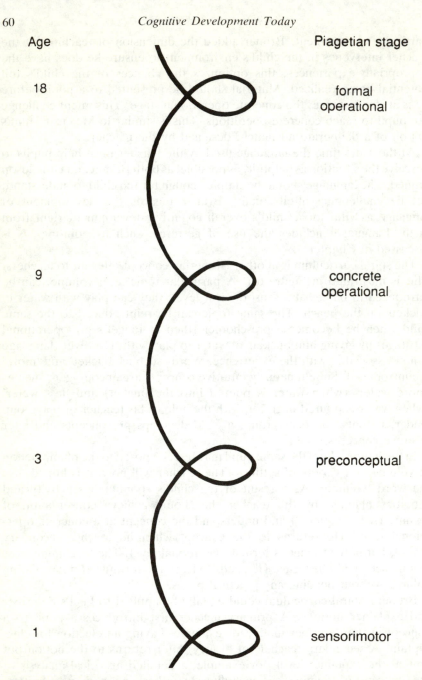

Age   Piagetian stage

18
                                         formal
                                         operational

9
                                         concrete
                                         operational

3   preconceptual

1   sensorimotor

Figure 6.1   Bruner's spiral model for the curriculum

Based on the principle of the spiral curriculum, Bruner made his famous challenge to teachers: any topic can be taught to children of any age in an intellectually respectable form.

Although Piaget's stages have been used in this illustration of the spiral curriculum, Bruner actually developed his own stage theory. It has received less prominence than Piaget's but is still worth the consideration of teachers and psychologists. There are three stages: *enactive* – learning is by doing; *iconic* – learning is by means of images and pictures; and *symbolic* – learning is by means of words or numbers.

At first glance Bruner's stage theory seems to cover a narrower age-range than Piaget's, applying mainly to babyhood and the preschool years. However, teachers of older children are reminded of the enactive and the iconic stages when pupils are involved with resource-based learning. They are then expected to learn by doing things with their hands. Similarly when an abstract problem is proving too difficult for pupils to solve, they can be encouraged to visualize the problem in terms of images. This may help to place the problem in an easier mode for the pupil to work in.

The enactive mode can be associated with another important Brunerian idea: the importance of play. Children should be encouraged to play with objects in order to build up understanding. Constructive play should be the dominant activity of the preschool years. Here Bruner agrees with Piaget.

The iconic is probably the most interesting of Bruner's stages since it is the least like Piaget's equivalent (although Piaget does write about figurative thinking, i.e. thinking in images). Like Piaget, Bruner advocates a child-centred approach to education linked to discovery learning. However, he differs from Piaget in advising a much more forceful role for teachers: they should not hesitate to intervene in classroom learning. For instance, when a teacher is using resource-based learning, she should be actively diagnosing difficulties in advance. This might pre-empt some of the problems. As the pupils go about their various assignments, the teacher should be trying to stimulate the thinking of the groups (or of the whole class).

In many inner-city areas, both in the USA and Britain, there is considerable academic under-achievement. Bruner was part of the optimistic movement of the 1960s that urged that special programmes should be developed. These should involve extra resources (by way of teachers and materials) being used to break the cycle of deprivation and under-achievement in pupils with poor self-esteem. The importance of pre-schooling was central: 3- and 4-year-olds must be stimulated in playgroup and nursery situations. Social workers need to get into the homes and teach parents how to stimulate children. It is not necessary to supply expensive equipment. Even simple pieces of urban junk can be stimulating to preschoolers.

This movement has been criticized from many quarters: by sociologists who do not accept the deprivation notion or positivist measures; by psychologists who do not accept the possibility of acceleration; and by right-wing governments who refuse to spend State money on such welfare programmes. However, the problem of inner-city deprivation has worsened since the 1960s: there is a higher degree of breakdown of family units. So Bruner's case would seem to be worth re-examining.

At first sight Bruner's ideas have similarities with those of Vygotsky, discussed in Chapter 4. Both emphasize an interventionist role for teachers. There is an obligation on teachers to make demands on their pupils. It is not acceptable for teachers to dismiss children's educational chances because of their environmental deprivation. Bruner and Vygotsky take issue with Piaget's readiness approach, whereby a teacher has to wait until a pupil is intellectually ready before he can be taught any particular topic. The teacher should rather be taking the initiative to stimulate the child to readiness.

Bruner also shares with Vygotsky a belief in the importance of cultural tools for children's development. These range from the pencil in the infant class to the microscope in the biology class. The computer is, of course, used right through school. And books are, of course, the prime tool for intellectual development in our culture. However, unlike Vygotsky, Bruner has a child-centred approach to the task. Children should be set tasks by teachers and encouraged to discover truths for themselves, whereas Vygotsky urged a teacher-centred approach with direct instruction.

To assess Bruner's contribution to cognitive development is not easy when he is still alive. However, when the considerable impact Piaget and Vygotsky had on him is taken into account, he may not be seen as a fundamentally original thinker. Nevertheless he has been a significant influence on such theoreticians as Margaret Donaldson. She (Grieve *et al.*, 1990) admires his emphasis on the child as a whole person rather than as just a mind. Additionally, Bruner has been a most stimulating influence on education (not least maths and science education) over the past thirty years.

Summary

Bruner urges that children should be challenged to reach as high a level of academic performance as possible. Society should aid this by providing remedial resources in order to overcome the problems of low achievement. In any classroom the teacher should intervene in the learning process to try to stimulate a child's growth. A spiral curriculum is one model for curriculum development.

Questions for discussion

1. To what extent should a teacher intervene in the learning process?
2. Should we try to accelerate children's development, as Bruner argues? Or should we wait for them to be 'ready', as Piaget implied?
3. Is Bruner's spiral curriculum of value to you as a teacher?
4. Does the spiral curriculum suggest more co-operation between infant, junior and secondary teachers?
5. How do Bruner's ideas compare with those of Vygotsky?
6. How can teachers encourage enactive and iconic activities in their pupils?
7. What role should play have in cognitive development?

Further reading

Bruner, J. S. (1963) *The Process of Education*, Harvard University Press, Cambridge, Mass.

Bruner, J. S. (1972) *The Relevance of Education*, Allen & Unwin, London.

Bruner, J. S. (1986) *Actual Minds, Possible Worlds*, Harvard University Press, Cambridge, Mass.

7
CRITICISMS OF SPECIFIC ASPECTS OF PIAGET'S WORK: BRYANT, DONALDSON AND OTHERS

Criticism of Piaget's theories has focused on specifics as well as on underlying assumptions. In this chapter we begin by mentioning criticisms of aspects of Piaget's stage theory, first discussed in Chapter 2.

Of the sensorimotor period by Bower and Butterworth

Stage 1 of the sensorimotor period has been largely superseded by subsequent work. During the past two decades many outstanding researchers have concentrated their focus on unravelling the capabilities of babies. Tom Bower (1977) is only one among many with his work on babies' early perception of shapes displayed above their heads.

More fundamental criticisms of the assumptions underlying Piaget's theory for the sensorimotor period were made by Butterworth (1981). One is that sensory perception cannot provide objective information about reality. A second is that a baby cannot tell the difference between sensory events independent of his own activity and sensory feedback contingent on his activity. From this is inferred that a baby cannot tell a change of place from a change of state of an object. Hence development starts from a position of profound adualism; the baby cannot tell the difference between his own perceptions and the 'reality' of the outside world. Butterworth argues that Piaget's theory is inadequate to account for the data we currently have. He propounds an alternative nativist view, similar to that expressed by Baldwin (1925), that there is a pre-established harmony between the baby and his environment. The baby is not confused by the sensory effects of his own activity. There exist prestructured feedback loops for the baby to use. In other words, there are inherited mechanisms that help the baby to adjust to the world. Hence Butterworth's alternative is even more biologically based than Piaget's, but with a greater emphasis on the baby's behaviour fitting into evolutionary patterns.

Of concrete operations by Bryant's school

Piaget's stage of concrete operations has elicited the greatest amount of follow-up work. Some current critics argue that it cannot be said that a child is at an overall concrete operational stage at any time. Rather, that he achieves operational thought separately in different domains. According to this domain-specific school, each domain has to be looked at in isolation (as discussed further in Chapter 9). Questions are asked to determine whether a child has achieved concretes or not. A number of leading British psychologists have argued that the phrasing of the questions should make it easier for children to understand the tasks they are set. They would then be able to do things at younger ages than those Piaget found.

Peter Bryant is one of the leading British psychologists who have taken up Piaget's ideas but modified some crucial points. Bryant differed from Piaget in the design of the experiments. Bryant uses the scientific tradition of experimental and control groups in order to investigate these problems, whereas Piaget used clinical studies of individual children in detail.

Bryant has focused on the attainment of concrete operations and more specifically on conservation tasks. When do children realize a quantity remains the same even though it has undergone an apparent change in appearance? The conservation of number is an important example of this for the child's understanding of maths. When does a child realize that, despite apparent differences in appearance (as between rows A and B in Figure 7.1), the same number is being represented? Bryant and Trabasso (1971) found that children of 4 (as against Piaget's 7) could do so. However, they must be given appropriate help. This consisted of giving the children matches and cueing them into the idea that they should successively pair off a bead from the top row with a bead from the bottom row. Hence this revolutionary study showed that Piaget had been far too pessimistic in the ages at which children could grasp 1:1 correspondence.

Bryant's work has in turn been criticized by Cowan (1979a and 1979b), who found the ability of young children to conserve number to be true only with small-number tasks and not with large-number tasks. So there would seem to be limitations among young children to the understanding of the principle of invariance, i.e. that the number 4 is the same whether represented by a longer row of beads or a shorter row. Nevertheless, Bryant's finding, as modified by Cowan, is still good news for teachers. It

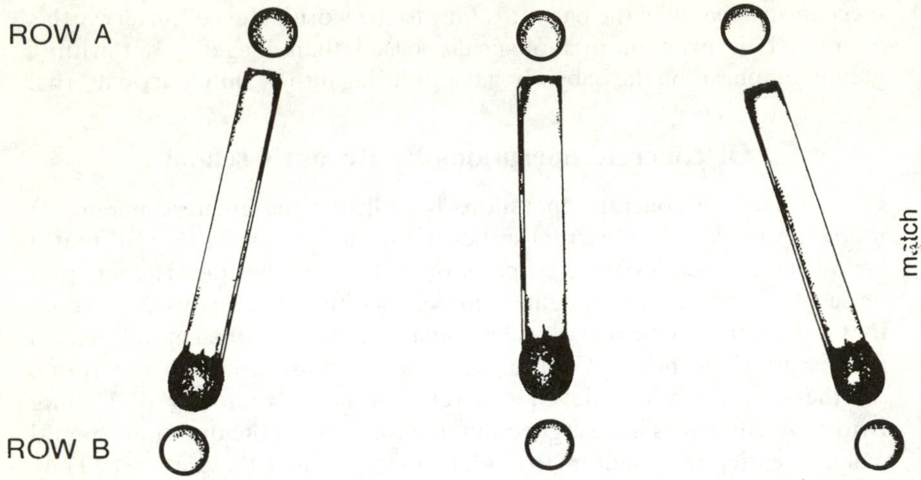

ROW A

ROW B

Figure 7.1 Bryant's method of teaching or acceleration of 1:1 correspondence

is up to teachers to find ways to help children understand things they would not otherwise have done. For example, in Figure 7.1, the teacher or psychological experimenter gives the child matches to link up the pairs of beads. By means of this technique, infant teachers can help children to understand that the same number can look different in different situations.

However, Cowan and Daniels (1989) think that Bryant's position should be modified. They found that a young child's ability to make 1:1 correspondences varies with the apparent density of the rows (called *numerosity*). The more closely the beads are packed in the row, the poorer the child's performance. Perhaps urging pupils to count the number in each row or to match pairs would overcome this understandable perceptual seduction. Cowan and Daniels (*ibid.*) also found other aspects of visual perception to be important in successful 1:1 correspondence (Figure 7.1). The child needed to see the whole situation (both sets of beads and the gap in between them) as a unit. Unsuccessful pupils tended to focus (or *fixate*) only on the gap between the rows.

When he examined the ability of 5-year-olds to make length judgements, Cowan (1982) found they could make absolute judgements, whereas Bryant had found they could make only relative judgements.

Another aspect of concrete operations Bryant has investigated in detail is *transitivity*. This means the ability to deduce that if A is larger than B and B larger than C, then A must be larger than C. Piaget had said that young pre-operational children could not draw this inference.

Bryant and Trabasso's (1971) study of the five-stick problem has aroused great interest among the information-processing (IP) school (Chapter 9). This involves a child comparing the length of five sticks of increasing length, as illustrated in Figure 7.2. The crucial comparison is that between B and D, since this can only be done with reference to C (whereas for the other sticks their position on the end or in the middle can be used). Children need to reason transitively. In other words, they need to argue: B is shorter than C; D is longer than C; therefore D is longer than B. This is a version of a classic Piagetian problem. However, the information processors point out that a child needs to *remember* the relations on which the inference is made.

This study had been criticized because of the long training period involved. This allowed children to memorize the process rather than working it out intellectually. However, in Bryant's recent study with Pears (Pears and Bryant, 1990), no memory was involved. Nevertheless, 4-year-old children could still draw the inference. A general point for all teachers is established here. We don't have to wait for a certain level to develop in a pupil, as Piaget had given us to understand. We don't have to wait for the pupil to become 'ready'. If we are sufficiently ingenious and enterprising in our teaching techniques, we can accelerate this readiness. We should reject Piaget's determinism.

In Figure 7.1 row B *looks* longer than row A. Bryant (1972) suggested asking questions such as 'Which row contains more counters?' This helps to cue children away from focusing on length. It also focuses on the vital issue of language use and, in particular, the adult's or teacher's language use, which should be aimed at giving maximum help to the child.

An emphasis on giving maximum language help to children is the common theme of this chapter. It is reiterated by the work of Margaret Donaldson, summarized below. The schools of Bryant and Donaldson have a common strand that provides a message for teachers and psychologists: we must examine very carefully the questions we ask children.

Many of the under-estimates of what young children can achieve are a result of faulty communication between the adult (whether teacher or psychologist) and the child. For instance, very young children are inclined to change their minds, but they often don't tell us they have done so. This may explain a child saying on one occasion that rows A and B contain the same number of beads and on another occasion saying they contain a different number of beads.

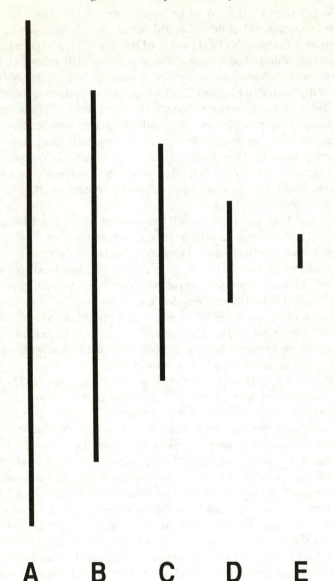

A   B   C   D   E

Figure 7.2 Bryant's modification of Piaget's transitivity problem

Of concrete operations by Donaldson and her school

During the 1970s a series of very significant challenges to Piaget's findings occurred. Besides the particular findings of various studies, the overall philosophy of Margaret Donaldson's school refuted the deterministic nature of the implications of Piaget's findings for teachers, i.e. that pupils can either solve or not solve a particular problem and that there is nothing much that teachers can do to help pupils or to accelerate their progress.

Donaldson gave a much more optimistic message: that most preschool children *are* capable of solving problems associated with operational thought *if they are given optimal help*. She was strongly critical of the way in which Piaget asked children questions in experimental situations. There was a tendency to try to 'catch children out' rather than to try to help them.

Let us take an example of the type she and her school showed young children could handle, if it is made meaningful to them: 'Jane is Mary's sister. Who is Mary's sister?' Nursery children can solve this problem when it is discussed in terms of themselves. In other words, the name of the nursery child being asked the problem should be substituted for Jane's and her sister's name for Mary's.

Perhaps the most important single experiment was done by Martin Hughes (1978). Piaget had said that young children could only think egotistically. They were not capable of seeing another's point of view, as illustrated by their replies to the mountains problem discussed in Chapter 2. Hughes devised (Figure 7.3) a cross-shaped screen to test this. A toy policeman was placed to the right of the child. To the left a doll was hidden from the policeman but was visible to the child. Nearly all children between 3½ and 5 years could say, after training, when the policeman could and could not see the doll. Thus nearly all were capable of seeing another's point of view. Young children are not cognitively egotistical, as Piaget had alleged.

A naughty teddy was used to 'interfere' with an experiment on the conservation of number in another vital piece of research by Donaldson, this time with James McGarrigle (McGarrigle and Donaldson, 1974). If this interfering was done by such a teddy, with whom the child could identify, rather than by an adult, most nursery children could conserve number. This led Donaldson to focus on how young children *perceive the adult's intentions*. This is a vital factor in determining whether the children can or cannot perform adequately by adult criteria. According to the findings of Donaldson's school, preschoolers are often not very good at

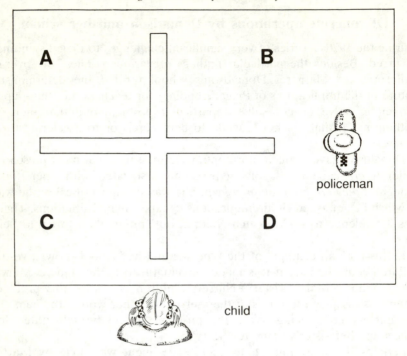

Figure 7.3 Hughes's screen

this, but they are good at problem-solving once they have understood the task requirements. Donaldson interpreted these results as indicating that children are capable of conservation at a much younger age than that Piaget found.

Donaldson also stressed that preschoolers understand things much better if they are presented in their natural settings. Events are embedded linguistically in overall contexts, not only physical but also personal and social. So a new toy not only has a name to match its physical reality but also the child's receiving the toy comes in a particular context, e.g. from the father on the child's birthday. Once a situation is disembedded from a natural into an artificial one of the laboratory or the classroom, it will be far more difficult for preschoolers to cope with. This point has obvious implications for psychologists and teachers working with young children. One of them is that we must make the learning situation as near to 'natural' as possible.

Donaldson focused particularly on reading. Children have to disembed the unvarying characteristics of the letter 'A' (for example) on a particular page and ignore the remainder of that particular context in order to read that letter efficiently. She argues that parents who are aware of this process give their children much more help in overcoming context-bound situations in order to reach disembedded ones than do other parents. Both she and Inhelder found that children from less privileged backgrounds tended to substitute a more 'natural' question when asked a more 'academic' one that implied the ability to disembed.

In another famous experiment McGarrigle, Grieve and Hughes (1978) claimed that preschool children were capable of class inclusion, thereby also contradicting Piaget. The Genevan had done numerous experiments of the type 'There are 3 red cows and 4 cows. Are there more red cows than cows?' McGarrigle, Grieve and Hughes arranged on a line of beads first a chair and then a table (Figure 7.4). They used, for instance, a line of red beads from the child to the chair, then a line of white beads from the chair to the table. They then asked the child: 'Does the teddy take more steps to the chair or to the table?' With these joint cues of the perceptual contrast of red and white (beads) and the helpful oral verbal wording, most preschoolers could solve the class-inclusion problem, i.e. say there are more steps to the table than to the chair.

In another version of this problem, the steps to the chair and the table are both the same colour, e.g. white. Children find this task much easier. The authors interpreted this in terms of the children misinterpreting the earlier mixed-colour (Figure 7.4) situation. The red steps from the child to the chair hindered rather than helped the child. But Gold (1987) interpreted the results in terms of reducing perceptual seduction by removing the colour contrast and his interpretation is therefore in accord with Piagetian theory.

Donaldson stressed it is vital for adults to express situations as helpfully and optimally as possible to children. She was very critical of this aspect of Piaget's original work. In the experiment with the cows, he gave the children two *wrong* answers to choose from, but *not the correct* one.

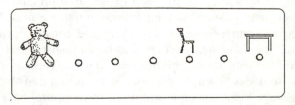

Figure 7.4 McGarrigle, Grieve and Hughes's test for the understanding of part and whole

Another set of studies examined children's understanding of a number of factors. In work done with Peter Lloyd (Donaldson and Lloyd, 1974), children were shown an array of four garages, joined together in a row, and a set of toy cars, sometimes three and sometimes five. The children were asked whether the following statements were true or not: 'All the cars are in the garages. All the garages have cars in them.' When three cars were considered, the first statement would be true and the second false. But when five cars were being considered, the first was false and the second true. However, some children did not use such logic. They held both statements to be false when there were three cars and both to be true when there were five. Donaldson and Lloyd denied the children did not understand the meaning of *all*. Rather the children were dealing with what they thought *ought* to be there. All the garages *ought* to have cars in them. They were focusing on the fullness of the garage rather than on the 1:1 correspondence (or non-correspondence) of the cars and garages. A panda was then introduced to the children. He was someone (unlike the adult questioners) who knew less than they did so that they could help him.

In a later development of this study with McGarrigle (McGarrigle and Donaldson, 1974), the cars were arranged on two shelves, five on one and four on the other in 1:1 correspondence so that an extra car stuck out. The four cars were covered by four garages. But the five cars were covered by six garages so that one was empty. When children were asked 'Are there more cars on this shelf (the row of four) or more cars on that shelf (the row of five cars covered by six garages)?' a third of them changed their judgements and said there were now more cars in the row of four than in the row of five. Yet before the garages were introduced, they had correctly said there were more cars in the row of five than in the row of four. McGarrigle and Donaldson interpreted this as the children again focusing on the dimension of fullness (were the garages full or not?) rather than on 1:1 correspondence between the cars and the garages.

A very important overall message emerges from this for teachers and psychologists. If we are going to teach or research on children in a way that will allow them to show us their full potential, we must be aware of how children are representing, interpreting and construing their experiences. Overall it is *language* teachers and psychologists must concentrate on if they wish to help young children to progress. This means help with grammatical subleties, such as the use of prepositions (Macrae, 1976), help with disembedding academic situations from natural ones and help in understanding the contexts in which children are acquiring language and therefore developing cognitively.

It is this central focus on language that distinguishes her approach from that of Bryant. Although both started with criticisms of Piaget's use of language, they have done so from fundamentally different perspectives. Despite the many criticisms he has made and reservations he holds, Bryant remains a neo-Piagetian. He accepts many of the fundamental assumptions of Piagetian study: for instance, that children's thought is best revealed by performing experiments on them and that children's thought proceeds through stages (in particular concrete operations). Donaldson does not accept any stage theory. She is not really interested in phenomena such as the various conservations (e.g. number, quantity, etc.). Rather, her central interest is in the development of a child's language *per se*, not as a means to the end of cognitive understanding, as Piaget and Bryant see it. It is not surprising she has been strongly influenced by the metacognitive movement. She is also very interested in how children construct their own concepts, so she could be included in the constructivist school. Much of the work of Donaldson's school was put together in her book, *Children's Minds* (1978).

Morag Donaldson (1986) is continuing this tradition of language-oriented research at the present time. She examined nursery and primary children's explanations of the actions of puppets and children in everyday life. She developed a taxonomy to classify them. An explanation is termed *empirical* if it explains an event in terms of another event, for example, 'The window broke because John threw a ball at it'. It is termed *intentional* if it explains actions in terms of the child's intentions, for example, 'John threw the ball because he wanted to break the window'. It is termed *deductive* if it uses evidence to justify a claim, for example, 'We can tell the window is broken because glass is on the ground'. On the whole children have more difficulties with the deductive mode, the most meta-cognitive of the three. This bears out a theme of this book — that it is unrealistic to expect pre-primary and primary children in general to be able to be aware of their own language and learning, as the metacognitive school implies.

Morag Donaldson did, however, find children to have a knowledge of the structure of causal sentences, which may well be implicit. Children have a knowledge of sentence structure when they start to learn to write. Teachers may be able to make use of this ability. She also compares young children's use of *because* and the conjunction *so*. She found that even children as young as 5 could use *because* correctly, but there was much more confusion with *so*. The ability to use 'because' means in linguistic terms that first-year primary children are capable of handling cause and effect successfully. Most young children could handle conjunc-

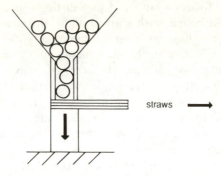

Figure 7.5   Morag Donaldson's kerplunk phenomenon

tions successfully, if they were given helpful contexts in which to do so
(pictures were particularly useful cues).

An interesting general methodological point that emerges from Morag
Donaldson's work is her use of videotapes. They give children a great
deal of help in working out causality, since a video actually shows the
movement whereas, with static pictures, a child has to try to imagine
movement for himself. Videos are of course an educational aid not
available in Piaget's day. Teachers make plenty of use of them but
perhaps developmental psychologists could make more use of videos to
clarify situations to children.

The kerplunk phenomenon is another stimulating innovation of Morag
Donaldson's. Marbles are kept in a funnel by straws, as illustrated in
Figure 7.5. Of course, if the straws are pulled out the marbles fall down
to the bottom of the flask. She used this device for investigating causality.
Although the solution seems obvious to us, some children found it useful
to have an audience of a toy panda in order to work out what they
needed to do.

Of the theory of knowledge by Bryant and his school

Ironically it is by a post-Piagetian, Peter Bryant (1972), that Piaget's
theory of knowledge (as outlined in Chapter 2) has been heavily criticized.
Bryant argues there is no acceptable empirical evidence for the detailed
steps of

1.   A disturbance that motivates;
2.   Regulation − modification of a particular bit of behaviour;

3. Compensation – whereby the child performs an opposite action to cancel out the effect of the first one;
4. Equilibration.

The training studies done by Inhelder, Sinclair and Bovet (1974) purport to demonstrate these mechanisms. Bryant rejects their findings on the grounds that the Genevans failed to have a control group with which the experimental group could be compared. Bryant regards Piaget's terms 'regulation' and 'compensation' as vague and reminiscent of the trial-and-error processes Piaget himself had initially reacted against.

Bryant's alternative (1982) stresses agreement rather than conflict as promoting developmental change. A child realizes a certain strategy is right when it consistently produces the same answers as another strategy. Bryant found this when children were asked to use, first, the strategy of *making direct judgements* and then, second, the strategy of *measurement*. Each strategy reinforced the other. For example, when children wish to know the length and breadth of objects, such as a carpet and a mat in their room, they first use the strategy of making intuitive judgements, e.g. the table is longer than the mat. The teacher then encourages them actually to measure the two lengths. When the pupils find the results are the same, they are learning by finding agreement. Piaget, on the other hand, had said that children learn from contradictions.

The philosopher–psychologist Boden (1979) criticized the terms Piaget uses – equilibrium, assimilation and accommodation – as being so vague as to be irrefutable. The terms are polysyllabic descriptions rather than explanations of cognitive growth. Neither does Piaget outline precisely what the transformations from one stage to another are, nor how they are to be effected.

The lack of individual differences

For teachers, one of Piaget's most serious weaknesses was a failure to take individual differences into account. By this is meant individual differences in personality, gender, intelligence and other factors that affect the ability to progress cognitively. For instance, it is possible that a particular personality type such as the introvert may reach the more 'advanced' stage earlier on average than its opposite personality type, the extrovert. However, Piaget did not consider such an issue worth researching. Nor was he interested in the sort of comments on personality differences within their classes teachers make on a more intuitive basis.

Piaget wrote little on gender differences – an issue that still could do with more systematic research. Sutherland (1980) found no significant differences between boys and girls in the achievement of concrete and formal operations, but this was based on only a small sample who were interviewed individually.

Piaget was also uninterested in individual differences in intelligence, i.e. the spread across the school population of, for example, the ability to conserve (or to think in an abstract formal operational way). To gauge this accurately a representative cross-section of the total school population of a country needs to be sampled. This could be turned into standardized scores, based on the average with variations both to the high (the more intelligent) and the low (the less intelligent) ends of the spectrum. This has been done for the British Ability Scales, using particular aspects of Piaget's work.

Piaget preferred to use his own children and other children of the staff at his research institute in Geneva. So both the genetic background and the environment of the children were very academic. This did not give a realistic idea of what the average working-class or lower-middle-class child is capable of. It is not surprising that the average ages of achievement of formal operations found by Sutherland (1983), Shayer, Kuchemann and Wylan (1976) and McNally (1970) were considerably higher than those of Inhelder and Piaget (1958), since all these workers were sampling the general population.

Strict, orthodox Piagetians would not have accepted these as criticisms. Piaget was not interested in how individuals differ. His interest was epistemological: how do we gain knowledge as a general process? He was a philosopher at heart, not a psychologist. The criticisms made in this section have been made by so many empirical and educational psychologists that they cannot all be named. However, Brown and Desforges (1979) synthesized many of the arguments.

The social critique of Schaffer and Hamlyn

Piaget's failure to take account of the social aspect of children's learning has long concerned teachers, who may have the responsibility for 25 children's learning simultaneously. It has also concerned psychologists, but the problems of utilizing the clinical method with more than one child in order to obtain reliable and valid data have not yet been solved. Classically, Piaget would study one child on his own in a 1:1 interaction, which would be recorded. This ignored the fact that most children are seldom learning on their own. The mother—baby interaction is a 1:1 situation for feeding, although the baby's siblings may create a larger social group for much of the time.

Schaffer (1989), in his work with preschool children, points out that children from 2 to 5 are in social groups most of the time: in various social settings such as playgroups, nurseries and mother-and-toddler groups. And at home most children are learning in the company of their siblings. Even the only child is in school for much of his time from 5 onwards. According to this critique, Piaget's ideas fit in better with a traditional educational model of pupils learning individually in rows of desks rather than the progressive one of pupils grouped at a table. This is a rare occasion of Piaget's ideas fitting the traditional paradigm of teaching. (Further criticisms by Schaffer as well as those by Doise and Mugny are discussed in Chapter 4.)

From a philosophical perspective, Hamlyn (1978) criticizes Piaget's view that social understanding develops eventually as a result of prior cognitive activity. Instead, Hamlyn argues that the social process is there from birth so that interaction with the mother (if not others) commences immediately. This initial interaction is more emotion rather than cognition. Bowlby (1953) claimed to have found the same thing.

Hamlyn sees that the acquisition of knowledge has an essential social aspect. Before any facet of knowledge can be established, there has to be an agreed norm as to what truth is. This implies a social group that agrees to that consensus. As a person is corrected by others for faulty grasp of knowledge, he or she is reminded of the social nature of the process of epistemology. By these and other means, Hamlyn builds up a strong counterargument to the notion that a child acquires knowledge in a social vacuum.

Summary

Both Bryant and Donaldson argue that Piaget was wrong in the way he questioned children. Rather than catching a child out, we should be giving him optimal language help by making questions and cues as clear and helpful as possible. In addition, Bryant found that children could be helped to an earlier understanding of number by skilfully created educational aids.

Margaret Donaldson's overall message for teachers and psychologists is that we must give children optimal help if we are to give them the opportunity to show what they are capable of. This help may take the form of (1) physical situations a child can relate to (for most children this means 'natural' situations); and (2) language he can understand. However, in 'academic' situations (often required in school by formal work), they are often required to disembed an abstract principle from the natural situation.

Questions for discussion

1. What pedagogical aids can be used in your teaching or research situation to help children to an earlier understanding?
2. How can a teacher or psychologist give a child better cues to help him give a better account of himself?
3. How can teachers give children more help with language, as Margaret Donaldson has recommended?
4. What equivalents of naughty teddy can teachers find that might help children to show latent understanding?
5. How can teachers help their pupils develop an understanding of causality?
6. Does Piaget's failure to take account of individual differences between children mean his ideas are not relevant to teachers?
7. In what way does the presence of other children shape the learning of a child? How can the teacher (or psychologist) make positive use of this peer influence?

Further reading

Bryant, P. (1974) *Perception and Understanding in Young Children*, Methuen, London.

Donaldson, M. (1978) *Children's Minds*, Fontana, Glasgow.

Grieve, R. and Hughes, M. (eds.) (1990) *Understanding Children: Essays in Honour of Margaret Donaldson*, Blackwell, Oxford.

Pumphrey, P. D. and Elliott, C. D. (eds.) (1990) *Children's Difficulties in Reading, Spelling and Writing: Challenges and Responses*, Falmer Press, Lewes.

8
THE CONSTRUCTIVIST MOVEMENT

Since Piaget's death, the constructivist movement has come to the fore. In some educational circles, the movement is known as the alternative framework in the sense of being alternative to the 'orthodox' Piagetian view presented at many colleges. However, it is also alternative in a school-based sense: it is an alternative to teacher-imposed formal learning where all pupils are supposed to learn the same thing at the same time. Constructivists would argue that few children do so.

The main constructivist proposition is that the child constructs his own version of reality from his own unique experiences. It is this construction he then uses to deal with any new experience in that field. The process of constructing his own knowledge is an active one. He does so by forming new relationships between ideas he already has. To these he incorporates new pieces of information. As he decides for himself rather than following a teacher's advice, it is difficult to predict what he will learn.

One of the main theoreticians drawn on by the movement is David Ausubel. Ausubel (1968) argues the case for the child's own personal constructs being the most important element in education: the most important thing for teachers to know at the outset of the teaching is what each pupil knows. The teacher can then plan a learning programme for each pupil, taking his initial knowledge and learning strategies as the starting-point.

Ausubel argues that pupils need guidance if they are to learn effectively. During the great debate with the advocates of discovery learning, such as Bruner, during the 1960s, Ausubel defended the notion of *meaningful verbal learning*. Instead of discovering for himself, the pupil is presented by the teacher with key concepts in a form easy for him to assimilate. An important part of the teacher's role is to modify the technical language of the subject and to present to the pupils only what they can cope with. Ausubel argues that we learn largely by means of language rather than by means of practical material. So a teacher's first priority should be helping pupils to grasp the appropriate language for that lesson.

However, this aspect of his views is not supported by British constructivists in maths and science education. They argue the contrary: that children learn primarily from practical experiences. Brown and Denvir (1985), however, warned against the dangers of practical work as an end in itself: the child must be able to strip the essential structure from the 'noise'.

Ausubel's *advanced organizers* have become particularly famous. They give a student a helpful conceptual framework to guide him through complex material. It is as though he was presented with a map or a set of pigeon holes to help him sort out the muddle of a mass of complex input. Shayer and Adey (1981) see his ideas as particularly valuable in introducing complex ideas, such as the periodic table, to fifth- and sixth-formers. Advanced organizers are also useful to teachers and curriculum planners in identifying what concepts need to be taught and at what level. From these, the subconcepts and the prior elements of knowledge required can be analysed.

Although the idea of meaningful verbal learning was greeted with relief by teachers who prefer the traditional didactic mode, it should not be seen as a mechanical form of learning where verbal material is passively accepted by a pupil without any real change in his cognitive structures. Ausubel advocated the opposite: that new ideas must be integrated into the cognitive structures the pupil already possesses. Otherwise they will have no meaning for him. They may be rote memorized in order to pass an exam but will then be forgotten.

He has been criticized, however, by White (1988) (and other learning theorists of the 1960s) for ignoring the context in which children learn. Ausubel assumed all children learn in the same way, regardless of the social and physical environment. By contrast, most current constructivists stress the importance of the specific context in which learning takes place, and look for ways by which each act of teaching and learning can be made meaningful for a specific child.

Another theoretical inspiration behind the constructivist movement, particularly that of Maureen Pope's group at Surrey University, is George Kelly's (1963) personal-construct theory. According to personal-construct theory, each concept poses a polar dichotomy. The pole the person chooses determines what sort of conceptual framework he will have for that particular concept. For instance, if the concept is 'environmental studies', the teacher might be asked to elaborate on her concepts of history and geography and ultimately to choose between them. So for each person a unique set of concepts evolves out of the way he resolves the dichotomies. The particular experiences of the person as well as his unique personality determine how he does so.

Kelly's original work was done on students and adults who could safely be expected to have concepts on most relevant areas. However, it seems doubtful children in school and younger children in psychology laboratories, representing as they do the whole range of ability and home background, have concepts in all relevant areas. There may be no concepts in the young child's mind to submit to the Kellyan dichotomy.

Another theoretical root of constructivism is Piaget himself. Piaget was a pioneer constructivist − in the sense that he believed a child constructed his own schemata (Piaget's term for constructs) from his own experiences in his immediate environments. But (according to proponents of this movement) he differed from current constructivists in that he laid some emphasis on the innate, genetically inherited ability of children, which they do not. Piaget also propounded his famous stage theory (outlined in Chapter 2), which many constructivists reject. They see cognitive development as a gradual process of modifying existing concepts rather than as one involving radical breakthroughs of the type Piaget indicated with his object constancy (tertiary circular reactions), operational thought and formal operations.

According to such constructivists as Ros Driver (1983), the child's understanding gradually moves from an instinctive 'gut' one at the time a child enters school to one that is academically acceptable within a subject by the time he leaves at 16 plus. This at least is the goal of constructivist educators. To what extent it is realized remains to be tested by empirical research.

Sutherland's (1989) case study of primary maths teachers in London and Scotland revealed no awareness whatsoever of constructivist ideas among teachers at those particular schools. One of the vital points for teachers to implement, if they do accept constructivist arguments, is that it is very difficult for children really to think in terms of the higher-order concepts expected at secondary-school level. They will continually tend to regress to the more 'common-sense' level. It may only be a minority of pupils that, by the time of GCSE assessment, really think at the theoretical level required by a particular subject.

The case for constructivism has been particularly strongly argued within science and maths education over the past decade. In the case of science, constructivism has largely triumphed at the university/college teacher-education level. Ros Driver at Leeds University and a number of academics at King's College, London, have been influential leaders of the movement.

A classic example for science teachers, both primary and secondary, is that children's common sense tells them that the sun goes round the earth. It will require the most skilful teaching for children really to think in terms of the Galilean explanation when they are *under pressure*, for instance, in a time-limited practical problem-solving situation or written exam. Pupils may rote learn the 'desired' responses in order to pass exams, but this may not affect their real thinking.

Driver (1983) has analysed this problem cogently in her book, *The Pupil as Scientist?* For those pupils who go on to become scientists, it is essential that their real thinking does change. Even for pupils who do not continue with science or maths after school, teaching will be a charade unless it provokes some real change in the pupils' cognitive structures. Teachers must leave pupils with some valid concepts of bacteria, viruses, inoculation and a vast range of others, in order for school-leavers to understand their own health situations and needs as adults. Simpler, non-abstract language such as 'germs' and 'stopping illness', will need to be used for the majority of the population. How this can be achieved by teachers in primary and secondary schools is discussed further in Chapter 14.

Like Piaget, constructivists see children building up their concepts from experiences of the world. However, the constructivists regard this simply as a response to the environment, with little genetic input. The similarity between the Piagetian and constructivist positions lies in the teacher being a facilitator rather than a didact. She should provide a suitable stimulating learning environment for the pupils. However, the constructivist teacher has a heavy responsibility to be aware of the previous learning experiences of each child in the class. Ideally she should know what conceptual framework and what learning strategies each child in the class possesses. One may ask how practical it is to expect this of a class-teacher responsible for 25 pupils.

Constructivists lay even more emphasis on learning experiences outside school than do Piagetians. Some of the most important learning outside school occurs during the first five years, before the start of formal schooling. Many basic concepts about language, animals, counting and the physical world around them will have built up. Infant teachers in particular need to be aware of this. These initial concepts will be resistant to the teachers' efforts to change them.

The child will also have evolved certain learning strategies that work effectively for him, such as counting on his fingers for number. These too will be resistant to change. Constructivists argue that teachers should use the pupils' initial strategies rather than simply impose more formal ones.

Why should a child be denied the use of a strategy that really works for him? Driver found that a pupil will tend to regress secretly to it anyway.

In the field of maths education, an extremely influential study was carried out in a remote area of Brazil by Carraher, Carraher and Schliemann (1985). It was not compulsory for children to attend school, and many youngsters spent their days working in the local produce market, helping their parents to run a stall. The researchers found that many of them had incredible abilities to calculate totals of goods bought, the change owed to the customer, etc. These were not strategies they had been taught in school but ones they had derived for themselves. They had no need to be taught algorithms they would calculate on paper, or even the use of an electronic calculator. Their informal learning in their own environment was adequate for their needs *in that society*.

Most of us do not live in such an informal society. Most adults are expected to pay their tax, many use banks to store money and the basic medium of numeracy is a paper one. In maths an element of teacher-centred learning is therefore essential. For instance in order to add and subtract two- (as opposed to one-) digit numbers, it is necessary for the child *not* to use his fingers but to rote learn the number bonds.

The work of Carraher, Carraher and Schliemann implies a passive form of constructivism. Teachers should neither intervene directly nor actually teach the pupils didactically. Instead, pupils should be given learning tasks appropriate to their current level of concepts and learning strategies. This case has been supported in Britain by such influential figures as Hilary Shuard, the director of Primary Initiatives in Maths Education (PRIME).

However, a more interventionist form of constructivism is advocated by Ros Driver, among others. Teachers should be aware of the strategies and concepts children bring to school, but should then actively intervene and build on these. This should help pupils master concepts and strategies that are adequate to work in that particular subject, for example, in chemistry to master the concepts involved in the periodic table in order to combine elements into compounds.

In the constructivist framework the job of the teacher becomes even more demanding than in the Piagetian one. The Piagetian framework implies the teacher should be aware of how well each pupil is progressing towards certain desirable goals (for *all* pupils, except those with the most severe learning difficulties) — for instance, the goal of conservation of number in maths. The child's previous learning experience can be assumed to be that outlined in Chapter 2. For the constructivist teacher, however, there is no such universal pattern. Brenda Denvir (1985) took the argument even further. Each child has a unique pattern of learning the teacher needs to know about. The constructivist pattern of learning of any concept is less hierarchical than the Piagetian one.

All this may seem to add up to a daunting task for the teacher. However, if teachers accept the constructivist evidence (and it is difficult not to), they have no alternative if their major concern is real and lasting learning by the children. The untenable alternative is to go through the motions of teaching prescribed syllabuses, regardless of whether pupils are actually learning anything or not.

Of course, an overwhelming implication of the constructivist case for society is for smaller classes, particularly if these are to be of mixed ability. Another implication *on purely cognitive grounds* is for some form of ability grouping. However, if class sizes are reduced radically, there will be less need for such ability grouping.

Bruner's ideas for teaching fall somewhere between those of Piaget and the current constructivists. Like both movements, he agrees that the role of the teacher is one of enabling and facilitating the learning of the pupils. Bruner is more of an interventionist than Piaget: the teacher must actively guide the learning of the pupils. He sees a stronger role for the teacher, compared to the constructivists. It is helpful for the teacher to have prior detailed knowledge of the pupils' existing concepts and strategies. But the teacher has more of an obligation directly to help pupils along. They cannot be allowed *laissez-faire* to learn as much (or as little) as they want to, as some constructivists suggest.

Summary

Constructivism starts from where the child is at present in terms of concepts and learning strategies. The child constructs his own unique set of concepts in order to cope with and explain the world he lives in. This will not occur if lessons have no meaning for him, but will occur if he is given relevant practical material to learn from. The teacher needs to know the conceptual level of each child in all her classes.

Although Piaget outlined a universal pattern of cognitive growth all children pass through, his ideas are reconcilable with those of the constructivists. Both emphasize each child learning from practical experiences.

Questions for discussion

1. What are the implications of the constructivist point of view for your teaching situation?

2. Can a teacher be aware of the initial learning strategies of all the pupils in her class?
3. Does Ausubel's idea of presenting key concepts to pupils in a form easily assimilable by them prevent genuine thinking and problem-solving?
4. Do children learn more effectively by discovering for themselves or by having key words presented to them?
5. Should teachers impose 'desirable' learning strategies on pupils?

Further reading

Driver, R. (1983) *The Pupil as Scientist?*, Open University Press, Milton Keynes.

9
OTHER IMPORTANT CONTEMPORARY SCHOOLS: ALTERNATIVES TO PIAGET

The information-processing (IP) school

As the name suggests, information processing (IP) focuses on the actual process of cognition. Questions are asked such as: 'How does a child learn a specific item, such as 3×4?' 'What are the factors involved?' Having a large capacity to memorize is one of the most important factors in successful IP.

The IP school differs from the Piagetian one in focusing on a single act of learning, taking place at one particular time. It also differs in not investigating whether learning differs for different age-groups. It is not interested in whether or not there are any qualitative differences in learning at different ages (even between mature adults and babies). IP does not accept that such qualitative differences exist. It is concerned with the process of learning rather than with the nature of the learner, whereas Piaget was interested in both.

At present, the IP movement dominates thinking on cognitive development in the USA. Various adherents of the movement have attempted to outline in detail what IP tries to achieve. Richard Sternberg is a highly influential member of the IP school. Sternberg (1977) has synthesized his ideas into a speculative theory of intelligence in which an attempt is made to quantify IP abilities. The various factors involved in IP make up intelligence. By definition, therefore, to be intelligent is to be able to process information efficiently.

Sternberg's six factors are as follows:

1. *Spatial ability* The ability to visualize a problem spatially in all its details.

2. *Perceptual speed* The ability to grasp a new visual field (or view) quickly.
3. *Inductive reasoning* The ability to generalize from evidence presented.
4. *Verbal comprehension ability* The ability to understand new words quickly.
5. *Memory* The ability to store visual material in the brain.
6. *Number ability* The ability to manipulate numbers according to certain rules.

It is a theory of competence yet it is also a theory that stresses the context in which learning takes place. This implies an adaptation by the learner to his environment. It sees considerable individual differences in learning arising. These may be due to differences in a number of factors:

1. The component processes.
2. The strategies into which these processes combine.
3. The mental representations on which the processes and strategies act.
4. The ways in which individuals allocate their attentional resources.

Sternberg (1986) has applied his cognitive theories to teaching, making the very useful distinction between teaching a whole class of mixed ability and teaching individuals. Since British teachers have to master both at the present time, his ideas may be of relevance here. However, it has to be admitted that Sternberg is dubious that cognitive theory can necessarily improve teaching. It can, if the teacher is aware of catering for the appropriate age of pupils for that particular lesson. Likewise, she should be aware whether the particular content of a lesson is relevant or not. It is hoped that the vast majority of teachers do fulfil these two criteria most of the time.

Oakhill (1988) offers the objectives for the IP movement of, first, giving a precise account of what happens in the cognitive system when a child performs a particular task and, second, giving a precise account of how developmental change can be accounted for in terms of changes in the developmental system. The theory should then explain why changes occur. Oakhill's model, as for most of the IP movement, is based on computers. She researched (1984) the way the use of negative comparisons can make it difficult for children to reason soundly, for example: 'Ann is not as bad as Betty. Betty is not as bad as Carol. Who is the best?'

In order to 'solve' such conundrums, Oakhill proposes there are certain crucial elements in a situation:

1. Perceiving and encoding the premisses.

2. Transferring them into the working memory.
3. Combining the premiss representations in the memory to form an integrated representation.
4. Encoding the question.
5. Scanning the representation of the premisses to answer the question or to formulate a conclusion.

However, putting such problems to children does not seem productive, unless one is testing only an intellectual élite.

Oakhill, like Sternberg and most other IP theorists, divided the cognitive system into components and explored the way these components transform and manipulate information. Johnson-Laird (1983) argues in terms of mental models: the reasoner builds a model of IP; he tries to formulate a valid conclusion from the model; he must then test his conclusion against alternatives. In Johnson-Laird's view, the development of reasoning ability depends on the acquisition of procedures for constructing and testing models, rather than on the development of formal rules of logic.

A revealing example of the IP approach given by Siegler (1978) is a balance. This is like a seesaw, except that the weight on either side can be moved nearer to the centre. In his rule assessment studies, Siegler showed that children have four different strategies of increasing complexity for making use of the possibilities of the scale. Ironically, the results can be explained in Piagetian terms: 5-year-olds took only the distance from the fulcrum (centre) into account. Piagetians say the same thing about 5-year-olds, i.e. they focus on just one aspect of a problem; 9-year-olds used both weight and length (Piagetians call this concrete operational thinking); and 13–17-year-olds took both length and weight into account simultaneously. The best thinkers of this age-range could actually quantify this in terms of a formula that would predict exactly what would happen. This is equivalent to Piaget's formal operational thought.

Siegler has stressed the interrelationship of three elements: problems, strategies and knowledge. An example of a problem is how to use a balance – pupils use their prior knowledge of the principles of balances to try to solve it. Simultaneously they develop strategies to deal with the problem. Together with the three elements is an over-arching metacognitive aspect: pupils' awareness of their own learning helps the process. The expert (adult/teacher) has a variety of strategies to try. From this repertoire she can seek the most appropriate one. The novice (child/pupil) has no strategies to begin with, but under the guidance of the teacher he can evolve an appropriate one.

Seymour Papert is an information theorist who has a favourable attitude towards Piaget. In his important book *Mindstorms* (1980), he argued that educationists should break down the schism between educating for the humanities *or* the sciences. This causes mathophobia in many humanities-oriented pupils, who categorize themselves as failures in maths. Both types of subject should instead be encouraged at school. Papert believes the computer gives teachers a maths-oriented machine to use. If pupils can become familiar with it and work fluently on it, they may overcome some of their basic mathophobia. He also believes that familiarity with artificial intelligence (AI) helps pupils to think about themselves.

Papert is interested in Piaget's epistemology rather than in his stages. This epistemology stresses the origin and growth of knowledge rather than its validity. Papert defines AI in both a narrow and a broad way. The narrow one is the capacity of machines to perform functions that would be considered intelligent if performed by people. The broad one is an interdisciplinary one, linking AI to linguistics and psychology. Both are relevant to teachers.

At times Papert seems more of a constructivist than an information processor. He advocates allowing children to develop transitional theories, even if they turn out to be wrong. In a similar way, constructivists advocate children developing learning strategies. However, Papert regards these transitional theories more as practice in the ability to formulate theories rather than strategies that would be of enduring value to the pupils. The 'learning how to learn' element of Papert's thought has a ring of the metacognitive approach to it.

IP contrasts with the Piagetian tradition in many ways. The Piagetian tradition looks for qualitative rather than quantitative change, and it has been criticized for not giving an account of what happens at any one moment of learning. This is the strength of the IP account. IP's primary research method is the scientific one of the controlled experiment, which has led information processors to criticize Piaget's clinical interview for its lack of scientific rigour. IP puts its emphasis on giving a precise, comprehensive, quantitative account of a single learning experience. However, by its very nature, this gives little insight into how any one child matures intellectually from babyhood to adulthood.

IP does, however, provide an explanation of why young children are poorer at single-focus tasks (such as memorizing) and complex multifocus tasks (such as reading). The young child has a limited capacity for memorizing, perhaps only three 'chunks' as opposed to the average adult's seven. Likewise, in the process of reading, the experienced school-leaver or adult can perceive and process larger units of text than the beginner. If a child cannot solve a problem (even after trying very hard), information processors argue that the demands of the task are greater than the child's capacity. Piagetians explain this in terms of the child not yet being at the appropriate stage.

In the IP account, short-term memory is of great importance in a person's ability to operate effectively. However, knowledge also has a considerable influence on the efficacy of the process of learning. The more a child knows about a situation, the more successful he will be in dealing with it. Chi (1978) gives the example of chess, where prior knowledge of possible moves can improve a person's performance in a match.

Since knowledge is generally contained within language, the skill of storing knowledge in some valid linguistic form (whether this be oral memory or written) is a vital prerequisite of successful IP performance. One of the teacher's main roles is to help children find strategies for reducing their memory load − for instance, to write down a list of the facts they need to solve a maths problem. Although a sharp contrast is drawn in this chapter between the IP school and Piaget, the computer was not, of course, as well developed as it is now when Piaget was in his formative years. If it had been, he might have been very interested in using it as a tool for developing epistemology.

IP may seem a mechanical model when compared to that of the Piagetians and constructivists. However, the IP model of learning is far more complex when compared to that of the behaviourists. IP is trying to build up a model of the mind − a concept such extreme behaviourists as Skinner (1969) do not believe exists. It also differs from the latter in allowing for individual differences. Most behaviourists see learning in terms of strictly limited responses to the stimuli teachers, psychologists and other adults present to children. Information processors, on the other hand, see learning more in terms of the individual: he has *goals* (to be able to write with a pen); he pays *attention* to the nature of a pen and how best to hold it; and he develops *skilful* behaviour patterns for doing so, which soon become automatic. This can return to conscious control if a problem arises − for instance, the pen is not working properly.

The domain-specific viewpoint

Is what children learn generalizable to other contexts or is it only usable within the 'domain' in which it was originally learnt? Piaget claimed that the ability to think in a particular way, such as concrete operational, applied to a wide range of areas. Brown and Desforges (1979) criticized Piaget's theory, particularly the problems of the validation of the theory, and they argued that the notion of *stage* creates more conceptual problems than it solves. Piaget's search for structure irrespective of content led to generalities that could not be sustained. Brown and Desforges believe the evidence shows that content must be located within specific subject domains.

Most investigators agree that children in general (and a child specifically) achieve different tasks at different ages. However, many leading contemporary authorities do not accept the Piagetian contention that there is a substantial correlation between the various achievements. They argue the contrary: each area of achievement (or *domain*) is entirely separate from the others. This viewpoint is hence known as the domain-specific one. This naturally requires a careful definition of the word 'domain', but no unambiguous definition in psychological terms has yet emerged.

The domain-specific viewpoint is not a school in the same sense as some of the other concepts that have been discussed: it is more of an opinion. Most of those who subscribe to it see IP as providing the best explanation of cognitive development. A child's improvement can be seen as an increase in his IP capacity rather than as a change in his inferential structure, i.e. a new stage. Carey (1988) argues the broad case against the Piagetians. Reviewing the evidence, she interprets domain-specific knowledge as accounting for most of the variance. A child is a novice in each domain and in each holds theories that differ from an adult's. For example, in the domain of language, 3–5-year-olds do not have a concept of a word. They know only what a word means. Hence they make the error of nominal realism, thinking a word has a physical reality. Papandropolou and Sinclair (1974) found preschool children denying that 'ghosts' is a word because there are no such things as ghosts.

If the domain-specific concept is applied to education, a child's cognitive development takes place only within a specific domain, such as English literature. Any progress in this domain will not transfer into other domains, such as history or chemistry. Piagetians believe, on the contrary, that there are universals in cognitive development. If a child achieves concrete operations in number (in other words, he can recognize five beads as being the same as five dolls), he will probably be capable of concrete operations in other domains, such as the conservation of volume, mass and transitivity. More difficult attainments follow some months later.

According to Carey (1988), 4-year-olds cannot in general do the following things: distinguish appearance from reality; focus on more than one dimension of a task at a time; have a notion of physical causality; represent linear orders; form representations of classes; and include classes. Piagetians and domain-specific theorists would agree on this list. However, the Piagetians explain the child's inability to do these things in terms of an inability to think operationally. Supporters of the domain—specific viewpoint argue that an explanation specific to each domain must be found. The ability to understand conservation of number has nothing to do with the ability to include a lower-order class, such as 'orange', within a higher-order class such as 'fruit'. Sternberg (1986) proposed the radical idea that some teachers (as well as pupils) are domain specific while others are domain general. One hopes primary teachers are domain general so that they can teach the huge range of the curriculum they are responsible for. College tutors will need to look for domain generality in selecting future primary teachers.

An approach to ability that fits in with domain specificity is that of multiple intelligence. This was outlined by Howard Gardner (1983), who denied the existence of general intelligence. Instead, Gardner argues in favour of seven specific abilities: musical, artistic, bodily kinaesthetic, linguistic, logico-mathematical, spatial and personal (sensitivity to the feelings of others). Thus a child might have a different innate ability for music compared to language or dance (bodily kinaesthetic). If teachers adopt Gardner's ideas as a basis for assessment of pupils they obtain a profile of different levels of performance for the seven different abilities.

The structuralists

The ideas of the neo- or post-Piagetians who are sympathetic to Piaget's stages of development are discussed in Chapter 10. However, there remain structuralists who offer alternatives to Piaget's ideas. Keil (1986) is one who believes young children do not differ qualitatively from older children in their thinking. This can be shown by implementing tasks carefully to reveal fine quantitative growth. He does see pervasive qualitative changes occurring in children but they are not dependent on general over-arching structures (stages). This is well illustrated by the example of language. Young children use a word to represent an object by referring to the characteristic features of the object (e.g. a *table* has four legs and a top). Older children, however, use words in a different way. They use various representations, such as defining features (e.g. a *mammal* feeds off the mother's milk at the baby stage), functions (e.g. a *word-processor* deals with words) or causal theories, depending on the category of the word.

Keil simultaneously upholds a domain-specific viewpoint and a structuralist one. Stage two in one domain is very different from stage two in another, unlike Piaget's generalized stages across domains. Hence stage transitions are at very different ages in different domains.

Fischer and Canfield (1986) see any single unit of behaviour as being ambiguous, whether it can be classified as part of an underlying structure or not. However, Fischer and Knight (in press) have derived a skill hierarchy that has four levels and seven stages, as illustrated in Table 9.1. The assumption is that each child has an *optimal* level (which gradually develops with age and experience). Specific behaviour varies widely across contexts, but only up to that particular optimum. It is only under optimal conditions of practice (a familiar context and high motivation) that a child reaches his optimum level. Normally a child performs only at a *functional* level. By means of this synthesis, Fischer and Knight believe they have, to some extent, resolved the conflict between the domain-specific and Piagetian viewpoints.

Level Rp 1 (Table 9.1) seems similar to both Sutherland—Peel's pre-describer and elementary describer stages (see Table 10.3). However, Fischer and Knight found Level Rp 1 at the age only of the pre-describers: 18—24 months. Level Rp 2 was found at nursery-school age. The authors gave the interesting example of a child knowing a secret Daddy does not know. Another example is two dolls representing Mummy and Daddy interacting. Fischer and Knight found Level Rp 3 from the age of 6 to 7 in middle-class children (the same as Piaget's concrete operations): a child pretends two dolls are both Mummy and Daddy as well as a doctor and a teacher at the same time.

Level Rp 4/A1 was found in children who (in Britain) would be at the transition between primary and secondary schooling (10—12 years). It is similar to Piaget's formal operations. An example given is of honesty as a general quality of an interaction between child and adult.

Level A2 was found at 14—16 years. Skills can either be purely intellectual or social. An example of a social skill is to integrate two social concepts, such as honesty and kindness, into the idea of a social life. (Levels A3 and A4 were found in young adults and so are beyond the scope of this book.)

Like Piaget, Fischer and Knight believe that a child's concepts derive from the learning environment as well as from the child himself. They evolve from an interaction between the nature of the task and the child's structure of knowledge. Fischer and Knight argue that their levels evolved out of the data and provide the best account of them. For a child to be at his optimum level, he should be well motivated and familiar with the task. Both individual children and groups of children (i.e. school classes) differ in the sequence in which they pass through the levels.

There are certain similarities between Fischer and Knight's four levels and Sutherland—Peel's eight stages (Table 10.3) in that both offer a wider and (it is hoped) more subtle range of levels than Piaget's. However, Sutherland—Peel's, like Piaget's, have to be passed through in a certain

Table 9.1   Fischer and Knight's levels and stages of development of reflective judgement

Skill level	Stage of reflective judgement
Level Rp 1 Single representations	*Stage 1* Single category of knowing: by direct observation without evaluation
Level Rp 2 Representational mappings	*Stage 2* Two categories of knowing: a child can be either right or wrong
Level Rp 3 Representational systems	*Stage 3* Three categories of knowing: a child can be right or wrong or knowledge may be incomplete
Level Rp 4/A1 Single abstractions	*Stage 4* Knowledge is an abstract process. It is uncertain
Level A2 Abstract mappings	*Stage 5* Knowledge is relative and subject to interpretation. Conclusions must be justified
Level A3 Abstract systems	*Stage 6* Despite knowledge being uncertain, it is possible to abstract some justified conclusions across domains or viewpoints
Level A4 Principles	*Stage 7* Knowledge occurs probabilistically via inquiry, which unifies concepts of knowledge

sequence. Fischer and Knight's variable-sequence order will depend in particular upon three factors about the children: their emotional state and motivation; their maturation; and their learning history. Both are, however, firmly developmental in their orientation.

The metacognitive influence

Metacognition is one of the dominant movements in developmental psychology in Britain at present. It carries an important message for teachers: pupils need to be made consciously aware of their own learning in order to improve the quality of that learning. This should include how and why they learn.

As a teacher I have considerable doubts about the practicality of applying these ideas to education, particularly to the primary school. I am not yet convinced the time a teacher needs to spend to make young children aware of their own learning is cost effective. I have doubts that 5-year-olds have a sufficiently developed self-concept to gain from this. The claim may well have been established in a laboratory setting, but practical ways of using the idea to teach 25 mixed-ability 5-year-olds have yet to be worked out. To find ways of helping teachers do this is a major task for educational psychologists.

These doubts are substantiated by a study by Brown, Campione and Barclay (1979). Young children in general were found to have major problems in regulating themselves and controlling their goal-directed activities. However, older children do pick up the basic strategies of learning and remembering from school without needing specific teaching. The researchers investigated children who were borderline between normal and ordinary school. The younger children (10 years old on average) did not gain from an intensive period of training, but the 13-year-olds did make significant progress in their ability to recall and (even more important-antly) in their ability to apply what they had learnt to real-life situations ('transfer of training' in psychological jargon).

The basic skills of metacognition are

1. Predicting the consequences of an action (what will happen if I do this?);
2. checking the results of one's own actions (did it work?);
3. monitoring one's ongoing activity (how am I doing?); and
4. reality testing (does it make sense?).

A number of other behaviours for overseeing attempts to learn and control problems are mentioned by Brown and DeLoache (1983). These children were lacking in all of them.

Children who were trained in the use of self-checking routines improved in a number of them: they took more time over a task; they recalled more ideas from a passage; and the ideas they did recall were more clearly related to the themes of the material.

The philosophy of Brown, Campione and Barclay (1979) is to develop the technique of a Socratic dialogue. Initially the experimenter/teacher asks the child questions that test the child's basic assumptions about his own learning. With an older, more intelligent child, this leads to an improvement. In the long term the hope is that the child will ask himself such questions. The process becomes one of self-interrogation, similar to Vygotsky's inner dialogues.

In teaching language, it is argued that there should be a particular focus on reading. It is while learning to read that children need help most to become consciously aware of their own learning. This argument applies most strongly to those who have difficulties in learning to read. Some of the questions a teacher might ask a pupil are 'What have you read today?', 'How did you read that? Did you have a ruler under the line you were reading?', 'Were you using the pictures to help you read?', 'Which are the letters you can't read?'

Brown and DeLoache (1983) believe children are capable of metacognition of a sort, even as early as babyhood. They admit it is not easy for children to apply these skills to new situations. It is here that adults are far more successful than children. Brown and DeLoache argue, however, that it is inexperience rather than youth that handicaps a person. They draw an analogy with a novice chess player of any age, who is unable to monitor his own performance effectively. Children are universal novices because they are not effective metacognitively. They fail to check and monitor their ongoing activities. They fail to make their own task analyses. Brown and DeLoache admit there are not enough developmental data to resolve the disagreement as to whether or not it is efficacious for young children to be taught the skills of metacognition.

It is important to check the results of an operation against an outside criterion of acceptability, whether one is following laboratory instructions or studying a poem. If secondary pupils are serious about their study, they need to learn this. But it is hard to imagine primary children having the sophistication to manage it. Teachers may need to coach younger children in this skill — for example, to be able to do simple primary-science experiments safely.

Brown and DeLoache put forward three main aspects of metacognition, all of which seem worth considering by teachers and psychologists:

1. The ability to get the gist of a message, whether written or oral.
2. Visual scanning.
3. Retrieval.

Aspect (1) is, of course, an invaluable skill for upper primary and secondary pupils. However, Brown and DeLoache (1983) found a vast improvement from 12 years upwards in the recall of important aspects of texts without a similar improvement in recall of less important details. Primary children showed no such distinction. Brown and DeLoache do not believe there is any breakthrough age for this improvement. Therefore they argue that the preschool child can gather the gist of practical situations. This is a skill where babies can perform competently with actual objects in front of them. Babies do, however, tend to look for an object at place A, where it was last seen, instead of at place B, where it was moved to. Older people soon learn to adjust to the new position, in a way babies find difficult.

Aspect (2) is a skill babies exhibit soon after birth. However, they tend to *fixate* on a small area of their visual field. As Piaget pointed out, children need to learn to *decentre* — in other words, to scan the whole visual field and, as a result, see the whole picture instead of just part of it. Mackworth and Bruner (1970) concluded that adults have an effective visual-search programme that enables them to co-ordinate central and peripheral vision, and that children do not. Children's retrieval processes (aspect (3)) become increasingly sophisticated as conscious, voluntary control over them intensifies. Cues are a big help in doing this. Here teachers can help their pupils enormously by giving them (or guiding them to discover for themselves) the cues they need.

Much effort has been put into applying metacognition specifically to language teaching. Making children aware of language can prove effective in improving their language performance. There is a close link between metacognition and language acquisition in the work of Annette Karmiloff-Smith (1986). Karmiloff-Smith rejects Chomsky's (1959) nativist explanation (outlined in Chapter 3) as inadequate to meet the data, although she admits having been influenced by the nativist position. She also agrees with post-Piagetians that some learning does take place through interaction with the environment. However, she believes young children are fundamentally theorists rather than inductionists. According to her, babies and toddlers have the ability to represent and be aware of their own representations. Just after a baby has been born, knowledge is implicit. Then the baby scans his immediate environment. Initially the baby focuses on external stimuli in order to get representations into his mind. Later he can eliminate the external stimuli and deal directly with internal representations, such as words or images, making self-repairs as he goes along. Later, knowledge becomes translatable into actual language. Unlike Fodor (1983), Karmiloff-Smith does not believe that there is a common representational system in very young children. She believes there is a multiplicity of means.

Thorpe (1991) examined motivation linked to metacognition. To what do children attribute their success or failure? Those who regard their failure as being due to lack of effort or the use of an inappropriate strategy are more likely to work harder or use an appropriate strategy the next time. However, children who regard their ability as low or the task as difficult are less likely to improve. In general those primary children with the greatest metacognitive awareness concentrated on the factors they could control — learning strategies in particular. In this way meta-cognitive theory stresses the role people have in affecting their own development.

This theory also focuses on the person—environment interaction, as Lerner, Hultsch and Dixon (1983) pointed out. For teachers, the relevance lies in pointing out the features of the environment. Primary teachers can usually be relied upon to know this, but secondary teachers in many subjects will need to improve radically the environmental stimulation they provide for their lessons: for example, English teachers could put up exciting visual stimuli for creative writing. This is why metacognitivists are also known as contextualists — a name derived from their emphasis on the child's need to adapt to the environment.

The metacognitive approach differs fundamentally from Piaget's. Learning proceeds quantitatively rather than qualitatively. There is no stage structure whereby learning is different in a young child to that of an adult. On the other hand, there are close ties with Vygotsky's ideas. Vygotsky could be considered a pioneer metacognitivist, with his emphasis on the child consciously controlling his learning. However, the metacog-nitive movement has not yet tackled the problem of the teacher's role: should she control the situation fairly strictly, as Vygotsky, Skinner and Feuerstein argue, or should she let the child decide his own leaning, as Piagetians, Bruner and the constructivists argue? Metacognition can be linked with constructivism, if children are made aware of their own learning and of the learning strategies on which the constructivists put so much emphasis.

There are closer links with the information processors. Information processors and metacognitivists are looking for the factors vital to learning and very often they agree (e.g. Brown and DeLoache (1983) referred to obtaining the gist of a message, visual scanning skills and retrieval). However, IP does not put the same emphasis on conscious *awareness* of learning; it is more concerned that the learning *does* take place.

To conclude, the philosophical underpinning of metacognition is re-ferred to briefly. Both the phenomenological and hermeneutic traditions are strong here, the former involving the ability to react personally to events and the latter involving the working out of meaning from texts.

The nativists

This radical (largely American) school argues that children have an innate potential for learning that will be realized provided they are exposed to an appropriate learning environment. Much of what young children learn is explained by their being biologically programmed to do so. Supporters of this position regard Piaget as a pioneer nativist. However, opponents put the emphasis of Piaget's position on the environmental side.

Chomsky (1959) was the first nativist to make a major impact, with his Language Acquisition Device (LAD − outlined further in Chapter 3). More recently, Gelman and Gallistel (1983) have put forward similar ideas for maths. Young children will learn counting and adding (and perhaps even other fundamental processes) merely by being exposed to appropriate number experiences, such as playing shop with money, and playing ludo and snakes and ladders, etc. The implications of this for preschool and primary teachers are discussed further in Chapter 14.

If all areas of cognitive activity are considered, not merely language and number, nativists reach similar conclusions. Fodor (1983) argued that there is little evidence for qualitative structural changes (i.e. stages) of the sort Piaget claimed; rather, the same representational and computational systems exist in all individuals. These are present from birth. What develops through childhood is an increasing ability to use these systems in an ever-wider range of tasks. However, Fodor's evidence, like Chomsky's, comes largely from the study of the acquisition of language.

Butterworth (1981) has researched on a broader front, arguing the genetic potential underlying most skills is present at birth. These innate skills will develop provided the baby is exposed to the appropriate environment. However, Butterworth's age-range for research is babyhood, so he has not investigated the case for children of 2 and over.

Mounod and Vintner (1985) have argued a largely nativist case, but one fused with elements of IP and Piagetian notions. Because of the Piagetian elements, their ideas are discussed further in Chapter 10. According to Campbell and Olsen (1990), the extreme nativist position would include formal operations within a baby's zone of proximal development (see Chapter 4). Overall, the nativists represent a radical biological orientation. Piaget was strongly influenced by his early experiences as a biologist, but the nativists are even more explicitly biological than this. They are at the opposite extreme to Vygotsky's emphasis on culture.

The implications for teachers are rather deterministic: the pupil has merely to be exposed to the appropriate environment in order to learn. However, this leaves little scope for the teacher to control the learning process. On this point nativists are in total disagreement with the behaviourists and Feuerstein.

As there is very little opportunity for conscious awareness of learning in the child, the nativist position is also irreconcilable with that of the metacognitivists. On the other hand, the nativist position is reconcilable with IP, as Mounod and Vintner (1985) have argued. The various abilities IP measures (such as storage capacity) are present from birth and merely require the appropriate stimulation to develop. Nativism offers an interesting perspective, but one that may be of more relevance to psychologists than to teachers.

Summary

The IP movement stresses the ability to process cognitive data at any one moment and in particular the use of short-term memory to do so. The domain-specific school argues that any ability a child has is specific to a particular domain and has no relation with any ability in any other domain. This may or may not coincide with a school subject. The structuralist, Keil, argues that children make qualitative progress without going through stages. Fischer puts forward a skills-based stage framework that, he argues, is not subject to the criticisms made of Piaget's.

The metacognitive movement puts the emphasis on children being made aware of their own learning processes. This implies that this very consciousness itself improves the quality of learning. The nativists argue that babies and children have an innate ability to learn, which has merely to be exposed to appropriate environmental stimuli to be activated.

Questions for discussion

1. Is the IP paradigm of use to teachers? If so, how?
2. What are the important factors for psychologists to bear in mind when carrying out experiments based on IP?
3. Which explanation best matches the evidence: that of the domain-specific viewpoint or that of the Piagetians?
4. Is it practical for all pupils (even nursery) to be made aware of their own learning in the way the metacognitive movement implies?
5. How does a teacher teach the individuals in a class (as opposed to whole-class teaching)?

Further reading

Richardson, K. and Sheldon, S. (eds.) (1988) *Cognitive Development to Adolescence*, Open University Press, Milton Keynes.

10
LOYAL TO THE FOUNDING FATHER: FUNDAMENTALIST, POST- AND NEO-PIAGETIANS

Despite the large number of critics of Piaget's work who have been active during the 1970s and 1980s and whose work is discussed in Chapters 4 to 9, there remains a core of cognitive developmentalists who are basically sympathetic to Piaget's original contribution, as summarized in Chapter 2. Of this, it is Piaget's stage theory that has attracted far more criticism than his theory of learning. Of those who support Piaget's ideas, the degree of support varies from the absolute to the qualified.

The fundamentalist Piagetians

Not surprisingly, the Geneva school has been the staunchest defender of the original Piagetian position. This has involved defending it against the domain-specific standpoint, particularly from the USA. Many of the Geneva school are still extending or testing some aspect of Piaget's ideas — for instance, Bovet (1974) examined an aspect of conservation but strictly within the Piagetian framework.

Les Smith (1982) has defended Piagetian interpretations from Donaldsonian attack. The Donaldsonians argue that a child can interrelate classes (such as cows and horses) on the basis of positive, observational properties alone, whereas Piaget had argued that the child must also be able to interrelate the negative, inferential properties in order to understand class inclusion. Take for example this array of 4 cows:

Class A consists of 3 black.
Class A' consists of 1 white.
Class B consists of 4 cows.
Class C consists of 4 sleeping cows.

Some children can calculate $A' = B - A$ without understanding why this is so. Thus they satisfy the Donaldsonian criteria, as investigated by McGarrigle, Grieve and Hughes (1978), who asked the children: 'Are there more black cows or more sleeping cows?' However, in order to satisfy the Piagetian criteria, the child has to be able to quantify both A and B. Piaget asked them: 'Are there more black cows or more cows?'

Smedslund has distanced himself rather more from Piaget than has Smith. On the other hand, he has not been strongly influenced by the information processing (IP) movement, as have all the authors in Chapter 9. Smedslund (1966b) had a particular role in expanding Piaget's original transitivity problem. In Piaget's original experiment, a child had to compare three sticks of varying length by comparing A and B and then B and C. Then, according to Piaget, he would make the transitivity inference and deduce that since $A > B$ and $B > C$, therefore $A > C$, without actually having to compare A and C physically. Smedslund showed that children could memorize the lengths of A and C and so they not actually make the transitive inference. He therefore made A and C both black, but had two B rods, both yellow but of slightly different length: one 19.5 cm and the other 20.5 cm, as illustrated in Figure 10.1. However, the 5−7-year-olds were presented with the problem as though there was only one yellow rod, i.e. they were shown the two different versions of the B rod as

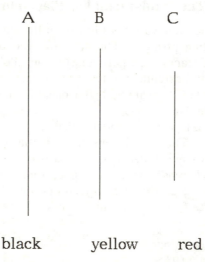

Figure 10.1   Smedslund's version of Piaget's original transitivity problem

though they were identical. So Smedslund was in fact tricking the children. This phrasing of questions in such a way as to 'trick' children is an element of Piaget's work that has been much criticized by Bryant (1974), Donaldson (1978) and other workers. In Smedslund's defence it has to be remembered that his work was published before the criticisms were made.

If they were to succeed in this problem, the children had to defy Smedslund and state there was more than one B rod and that the two were of different lengths. Expecting 5-year-olds to say this to an adult male psychologist whom they did not know seems most unlikely. It is more a test of self-confidence than of ability to make transitive inferences. Nevertheless, Smedslund concluded that Piaget was correct: children of 5—7 cannot make such inferences.

Smedslund (1961) played another 'trick' on young children. In Piagetian jargon, the children had previously shown understanding of the conservation-of-quantity principle. Initially he showed children two weights of clay, which they recognized as equivalent. He then secretly took some of the weight off. What reasons would young children give for the now different weights demonstrated to them? None of the eleven conservers trained by Smedslund could account for the new situation. However, six out of the thirteen natural conservers (i.e. they had come to this state of thinking without training) did state that 'something must have dropped on the floor'. In other words, these six were not deceived by the 'trick'.

This finding seems to favour Piaget's idea of readiness rather than Bruner's idea of intervention. Children are more likely to master an aspect of concrete operations effectively when they have realized it for themselves rather than being trained to do so (or accelerated). By implication, this applies to any other principle. If the children have internalized the principle for themselves, they can see through 'tricks'.

In his later work, Smedslund (1977) also drew our attention to the problem of how we know whether or not a child has understood the task requirements correctly. We must not assume that, if a child fails to perform a certain task 'correctly', it is because he is incapable of doing so. It may be because he has not understood what he is required to do. Smedslund saw a circular argument here: in order to deduce whether a child has a particular logical structure or not, we assume he has understood the (logical) task instructions. But we have to assume the child has understood the instructions in order to study his degree of logicality.

Smedslund (1966a) made an even more fundamental criticism of Piaget's failure to consider the social dimension of children's learning. From 5 years onwards, children spend most of the day in the presence of their peers in the school classroom and most children have at least one brother or sister at home. Smedslund (*ibid.*) showed that it is *not* only the inanimate environment that interests the child: 'It is well known that the child's interests (and consequently the majority of his experiences) are concentrated on the principal aspects of the social life, notably roles, values and symbols. Even when the child plays alone, his play causes roles, symbols and social products to intervene.' For this reason alone, social interaction is a major factor in cognitive development. This criticism has been extended by various other authors, as discussed in Chapter 7.

The neo-Piagetians

Neo-Piagetians have accepted the main ideas of IP (Chapter 9) in terms of its emphasis on cognitive processing or short-term memory capacity. An improvement in a child's cognitive capacity results from an increase in his IP ability rather than in his inferential structure or power. Unlike the IP and domain-specific viewpoints, however, neo-Piagetians do see changes as domain general. Translating this into the school curriculum, a child who has demonstrated cognitive development in one subject should make improvements across various subjects.

The neo-Piagetians are reconciled to some of Piaget's ideas while being critical of others. Pascual-Leone (1976) has moved from pure Piagetian theory to a synthesis of Piagetian and IP theories. He de-emphasizes the role of general logical structures and equilibrium while retaining most core Piagetian constructs and postulates. From IP he evolved the concept of M power: the ability of a child to store instructions and to scan his perceptual scene for relevant elements to focus on. Any task can only be achieved when the appropriate M power has been developed.

Pascual-Leone's revision of Piaget's stages involved a synthesis of Piaget's stages with his own M value, as illustrated in Table 10.1. Pascual-

Table 10.1   Pascual-Leone's revision of Piaget's stages

Stage	Age in years	M value
Early pre-operations	3–4	a + 1
Late pre-operations – early concrete operations	5–6	a + 2
Mid-concrete operations	7–8	a + 3
Late concrete operations	9–10	a + 4
Early formal operations	11–12	a + 5
Mid-formal operations	13–14	a + 6
Late formal operations	15–16	a + 7

Leone argues that his M power successfully explains horizontal *décalage* (or lag). A child achieves different stages in different areas. Pascual-Leone argues that the M power needed in the various situations is the same. In other words, for a child to reach a higher stage in, say, history, requires the same M power as to reach a lower stage in, say, physical education.

Case (1985) has evolved still further from Piaget's original ideas while building on those of Pascual-Leone. He sees development as the acquisition of increasingly complex cognitive structures constant across many content domains. In this way he remains a neo-Piagetian. He rejects the extreme domain-specific notion that there is no correlation between a child's performance in different domains. However, he has been much influenced by the IP movement and its crucial concept of working memory capacity. Case calls this short-term storage space (STSS). Unlike Pascual-Leone, Case argues that growth in STSS can be achieved by greater operational efficiency. This implies that teachers can help children to use their capacities more efficiently.

Like Pascual-Leone, Case evolved his own stage-based theory, in his case combining the memory-capacity idea of the IP school with a modified version of Piaget's stages. Case believes that his version overcomes several of the major criticisms of Piaget, e.g. the precise role of equilibration and how it can be quantified. Case operationalizes this in terms of his STSS so that equilibration can actually be used and measured. In Case's alternative stage theory, there are four major stages of development. Within each there are three possibilities: unifocal, bifocal or elaborated. In essence it is a more complex version of Pascual-Leone's. At each level a Piagetian type of stage is combined with an increasing ability to perceive and store the immediate situation (or STSS in his language).

Halford (1978) came to very similar conclusions to Pascual-Leone. IP concepts need to be combined with Piagetian ones in order to provide an adequate explanation of cognitive development, but the balance is very much in favour of IP. Halford studied how a model helps a child to solve problems. He found three stages:

1. Translation into a model.
2. Operation on the model in order to make deductions.
3. Retranslation back into the problem-solving situation.

His results were classified at one or other of three levels:

Level 1 Unable to code anything more complex than binary relations, univariate functions or unitary operations.

Level 2 Able to handle concepts that can be encoded as binary operations.

Level 3 Being able to handle concepts that can be expressed as compositions of binary operations, such as dysfunction, conjunction and implication.

These are all classic Piagetian logical operations. The sort of things Halford studies are: symbol—symbol relations (for instance, a man is taller than a boy); symbol—object relations (for example, naming the man as 'Daddy' and the boy as 'Billy'); and object—object relations (the actual size of the man is 5 ft 8 in and of the boy is 3 ft 3 in).

Halford looked to IP rather than structure for an explanation as to why a certain child's performance should be limited to a particular level. He found children's level of cognitive development accounted for only a small part of the variance. He agreed with Pascual-Leone (1976) that IP capacity is the main limiting factor. This must reach the required magnitude if that child is going to be able to operate at level 2 or 3. Once the minimum capacity for IP is available, learning will be a function of experience and task variables. Concepts would thus emerge across a population of children, such as British 11-year-olds, gradually rather than synchronously or in a defined sequence. Unlike Piaget, Halford does not find evidence for stages that have abrupt transitions.

Mounod and Vintner (1985) have also developed a synthesis of IP and Piagetian notions, but added to this a nativist element. They deny Piaget's ideas that the child constructs new concepts for himself during the course of his development. Instead they believe that formal structures are preformed, in other words, biologically predetermined at birth. As the child grows up, his internal representations are elaborated. The child's concepts, which seem to be present at birth, are broadened by experience.

Simultaneously, Mounod and Vintner reject Piaget's notion of equilibration. Instead they see a system for IP present at birth, which changes over time in the course of a series of cognitive 'revolutions'. Mounod and Vintner believe the child should have a more independent role in his interaction with a psychologist or teacher — any learning situation should not be too rigorously defined. The child should define the situation for himself rather than having it defined for him.

The post-Piagetians

Peel and his Students

During the 1960s E. A. Peel evolved an alternative classification to Piaget's in terms of describer and explainer thinking. The terms are more or less self-explanatory. Like Piaget's, Peel's is a hierarchical system with explainer being the 'desirable' stage from an academic point of view. *Describer thinking* involves a complete immersion in the immediate situation around the child. It follows there is very little predictive ability from the situations, whereas the explainer can predict the outcome from superficially different situations.

In place of formal operational thought Peel uses the term *explainer thought*. This denotes the ability to attribute causality as opposed to merely describing phenomena. After attaining this the adolescent can work easily within the cognitive expectations of abstract thought traditionally expected in the secondary school. Peel, with his science background, put particular emphasis on the criterion of an adolescent being able to hypothesize and to be able to test the various hypotheses. The differences between the two are encapsulated in Table 10.2.

More generally, the adolescent who thinks at an explainer level realizes that reality is only one of the possibilities. This gives abundant scope to the imagination to conjure up other possibilities. As illustrated in Table 10.3, Sutherland (1982) expanded Peel's two-category system into a more comprehensive nine-category one, to delineate finer nuances of development, particularly in the primary school.

The ages quoted are averages obtained in infant, junior and comprehensive schools in a large English city, which catered for a representative sample of the IQ range. It was pointed out by Hazel Francis (at a conference) that these stages represent a development more of language than of thought. The subdivisions of describer replies especially indicate a growing linguistic capacity to use more complex grammatical structures and a greater vocabulary.

Peel's second major classification of responses is in terms of the pupil's *awareness of events outside the written passage* presented to him. In some ways it is a variation on the describer−explainer theme. This time the hierarchical classification is in four stages. Examples are given of responses to the following passage:

> All large cities have art galleries and Italy is exceptionally rich in art treasures. Many people travel to Italy, especially to enjoy these old paintings, books and sculptures. Floods in the Florence area recently damaged many of these great works. Old paintings are rare, valuable and beautiful and should be kept safely stored.
>
> *Question* Are the Italians to blame for the loss of the paintings and art treasures?

1. *Restricted* This term applies to the logic used. Responses tend to be tautological, merely repeating parts of the passage verbatim or in a

slightly modified form. Alternatively, irrelevant guesses are made. Example: 'No, because they've got lots of treasures.'

2. *Circumstantial* Judgements made are now relevant, but the content of a passage dominates the reply with very little attention to its

Table 10.2 The differences between Peel's describer and explainer thinking

Describer thinking	Explainer thinking
1. The child cannot hypothesize	The adolescent can hypothesize
2. Inductive thinking is dominant	Deductive thinking is dominant
3. Answers the questions: How is this made up? What are its features?	Answers the questions: Why is this so? What is this an instance of? In what context does it fit?
4. Responses are content dominated	Responses are imaginative and possibility invoking
5. Observations are partial and circumstantial	Judgements are comprehensive
6. Solutions have to be physically present	Solutions do not have to be physically present, but can be conjured up mentally
7. Predictions are very limited	It is possible to predict outcomes from superficially different situations
8. 'a relating of the parts of a phenomenon with each other'	'involves referring the phenomena to other previously experienced phenomena and to generalizations and to concepts independently formed' (Peel, 1971, p. 26)
9. Applies largely to primary-age children	Applies largely to adolescents
Summary 'particularistic, perceptual, circumstantial and largely inductive ways of thinking'	'the invocation of imagined possibilities which gradually become more articulate in form to warrant the term: hypotheses and propositions. This articulateness is shown in the increased use of deduction and the power to eliminate unsupported alternatives'

meaning. Analysis, such as exists, is partial and takes account of only one element in the passage. Example: 'Well, I shouldn't think so, not really, because of the floods, I mean they didn't let the flood come, did they?'

3. *Comprehensive circumstantial* More than one piece of evidence can be taken into account at the same time. The pupil now shows a clear awareness of cause and effect.

4. *Imaginative* The pupil's thinking now goes beyond the limited circumstances of the passage. He shows an awareness of abstract gener-

Table 10.3 The Sutherland–Peel category system

---

0. No knowledge of the concept area
1. Pre-describer (5 y.): The child has some awareness of a phenomenon, but expresses this in an illogical or irrelevant way. An example is snow lying on a bridge – the pre-describer thinks the snow came out of the bridge
2. One-phrase describer (5 y.): The child uses short constructions, which indicate some slight understanding that cannot yet be called a concept. For example, a cloud is called 'fluffy'
3. Elementary describer (7 y.): Very simple sentences are now used, concentrating on the immediately perceivable. For example, dew is spoken of as 'sort of water that comes up in the morning'
4. Middle describer (10 y.): There is now some understanding of concepts and the parts of a phenomenon are linked up. For example: 'The fire went hot because I blew on it'
5. Extended describer (12 y.): A more comprehensive description is now given, complex concepts are now used and, for the first time, invisible causality is now understood, e.g. cold. Another example is describing a car window in winter: 'You can see it because the frost has got onto it and made it visible'
6. Elementary explainer (or transitional) (13–15 y.): Explanation enters replies for the first time, but they are still limited. There is still a fair degree of description. There is limited ability to use inference or analogy. For example, a pupil giving her idea of ice says 'If it is not the right temperature, it would melt'
7. Full explainer (less than half of 15–16-year-olds): This is Peel's original conception of explainer thought. Replies are comprehensive and explicit. A general principle is used and hypotheses can be formulated. The emphasis is now on 'Why?' rather than 'How?' questions. For example a pupil explains boiling as 'when water starts changing from liquid to steam'
8. Extended or theoretical explainer (18 y.): There is now a theory underlying pupils' replies. In biology this might be cell theory or evolution; in literature, structuralism; and in sociology, interactionism or Marxism. In higher education this level of response is expected. However, Piaget made no provision for a stage beyond formal operations. That is what is claimed for it. For example, a sixth-form science pupil explains air in terms of 'molecules loosely bonded together'

---

alizations. Independent experience and ideas are drawn upon. Extenuating possibilities are invoked to cover the behaviour of a character in the passage. Possible causes are mentioned and related to effects in an explicit way. Overall a mature, balanced judgement is made. Example: 'Well, not completely, they could have been kept safe, unless the floods took them completely by surprise. I suppose they did, but it might be best to protect them in glass cages.'

These alternative formulations of Peel's ideas were applied to most subjects of the secondary curriculum. A summary of some of the more interesting pieces of research relevant to teachers today is given in Chapter 16.

The Average Ages of Piaget's Stages

There have been a number of searching critiques of the ages Piaget gave for the attainment of his stages even from within the Piagetian framework. Sutherland (1980), investigating the age of attainment across the whole school age-range, found that both biology and physical-science pupils in a comprehensive school understood respiration and the water cycle in formal operational terms only at the age of 16. Even then, less than half the age-group could do so. Shayer, Kuchemann and Wylan (1976) and Shayer and Wylan (1978) had similar findings with representative samples of school-age pupils in England. McNally (1970), working at more or less the same time in Australia, also had similar results. These findings indicate that most secondary pupils are transitional between describer and explainer thinking. This has major implications for the secondary teacher, which are developed in Chapter 16.

So there is evidence that Inhelder and Piaget gave an inaccurate picture of the age at which youngsters are capable of formal operational thought. No doubt the children of the lecturers at the university clinic in Geneva could master this type of thinking by the age of 11. But only a tiny minority of children in comprehensive schools have anything approaching this environment and hereditary background. As Shayer, Kuchemann and Wylan (1976) pointed out, if grammar-school and public-school pupils are tested, they do show this ability from the beginning of secondary schooling.

Similarly, Sutherland (1982) found that concrete operations was attained only at an average age of 12. Shayer, Kuchemann and Wylan (1976) found the same thing. It seems that pupils, on average, only attain concrete operations in the first year of secondary school. On the other hand, workers such as Bryant (1972) and Donaldson (1978) found concrete operations in different areas being attained at much younger ages than did Piaget. These are discussed in Chapter 7.

Can Development be Accelerated?

Adey, Shayer and Yates (1989) have investigated this question in science education. Their findings have a particular relevance to science education but an even stronger general relevance to cognitive development and so are reported in this chapter rather than Chapter 16.

Adey's King's College, London, team set up a study involving experimental and control groups at comprehensive schools. The same teachers taught CASE (Cognitive Acceleration Science Education) material to the experimental classes and standard material to the control classes. The teachers were given a minimal in-service training on the CASE approach of one day per term for six years. The criterion for cognitive understanding was the onset of formal operational thinking as measured by Piagetian reasoning tests. The CASE material involves practical problems that require the use of formal schemata for their solution. For example, pupils are given a set of tubes of different lengths. They are encouraged to blow across them. They are expected to work out which variable affects the note. They are then expected to be able to transfer this to other tasks. Other formal operational schemata taught include probability, ratio and compensation among the physical-mathematical concepts. Biological concepts were also taught. After three years of such intervention, the boys (but not the girls) in the experimental class were significantly better than the control class (boys and girls) on the Piagetian reasoning tests. This applied only to the 12-year-olds (second-formers), not to the 11-year-olds (first-formers).

These results would seem to show that acceleration by means of specially designed curriculum material is possible in principle. However, it must be aimed at an amenable target, i.e. pupils who are 'ready' to be accelerated. Of course, these particular findings applied only to science. It is highly likely that a different pattern of results might be obtained in other subjects. Two other points should be borne in mind when interpreting the results. First, there is the risk of the Hawthorne effect operating: teachers teach the new material more enthusiastically than the old. (However, Adey and his colleagues argue that the Hawthorne effect wore off over the three-year period of the study.) Second, they found the convergent type of answers of the Piagetian reasoning tests favoured boys rather than girls.

American Post-Piagetians

Some theorists such as Feldman (1986), who are sympathetic to Piaget's outlook, have attempted to overcome criticisms of Piaget's statistical inadequacies. Feldman has also argued we should study *non*-universally attained competencies as well as the universal ones, such as conservation of number. Based on his longitudinal study of children's drawing of maps, he came to various conclusions on the nature of cognitive development. Whether the competency be universally achieved or not, Feldman sees development as an alternating sequence between periods of relative internal stability and periods of radical change. With each successive period the stable periods become more and more stable. At a peak period for change, many elements in the situation progress, but at the same time many elements regress to a 'lower' order.

Summary

Despite the many critiques mounted, there remains a core of cognitive developmentalists who are fundamentally positive towards Piaget's outline and who accept his stages. The degree of support varies from the hardline fundamentalists to those who accept a modified Piagetian position. The latter includes the post-Piagetians who accept many of the criticisms made but who believe a modified form of the Piagetian case is the nearest we have to the truth. The latter also includes the neo-Piagetians, such as Pascual-Leone and Case, who compromise between the IP and Piagetian movements and offer a synthesis of the two.

Smedslund claimed to have confirmed Piaget's finding that young children are not capable of making transitive inferences while claiming to have improved on a number of Piaget's original experiments, in particular transitivity and the conservation of quantity. He also claimed to have confirmed Piaget's claim that children cannot be trained to become conservers; rather the children have to be 'ready'. However, he was critical of the lack of the social dimension in Piaget's work.

Peel distinguished describer from explainer thinking or alternatively circumstantial from imaginative thinking. Sutherland expanded this into eight substages. Both Sutherland and Shayer, Küchemann and Wylan (1976) challenged the ages at which Piaget said his stages were attained. Both teams of British workers found it was only in the first year of secondary school that the average pupil is concrete operational and it is only at 16 that a minority of the age-group achieve formal operational.

Questions for discussion

1. How can describer and explainer thinking be applied to your type of teaching?

2. If Sutherland and Shayer, Küchemann and Wylan are correct that most children are not capable of abstract thinking, what are the implications for secondary teachers?
3. How important for learning is short-term memory (or short-term storage space, as Case calls it)?
4. Are M power and STSS really developmental concepts?
5. How can teachers make use of the idea supported by Smedslund that children can help each other?
6. How can teachers taking a lesson and psychologists conducting an experiment be sure children have understood the task requirements correctly?
7. What should we as a society do to help those whose home environment is inadequate to cope with formal schooling?

Further reading

Entwistle, N. E. (ed.) (1985) *New Directions in Educational Psychology: 1 Learning and Teaching*, Falmer Press, Lewes.

Peel, E. A. (1972) *The Nature of Adolescent Judgement*, Staples Press, London.

11
WHERE ARE WE NOW IN COGNITIVE DEVELOPMENT?

A wide and conflicting range of viewpoints has been presented and conclusions drawn. Wherever we are, it is clear we are not yet at the end. In this chapter we consider some of the remaining unresolved issues in developmental psychology. Is Piaget *passé*, or does he still have something to offer to both developmental psychologists and teachers?

Such recent critics as Cohen (1983) have argued that, since Piaget did most of his important work in the 1920s and 1930s, this has been invalidated by subsequent work. The contrary is argued here: much of his work is still relevant today. This applies, first, to the broad theory of development from birth to adolescence, and it applies also to particular ideas, such as a baby discovering that an object continues to exist when he can no longer see it (tertiary circular reactions), concrete operational thinking and abstract thinking (or formal operations).

Cohen also maintains that the criticisms of Piaget's work have been so damaging it no longer stands up to scrutiny. The counterargument is that this applies only to limited aspects, such as his first stage of reflexes in sensorimotor thought. Criticism of other aspects seems to lead to a modified version of Piaget's ideas still being valid today: a post- or neo-Piagetian position.

Let us take the example of the acquisition of (concrete) operational thought. There have been many investigations of this, and these investigations have led to Piaget's initial ideas being no longer acceptable for the reasons given in Chapter 7. However, a modified version is tenable – that the phenomenon of operational thinking does exist and that this is sometimes attained at an earlier age than Piaget indicated.

However, in order to attain operational thought, children need optimal help from teachers, psychologists or other adults. This should take the form of making the learning situation as stimulating as possible. There should be verbal cues to assist children to understand the task requirements as clearly and unambiguously as possible. Teachers should try to devise educational aids to help them solve problems. And, most important of all, the language in which the question is phrased to the children should be as helpful as possible. The correct answer should certainly be among the options put to them. For example, in the conservation-of-quantity experiment (Figure 2.3), children should be asked: 'Does the tall jar have more water in it or less water in it than the wide jar, *or are they both the same?*'

Do Piaget's developmental stages (or periods) actually exist? And even if empirical evidence is given in support of the system as a whole, can each of them stand up to criticism? Both the overall system and individual stages have been much criticized. The sensorimotor period was criticized by Butterworth (1981), who regards Piaget's concepts as insufficiently biological. Butterworth argues that we should see babyhood in a more evolutionary perspective. Since he confines himself to babies and sensorimotor activity, Butterworth does not cover the way sensorimotor activity leads into language (or symbolic activity) and all that follows from the impact of language on children's cognitive development over the next two decades until adulthood. Recent research has shown babies to be far more capable at a far earlier age than Piaget indicated. As noted in Chapter 2, Piaget's ideas about very young babies are probably no longer relevant, but his later stages of sensorimotor activity are still worth further investigation, particularly his object constancy studies.

The period of pre-operational thought has been the least criticized, probably because it has been the least researched. In academic circles criticism is often an inverted form of commendation: work has to be of a certain stature to be worth criticizing. By this logic, pre-operational thinking is the stage with the least psychological explanatory power.

With 4- and even 3-year-olds understanding the conservation of number, the time between the acquisition of the first word and the acquisition of operational thinking has become shorter and shorter, perhaps only a year or two. Nevertheless, there is a great need for further research into pre-operational thinking, however difficult the methodological problems. As argued in Chapter 2, the very term *preconceptual* is insulting to toddlers and needs renaming, perhaps as *striving for concepts*.

The attainment of operational thought has been the most criticized of Piaget's ideas. As Bryant (1972), Donaldson (1978), Hughes (1981) and many other workers have shown, children are capable of many of the aspects of operational thought at much earlier ages than Piaget indicated. The frontiers of operational thinking have been successively reduced.

On the other hand, British workers researching into children's understanding of science found that Piaget had been optimistic about age achievement. Sutherland (1982, 1983), Shayer, Kuchemann and Wylan (1976) and Shayer and Wylan (1978) found concrete operations to be achieved on average only at 12, i.e. during the first year at secondary school. This finding, since it conflicts with those of Bryant (1972) would fit a domain-specific interpretation: a child shows different levels of achievement in different subjects. Piagetians might explain the differences in terms of the horizontal lag (or *décalage*) between attainment of the same type of thinking in different subjects. Donaldson goes further than Bryant. Donaldson (1978) casts doubt on the very existence of operational thought. Formal operational thinking has not attracted the same amount of criticism as concrete operations. Nevertheless, it has been subject to a searching critique by Wason and Johnson-Laird (1972), who also investigated specific aspects, as did Smedslund (1977) with his study of correlation.

One universal criticism of educationists is the manner in which Piaget asked children questions: giving them alternative answers that did not include the 'correct' one. The precise wording of Piaget's questions is impossible for non-French readers to ascertain. However, Smith (1986) reports there has been a great deal of inaccurate translation.

When Piaget's learning theory is appraised critically, critics focus on equilibration. Some regard this as controversial. For example, Haroutounian (1983) sees no logical need for it: others are more positive, e.g. Bryant (1985). They see it as a vital concept, but want its precise role clarified and a way found to quantify it.

Not all cognitive developmentalists have been critical of Piaget's ideas. In Britain such pioneers as Peel (Chapter 10), Lunzer (1960) and Lovell (1964) were largely supportive during the 1960s and early 1970s. However, the scale of criticism has mounted since the 1970s and even more so since Piaget's death in 1980. However, some of the critics, such as Bryant (unpublished speech on Piaget's death), nevertheless admire certain aspects of Piaget's work.

Not all workers favour a reconciliation with Piaget that could be included within a post- or neo-Piagetian theoretical framework. Certainly there remain big issues awaiting conclusive answers. Are there general thinking abilities, such as operational thinking, that exhibit themselves in the same child in a wide range of different situations, or are there rather specific abilities that do not transfer to other domains?

We are not yet in a position to state categorically who is right in the dispute between the Piagetians and the domain-specific movement. Piagetians argue the domain-general position: there are such generalized abilities, which manifest themselves in a number of different activities.

The domain-specific adherents argue that children show abilities specific to that domain. Intercorrelations of tasks have so far been on the low side and this has given substance to the domain-specific movement. However, if longitudinal research were to be done on the actual development of the same children over many years, results might favour the Piagetian cause. Levin (1986) wondered whether the whole question is really a level-of-theory problem or a level-of-analysis problem.

Should cognitive developmentalists focus on qualitative breakthroughs of the type Piaget claimed to have revealed, or on individual acts of learning that gradually accumulate quantitatively, as recommended by the information processors, the behaviourists and the structuralists, who do not support stage theory? Or should the focus be on encouraging children to be more aware of their own learning, as the metacognitive school advocates? Neo-Piagetians, such as Pascual-Leone (1976) and Case (1985), evolved compromises between Piagetian stage structure and IP. It will be interesting to see whether these compromises will survive the replication studies to which they may be subjected in the next decade.

There are alternative stage theories. Fischer and Canfield (1986) have put forward their own skill-based stage sequence. These too may be replicated. Another fundamental question has been pointed out by Beilin (1987): how is experience incorporated and properly represented in the mind? Is it directly registered, as the information processors would have us believe, or is it reconstructed by the child, as the post-Piagetians and constructivists argue?

The constructivists have been particularly critical of stage theory. Can these two conflicting child-centred movements be reconciled, or are the Piagetian and constructivist positions irreconcilably far apart? The two positions grew from a common Piagetian origin. Piaget was a pioneer constructivist. There have been 'family quarrels' between the two (for example, between the post-Piagetian Shayer and the early constructivists during the late 1970s), but these can be and have been patched up.

Not all cognitive developmentalists have been converted by one of the alternatives. Smith (1982) and others remain fundamentalist Piagetians, although not without making some criticisms. In the last analysis they favour the Piagetian interpretation of events over the alternatives.

If we are to be fair to children when we assess their attainment, many of the criticisms of Piaget's methodology must be accepted. In particular, his use of language to 'catch out' children is unacceptable. But there remains an explanatory power to Piaget's stage theory that seems to survive criticism. It provides the best insight we have into children's thinking, particularly in abstract subjects such as maths and science. What is needed are broadly based investigations of the alleged phenomena, instead of detailed replications of Piaget's original experiments, accompanied by criticisms of his methodology.

Information processing (IP) has its own methodology, focusing on the individual act of learning, but its orientation is not developmental. For instance, in the conservation-of-quantity experiment (Figure 2.3), it would be focusing on the amount of information the child has to hold in short-term memory before answering rather than on the child's understanding.

IP and metacognition had become the dominant perspectives in psychological circles by the early 1990s. However, neither has yet demonstrated that it can offer something distinctive to cognitive *development* over the whole sweep from babyhood to adulthood in the way Piaget has. IP can, however, give a more precise account of an individual act of learning than Piaget or Vygotsky could. Every possible variable is quantified. The importance of short-term memory has been rightly stressed. Perhaps in the future there may be more focus on the improvement of long-term memory and how this could aid the development of concepts.

Behaviourism still seems to have a useful role in certain situations, particularly with children with learning and behaviour difficulties. Vygotsky's influence has also revived recently. The immediate future may belong to him as cognitive developmentalists attempt to account for the *social* aspects of learning. These were largely ignored by Piaget in his work although he was, of course, aware of them.

Pascual-Leone (1976) and Case (1985) have each developed a synthesis of neo-Piagetian stage theory and IP. However, some sort of new, even broader, synthesis is required to incorporate metacognitive ideas with Piagetian, Vygotskyan and IP concepts. This takes as its premiss that an approach is needed that draws on *all* the perspectives presented rather than considering the newer ones as being in conflict with Piaget (and others). Feuerstein has been a pioneer here, although he sees himself as a practical educationalist rather than as a theorist. Margaret Donaldson (1978) and Schaffer (1971) have both drawn on a variety of these viewpoints.

Summary

Criticism of Piaget began with Vygotsky in the 1920s and continued with Bruner in the 1960s but only really mounted in the 1970s and 1980s. Does he still have anything to offer? Different critics have attacked the stages individually. Others, such as the constructivists and domain-specific adherents, deny the existence of stages as such. If this issue is resolved in favour of the existence of general abilities, Piagetians will argue that Piaget still provides the most powerful explanatory theory for developmental changes we have.

Another major issue is whether knowledge is registered immediately in the child's mind, as the information processors and behaviourists contend, or is constructed by the child, as the Piagetians and constructivists argue.

Questions for discussion

1. Is Piaget *passé*?
2. If not, what has he to offer to psychologists?
3. Are Piaget's ideas still relevant to teachers? If so, how?
4. How can the discrepancy between the different ages of attainment for concrete operations be resolved?
5. Can the Piagetian and constructivist views be reconciled?
6. What new syntheses between viewpoints can be made?

12
GENERAL IMPLICATIONS OF THEORIES OF COGNITIVE DEVELOPMENT FOR TEACHERS

Piaget outlined his ideas on learning over a period of nearly sixty years. It is now a decade or more since Piaget's death. With his influence in psychology fading, perhaps it is time for a reassessment of his influence in education. In Britain this comes at a time when the Education Reform Act 1988 (ERA) is being implemented.

The framework of the National Curriculum implies a need for formal teaching methods. Vygotsky (1986) was one of the first cognitive developmentalists to take a formal teacher's point of view. However, he was strongly opposed to learning being mechanical; on the contrary, it must be active. There has been very little support for formal class teaching as such from psychologists in English-speaking countries. The American David Ausubel (1968) is an exception, but he also does not approve of any mechanistic model. Another American, Jerome Bruner (1986), drew on many of Vygotsky's ideas to develop his interventionist alternative. Teachers must have a direct influence − it is not sufficient for teachers to wait for their pupils to become ready for a certain lesson, they must *make* their pupils ready by helping them with language, stimulating their underlying concepts with appropriate experiences and spurring them on with well-cued questions.

At present the child-centred movements include both the Piagetians and the constructivists. The post-Piagetian standpoint accepts many of the criticisms made by Bryant and Donaldson, as outlined in Chapter 7, but remains convinced that generalization across various attainments is possible. This means a child can be said to be, for instance, concrete operational in the broad combined area of maths and science. Those children who are successful at number conservation are considered to be more likely to be good at quantity conservation.

Most constructivists go further than Piaget in stressing the importance of a stimulating home environment, leading to informal learning of concepts and strategies for learning. Most constructivists reject Piaget's stages while retaining some sympathy for his theory of learning. However, both the Piagetians and the constructivists agree that teachers should be in an enabling role and provide children with as stimulating an environment as possible. This has been the dominant ethos in British primary education for the past two decades. It is now extending to the secondary school with the widespread introduction of resource-based learning for GCSE. Both the Piagetians and the constructivists agree that teachers must know exactly where a child is in terms of his present concepts and start from there. Constructivists also believe teachers must be aware of their pupils' existing learning strategies and use them. Some post-Piagetians, e.g. Sutherland (1989), then offer a compromise to formal teachers: children can also be given formal strategies by teachers, which will help them in formal subjects, such as maths. Many constructivists would probably not approve of this.

In maths and science education, Piaget has had an enormous influence. However, in subject areas outside maths and science the various Piagetian conservations (which signal the achievement of concrete operations) are often not relevant. For the teaching of English, history, art and craft and foreign languages, therefore, Piagetians stress the teacher being aware of

1. the previous learning experiences of the children;
2. the range of levels of concept attainment consequently attained by them;
3. the need for stimulating experiences to be given to the pupils, based on their various concept levels.

All this implies a non-interventionist, non-didactic role for the teacher. Some extreme constructivists have argued that the teacher must never interfere with what has been mastered outside school. However, the alternative argument is that it is sometimes essential for teachers to intervene and offer a direct input that will help the pupils' understanding. This might take the form of a discussion on Galileo's theory in order to help overcome the 'natural' gut concept that the earth is the centre of the universe.

For educational reasons a compromise between the post-Piagetian and constructivist views is argued here. Teachers must know about and appreciate children's ideas and the learning strategies they bring from home; yet teachers still need to teach. It is unacceptable for teachers to have the extreme background role implied by the Constructivists. There is not much ordinary children can learn without teaching.

The domain-specific standpoint, however, implies there is nothing a teacher can do to help a child transfer a way of thinking learnt in one subject to other subject areas, because this is not possible. For the secondary teacher this may be convenient. She can encourage a child to develop his understanding to the utmost within the specialist subject for which she is responsible. For the primary teacher, however, adherence to the domain-specific standpoint could make life very difficult. It implies she needs to think in pigeon-hole terms. When she is teaching technology, she may develop a certain picture of the capacity and attainment of a child, but when she is teaching art there will be no significant relationship between the child's performances in technology and in art. The primary teacher may find solace in the National Curriculum, which defines the primary curriculum in terms of subjects rather than themes.

Teacher-centred movements have long been in opposition to Piaget's ideas. According to the behaviourists, the teacher should be in absolute command of the situation and decide exactly what the child learns and where he is going. Behaviourism focuses on individual learning. Each child learns at his own pace. This fits in with the current focus of both primary and secondary teaching.

According to behaviourism, all children learn the same content in the same way, i.e. they are conditioned by the teacher. This does not fit with the current focus in teaching, whereby the pupil shows some initiative in determining his own learning. Therefore teaching a whole class of mixed ability to learn the same thing at the same rate is not possible. Whereas constructivists stress learning at home, behaviourists are concerned only with learning at school. Similarly, information processing (IP) implies a teacher-centred approach. Many of its principles are similar to those of behaviourism. Oakhill (1988) made a comparison between the educational implications of IP and the Piagetian view. Both agree that, first, the teacher must start with the child's current level; second, that the child must be active in the learning process; and, third, that the need for promoting high-level cognitive growth be stressed. However, there are contrasting views on the nature of higher-level operations and the processes by which they occur. Piagetians see this in terms of formal operational thought whereas IP sees it in terms of an increased capacity for working out problems. According to the information processors, the pupil develops increasingly complex strategies. Coaching and instruction are important. IP gives teachers a much more direct role to play than do most other paradigms. It is perhaps the most appropriate model for traditional teachers to use.

The IP approach has certain strengths and weaknesses. It provides insight into the individual act of learning at any one age; it stresses the role of short-term memory and reminds teachers (and psychologists) of young children's limited capacity to process information. There is great potential for education in this movement. Perhaps, over the next decade, the computer could be used as a teacher to revolutionize learning in schools.

Metacognition focuses on making children aware of their own learning. This has enormous implications for teachers − if it is feasible. The metacognitive approach would seem to imply a child-centred approach, but this is not inevitable; it could also imply a teacher-centred strategy along Vygotskyan lines. The teacher would draw the pupils' attention to their own learning. Teachers should not just ensure children learn but also ensure they are aware of the learning. This applies most potently to the learning of the home language. This suggests that learning the home language should follow the model of learning a foreign language. Here a child has, of necessity, to be aware of the process of learning, unless an entirely natural situation can be successfully created. At a more practical level, metacognition for teachers means telling their pupils to check their answers and to think over what they have just read, etc.

Vygotsky (1986) is having a revival of influence within cognitive development at present, both in Europe and in America. He argued that teachers must *instruct*. An indirect role is not enough. However, this instruction must not be merely the mechanical iterating of material; there must be an interaction between teacher and pupils.

The nativists argue that children have an innate potential for learning that teachers and psychologists need to be aware of. This potential must be stimulated by appropriate experiences in the environment or else it will be lost or stunted. This applies again most especially to the learning of the home language. According to the Chomskyan model (outlined in Chapter 3), if the child is not exposed to the home language at the age of 1−3, he will never learn to speak it adequately. There do not seem to be many applications to nativism to school teaching.

Despite the difference between the child-centred and the teacher-centred approaches drawn here, there is a vital strand of consensus: whichever approach to learning she chooses, the teacher should start from where each child is.

After many years, formal teaching linked to mechanical learning (based on the behaviourist model) has been rejected. In its place was substituted a concept known as discovery learning or resource-based learning. Teachers must only guide, help and enable their pupils to learn for themselves. In doing so, teachers cut themselves off from any relevance to education that all the other schools of thought outlined in this book may have.

Surely a fully graduate teaching profession will use whichever method is appropriate to a particular teaching situation. Some teachers will be far more receptive to open-ended approaches than others. The current debate about falling standards of reading only emphasizes the need for occasional direct teaching. Children with special learning difficulties may thrive on a resurrection of formal teaching. On the other hand, the very bright should not be bored and may need the challenge of resource-based learning. Those intellectually able pupils who became psychologists, teachers or educationists tend to be the most critical of 'old-fashioned' formal teaching. Yet they should not deny the less intellectually favoured children the chance to learn in a more structured way.

Summary

The various schools of cognitive development fall into one of two approaches in their relevance to teaching. The Piagetians and constructivists imply a child-centred approach, the behaviourists and information processors a teacher-centred one, based on individualized learning. Vygotsky and the Russian school offer a cognitive-developmental justification of class teaching, based on active learning by the pupils. Metacognition stresses that children should be helped by teachers to be aware of their own learning, particularly of the home language. The conclusion is that teachers should use the appropriate cognitive-development model for the needs of particular pupils.

Questions for discussion

1. Which psychological school has the most to offer teachers?
2. Can formal teaching be justified by any psychological theory?
3. Which theories are most relevant to the teaching of children with learning difficulties?
4. Which theories are most relevant to the teaching of the bright?
5. Which theories are most relevant to the teaching of the average?
6. How can the bright, the average and the slow all be taught in the same mixed-ability class?

Further reading

Richardson, K. and Sheldon, S. (eds.) (1986) *Cognitive Development to Adolescence*, Lawrence Erlbaum Associates, Hove.

13
FEUERSTEIN

Reuven Feuerstein (the Israeli remedial educationist) has made one of
the strongest responses to the determinism implied by Piaget's theory. 'If
there are limits, I don't know them', he claimed when interviewed on
BBC television. He argues that intelligence can be improved at any age.
His work has concentrated mainly on disturbed adolescents from 12 to 14.
He has concentrated his efforts on helping those with learning difficulties
rather than offering ideas for all pupils. But there is no reason why his
ideas should not be applied to pupils who are at an average level or who
are doing well. His concepts have been used to stimulate gifted pupils.

Feuerstein's is not a deficit theory: he claims to be able to help the
slow learner to catch up with the average. These difficulties can arise
either from organic deformity (such as Down's syndrome) or from a
situation where the youngster has failed to learn how to learn. Feuerstein
then applies the metacognitive message: helping adolescents to understand
how they are learning. However, because Feuerstein is eclectic in the
theories he draws on, his ideas are discussed here rather than in Chapter
9. He also draws on the information processing (IP) school: for its stress
on the need for information gathering, solution finding and communicating
the solution. Despite his current opposition to some of Piaget's ideas, he
did study in Geneva. This may have had some residual influence on
him, such as the importance of abstract or formal operational thinking.
Feuerstein forces pupils to think in the abstract.

We now turn from the theoretical influences on him to how Feuerstein
actually helps a child. The capacity to learn is measured by the Learning
Potential Assessment Device (LPAD) (1980). The success of this depends
on the tester establishing a rapport with the pupil, as part of dynamic
assessment. LPAD is a diagnostic test of learning difficulties as well as a
measure of potential. The result gives an assessment of the modifiability
of the pupil, i.e. of his capacity to learn, including the ability to accommodate – another Piagetian influence.

Feuerstein abolishes the distinction between testing and teaching. The diagnosis or pretesting is carried out by the teacher. A particular result implies an appropriate programme of teaching to follow from it. The teaching itself is then followed by post-testing to measure the effectiveness of the teaching. The integrated approach has been criticized by Campione *et al.* (1982) as teaching in order to test. However, supporters of national testing in Britain might praise it as a fine model for teachers.

Feuerstein's general teaching technique is called instrumental enrichment (1979), often abbreviated to IE. This is based on an interactionist theory of learning between the teacher and the pupil(s). The size of the class is ideally in single figures. IE involves a strenuous programme of mental activities, with an emphasis on the nonverbal, such as patterns of shapes. However, it also includes language, numbers and pictures. There are fifteen separate sequenced sets of tasks; each one is claimed to develop a particular mental skill. These involve comparison, classification, sequencing and understanding relationships in space and time. Feuerstein tries to avoid content that is associated by a pupil with previous failure.

Burden (1990) has pointed out that the success of the programme will depend to a large extent on how the adolescent interprets the strange new experience. An initial positive perception is crucial. As the pupil works on these problems, the teacher guides him away from unproductive strategies. The teacher has to have the skill to intervene at exactly the right moment. The pupil discusses his successes and difficulties with his teacher and decides what he has learnt and how he has learnt it. In other words, he is taught to apply metacognition. However, Burden (*ibid.*) argues that pupils need a full two-year programme to appreciate the metacognitive aspects.

Pupils are encouraged to invent their own strategies both in and out of school. Here there is an element of constructivism in the use of strategies learnt out of school. However, the ethos of IE is far from that of constructivism, since a tight control of the learning environment is preferred (ideally in a boarding school). The ethos of control is similar to Skinner's behaviourism (Chapter 5).

Feuerstein claims that a course in IE helps to release and utilize the native latent intelligence, which can then be applied to verbal activities in school. Since his techniques involve a high degree of intervention on the native intelligence, it is a form of mediated learning. He claims that IE helps youngsters to learn more effectively. The claim of transferability is an important yet contentious one. Many critics (e.g. Shayer and Beasley, 1987) do not accept that Feuerstein has proved the case for transferability of progress generally. Shayer and Beasley did, however, find that retarded adolescents made statistically significant gains on tests of *fluid* intelligence, e.g. Piagetian tests and Raven's Progressive Matrices (patterns of shapes), but not on tests of *crystallized* intelligence, e.g. vocabulary.

The evaluation studies in general indicate that, for IE to be effective, two conditions need to be fulfilled: adolescents need to be specially selected and they need to learn under optimum conditions. According to Feuerstein, IE works not only by developing specific thinking skills but also by changing attitudes. So he works simultaneously on the cognitive and the emotional aspects. The teacher acts very much as a mediator. She mediates between the pupil and his learning. The teacher is cast by Feuerstein in the role of a personal saviour of such children's minds.

He sees three crucial aspects to the success of the enterprise: belief, teaching and environment. A passionate belief by teachers that they will succeed is the most important of these. Second, IE's appropriate teaching technique should be used. Third, however, the right environment has to be created. Ideally this is at such a place as Feuerstein's boarding school at the Hadassar Institute near Jerusalem, which acts as an intensive-care unit for deprived children.

An example of such deprived children was a pair of 'ineducable', illiterate, Indian immigrant twin boys of 9 who had considerable aggressive behaviour problems. Immediately after the twins were admitted to the institute they were separated from each other. A programme of help was then initiated for them. After five months of Feuersteinian treatment from his team, the boys were able to read and were ready to cope with normal schooling.

Feuerstein claims to be able to reveal new abilities in a whole range of pupils and, in particular, to aid the late developer by uncovering his hidden ability to learn. Categories which American disciples of Feuerstein's claim to be able to help include the deaf, Down's syndrome children, the emotionally disturbed and the learning disabled. His programme demands 100-per-cent involvement from both teachers and pupils. It is not a matter of a weekly remedial lesson. Ideally children should stay in a special boarding school for two years where sustained daily IE exercise takes place, under the supervision of dedicated teachers. All such teachers must have been trained by Feuerstein in his methods and be convinced followers of his philosophy. He claims that 80 per cent of his pupils are ready to return to ordinary schools after the two years of treatment. Feuerstein claims the results of a course of IE include a greater enjoyment of learning by pupils, an improved concentration span, a more careful approach, an improvement in analytical powers and a better self-image. The last point has been disputed in a number of American replication studies.

However, the tests of self-image used have themselves been criticized as inadequate.

Feuerstein's ideas evolved in an Israeli context, in a new country made up of immigrants from Arab and European countries. All need to master Hebrew. It is the Sephardic Jews from the Arab countries who tend to struggle to achieve the standards set by the pioneer Ashkenazy children from European countries. Feuerstein has concentrated his efforts on these Sephardic children: they suffer from a cultural deprivation Feuerstein believes can be overcome by mediated learning experiences. Consequently there is a strong cultural dimension to his ideas on learning, as there is also to Vygotsky's. Feuerstein tries to supply the elements that are missing in the particular subculture (e.g. Moroccan) from which the pupils come.

Britain has similar problems but on a smaller scale with ethnic-minority children from the Indian subcontinent, the Caribbean and elsewhere. However, the lack of a kibbutz-like enclosed community makes it difficult to apply Feuerstein's ideas. In fact the opposite is the norm, with ethnic minorities generally living in mixed communities in inner cities. There is not the unified value system that prevails in the Jewish community in Israel. There, immigrants are Jews and are committed to Israeli values. Those who want to stay in Israel are committed to mastering Hebrew.

Israel also benefits from the lack of the class conflict still dominant in British education. In Britain the children of the unskilled working class are the major 'problem' group. Unless they can be persuaded to accept that education is worthwhile it does not seem possible to help them with Feuerstein's methods. However, it should be remembered that Feuerstein has taught children other than Jews successfully, in particular Arab children. This gives some evidence that his techniques are usable in other contexts.

The biggest unanswered question is whether a teacher in an ordinary day school in Britain, teaching the full range of children (as opposed to those diagnosed as backward) can utilize Feuerstein's ideas and, if so, how? Feuerstein's selection of suitable pupils for his treatment casts doubt on this. However, there have been hopeful results from Feuerstein supporters using his ideas in American schools. In British schools there have been mixed results. Kirkman (1986), reporting on a school in Bridgwater (Somerset), found Feuerstein's techniques to be particularly successful with low-ability pupils. The main problem, however, lay with the teachers. Despite a short training course, they understood neither Feuerstein's philosophy nor how to teach IE. They tended to mistake its teaching material for 'worksheets'. Another problem was that some of the IE material was found to be too easy by many British pupils.

It is also not yet clear whether Feuerstein's ideas apply to the primary school, particularly to the infant classes. However, the optimistic overall message for teachers, and even more for pupils, is that failure and deficiencies can be compensated for.

Summary

Feuerstein's intervention was initially intended to help immigrant adolescent pupils who are (often due to cultural factors) struggling to master Hebrew. He advocates the diagnosis of the pupil's difficulties by means of his LPAD. Teachers should then use his learning method, IE, in order to make up the cognitive deficit. For his theoretical sources, Feuerstein draws on metacognition, IP, Piaget, constructivism and Vygotsky. It is claimed that Feuerstein's methods help adolescents who have fallen behind at school, both in Britain and the USA.

Questions for discussion

1. Should Feuerstein's IE be used to help backward pupils?
2. If not, how can latent intellectual talent be revealed?
3. Can Feuerstein's technique for overcoming cultural deficit be applied in Britain?
4. Should Feuerstein's ideas be used by learning-support teachers in Britain?

Further reading

Sharron, H. (1987) *Changing Children's Minds*, Souvenir Press, London.

14
THE EFFECT ON EDUCATION OF THESE VIEWPOINTS

The National Curriculum

Pupils are now faced with a wide range of compulsory subjects from the beginning of primary school. From the point of view of cognitive development, how can they be expected to cope with this? From a post-Piagetian standpoint a pupil would be expected to achieve different levels in different subjects. Piaget wrote about horizontal *décalage* (or lag), meaning that a child reaches any one important cognitive breakthrough (such as operational thought) at different ages for different tasks. So it is unrealistic to expect uniform attainment by any one child in the different subjects or by the whole national year group of children in any one subject (let alone the whole National Curriculum).

The domain-specific school might approve of the way knowledge is divided up into discrete subject areas in the National Curriculum. Domain-specific adherents might argue that, for any particular pupil, there will be no correlation between attainment in the different subjects of the National Curriculum. Each ability is so specific it has to be seen in isolation. This is a strong argument for profiling and criterion-related assessment as both the formative (ongoing, year-by-year) and summative (at 16 plus or 18 plus) forms of assessment of a pupil's achievement at school. (Criterion-related assessment is explained in Chapter 14.)

The constructivists might be the most critical of the National Curriculum, at least in the sense that it is linked to standardized testing. Instead each pupil should be seen as unique. We should certainly not impose any uniform expectations of attainment. Teachers should encourage and stimulate the pupil to build on those concepts and learning strategies he brings to school with the aim of maximizing his learning, without any comparison with others. For this reason constructivists approve of criterion-related assessment. The National Curriculum as such might be seen as somewhat limiting in that the choice of options outside the compulsory subjects is so limited. The constructivist case is one for breaking down subject barriers.

The metacognitive movement also seems to be excluded from the National Curriculum, at least by the way it is conceptualized at present. The emphasis on both product (rather than process) and pressure to obtain satisfactory results in exams and tests seem to preclude metacognition. This needs pupils to be consciously aware of their own learning.

National attainment tests

The UK government is introducing tests of attainment at 7, 11, 14 and 16 (8 and 12 in Scotland). In theory these should measure the effectiveness with which the National Curriculum is being taught. The tests are to be based on the principle of *criterion referencing*. This means a pupil should achieve the highest level of which he is capable regardless of the attainment of the other pupils in the class. Music has long used this form of assessment. A child learning the piano is given grade 1 as soon as he has fulfilled the criteria for that grade. Whether he passes or not does not depend on the percentage of the entrants being given grade 1 that year. Nor does it depend on the age of the pupil: an able pianist will soon reach grade 1, a slow one may take many years to do so.

In practice there will be ten levels to cover the age-range of compulsory education from 5 to 16. There will be four or five SATs (standard assessment tasks) for each of the three core subjects: English, maths, and science. These will be defined in such a way that a teacher can allocate each pupil's response to a task to one of the ten levels. If a child can fulfil the demands of that task at level x, he will then be said to be at level x, whatever his age might be. In other words, a very able young pupil may be able to succeed at a high level of attainment. However, a very weak pupil of 14 may not be able to get beyond the first level.

This is a different concept of testing from the old *norm-referenced* system where all children of a certain age were tested simultaneously and compared with one another. Under criterion referencing the child is compared only with the criteria and himself.

In reality much depends on what level a pupil is entered for in the first place. A bright child may be entered for a much lower test than he is capable of. He may get the top mark within the band of levels he is entered for, but may be capable of achieving a higher level. On the other hand, ambitious parents may put pressure on a school to have their child assessed at a higher level than the teacher would otherwise have recommended. In other words, the pressure from parents is to turn the supposed criterion referencing back into norm referencing.

Teachers at key stages 1, 2, 3 and 4 will test their pupils within certain bands of the ten levels: levels 1–3 for key stage 1 (7-year-olds); 2–5 for key stage 2 (11-year-olds); 3–8 for key stage 3 (14-year-olds); and 3–10 for key stage 4 (16-year-olds). Giving discretion to the teacher to decide the level a pupil is entered for negates a major purpose of national testing: an objective test of each child's attainment, independent of the subjective assessment of the class teacher.

At present, the government expects of a teacher that all her pupils should reach the average for that age. This conflicts with a fundamental principle of criterion referencing. These expectations also conflict with the findings of cognitive development. From a post-Piagetian standpoint such expectations are realistic for the average pupils. Those at a 'higher' Piagetian stage of cognitive development (e.g. formal operations) should be attaining a higher level than the average (e.g. concrete operations in the lower secondary school). According to this view, it is desirable that advanced pupils should not be held back to the average; they should rather be challenged and encouraged to reach as high a level as possible. Various arrangements are being tried to facilitate this, e.g. taking GCSE a year early or narrowing the range of National Curriculum subjects to allow the brighter pupil to take more options.

It may, however, be counterproductive to expect those at a 'lower' stage of cognitive development (e.g. intuitive) to attain the average level. This may put debilitating pressure on them. However, let us assume that the teacher realizes a child is at a 'lower' stage and enters him for a lower test. This may be realistic, but at the same time the child is labelled negatively as far as he, his peers, his parents and (perhaps most important of all) his teacher are concerned.

Supporters of teaching through mastery learning believe uniform attainment of targets by pupils of the same age is possible in specific areas. Mastery learning means all (or at least most) of a mixed-ability year group can reach a reasonable target, provided they are given appropriate teaching.

The problem of the very low-stage children seems to have been solved by exempting statemented children from national testing. These are children with learning and other difficulties who, under the Warnock proposals of the Education Act 1981, have their learning and other needs recorded as requiring special provision. However, not all such children will necessarily be statemented if a particular local authority does not have (or wish to provide) the resources to provide the appropriate support.

Schools in England and Wales now have to market themselves in order to attract pupils. The results of national testing may well be used for this purpose, just as exam results have long been used by independent schools as a major advertising gambit. This could mean schools' goals might become achieving higher attainment levels than competitors. Instead of testing following teaching, testing may well dominate teaching. The assessment tail will wag the teaching dog.

In terms of cognitive development, this process would focus teaching on the needs of the school rather than on the needs of the child. With testing commencing as early as 7, schools may well want to start preparing their children from the moment they enter at 5. There would be hardly a school year that would not be dominated by the need for 'good' results on the national tests. This would be following the model of the independent schools where, from the age of 8, preparatory-school pupils are prepared for the common entrance examination and, from 13, public-school pupils for GCSEs. Teachers' promotion may depend on their classes achieving 'good' results.

Although the concept of ten levels is developmental and Piagetian, the way in which they are being implemented is behaviourist. It is the pupil's performance in a test situation that is of major importance. The teacher's role is to create the learning conditions that maximize pupil performance. So the stimuli teachers provide must be geared towards test performance rather than towards creativity and personal development.

It is perhaps forgotten by the government that State schools, unlike independent schools, have to cater for the whole of the ability range. Developmentalists may argue that many children at a 'lower' stage would be helped more by encouragement than by being told they can only perform competently on much easier tasks than the rest of the class – in other words, they are 'failures'.

Mixed-stage/mixed-ability teaching

Any year group consists of pupils at a mixture of stages of cognitive development, if the work of Sutherland and Shayer outlined in Chapter 10 is accepted. However, the older the pupils are, the greater the number of different stages that exists in a class, and the greater too is the difference between the 'highest' and 'lowest' stage. So secondary teachers have an even tougher task than primary teachers in implementing mixed-stage teaching.

It is generally acknowledged that mixed-ability teaching is a challenge for teachers. This is even greater if they have been used to teaching in such an ability grouping system as streaming. What general advice can a cognitive developmentalist give teachers? It may be possible to modify ability grouping. A year group in any 'typical' secondary school could be team taught during the same period: the smaller number at a stage below the average could be taught separately by a learning-support teacher. She would provide learning experiences and guidance at a simpler level. The larger middle group at the average stage could be taught in a more demanding way by another teacher, while a third teacher could challenge those at (or in the transition to) a higher stage with more abstract work. This system is also known as *setting*. The principle of grouping in this way is used in many schools for subjects that tend to be learnt in a step-by-step fashion, e.g. maths and foreign languages. Alternatively, streaming could be used. In other words, pupils would be put in the same class (A, B or C stream) for all subjects.

If setting or streaming is not possible and the mixed-stage class has to be taught as such, the pupils can still be grouped within the class in a similar way to setting. Many primary teachers have done this generally for the past two decades. A learning-support teacher or teacher's assistant may often help with the 'lowest' stage group. Each group may work on a group task set by the teacher.

Individualized learning can also be used. In theory each pupil works at his own level and pace. Material needs to be prepared across the whole ability range so that each pupil can work from his present level to the maximum of which he is capable. Such a major task cannot easily be achieved by teachers during their meagre preparation time, so commercial publishers have prepared schemes to fill the gaps, most notably in two of the core subjects of the National Curriculum, English and maths. Computer packages are another means of achieving this. The computer can be an invaluable educational tool, particularly for motivating those pupils at a lower stage who find most academic work difficult and frustrating.

Some critics argue that the aims of individualized learning are still not being realized by some of the schemes. In particular, ambitious parents may think their bright children are not being sufficiently challenged by the workcards provided. In theory it is this upper end of the ability range that should benefit most from individualized learning: they have the superior ability in reading the task for themselves in order to understand what is expected of them, the very skill the system depends on. It may be that the questions being asked are not sufficiently demanding.

Here the work of Peel and his students (covered in Chapters 10 and 16) provides a lead as to what should be done. 'Why?' questions should be asked, rather than 'What happens?' questions. In Peelian terminology, *explainer* level rather than *describer* level answers should be encouraged.

The pupil should be helped to go beyond the passage presented and to use his outside experiences and imagination. This would avoid comprehension-type exercises becoming simply mechanical routines whereby pupils just give answers consisting of material from the text. When individualized learning is used, the subgrouping would be in the mind and the records of the teacher rather than in the physical placing of pupils and desks. (It is difficult, of course, to prevent even this subtle form of subgrouping from entering the minds of the pupils).

The secondary teacher

Teachers in comprehensive schools have complained loudest about the pressure on them to teach their pupils in mixed-ability groups. If the developmental point made above about the greater number of stages in a secondary class is accepted, they have more reason than primary teachers to see a challenge.

Now GCSE is in operation there is a universal form of assessment for all school-leavers at 16 plus. This is geared to the whole stage range rather than an élite exam (O-level) just for those capable of abstract or formal operational thinking. GCSE (Standard Grade in Scotland) caters for the complete range by means of criterion-referenced assessment. In theory, each pupil should achieve his highest grade (or stage) regardless of any other pupil or average. This will be represented on the GCSE certificate. In practice, chief examiners and moderators seem reluctant to vary the number of grade 1s in different years.

Now the system of assessment is geared to the whole stage range, some strategies need to be evolved for coping with the mixed-stage nature of each year group. In Scotland a form of banding is in widespread use. The above-average and some of the average pupils are taught in one class (Credit-General) while the below-average and the rest of the average are taught in another (Foundation-General). At least this system means that in any one class the teacher does not have to cope with pupils at both extremes of the ability range (either the brighter or the less able are in another class).

If the stage developmentalists offer a gloomy diagnosis, the information processors offer a happy one. The secondary pupil is more skilled in perception, memorizing, orienting himself to problems, reasoning and computation than his primary counterpart. So the task of the secondary teacher should be easier than that of the primary teacher, since her pupils are more competent.

Likewise it may be easier to apply metacognitive ideas to secondary than to primary pupils. Secondary pupils may prove to be more receptive to becoming consciously aware of their own learning because of their greater degree of cognitive maturity and the self-consciousness of adolescence. (The teaching of particular subjects in the secondary school is discussed further in Chapter 16.)

The junior teacher

The role of the junior teacher is not changing as much as that of the secondary teacher at present. The transition to mixed-ability teaching took place some twenty years ago when selection for grammar schools was largely abolished. During this time progressive junior teachers established strategies for coping with the full ability range. Many of these are now being adopted by colleagues in secondary schools. These include some categorization of the class into above-average, average and below-average subgroups. If possible this is done without the pupils realizing it, using neutral labels such as 'robins' and 'sparrows', although upper-primary pupils are seldom deceived by these euphemisms.

It was argued above that pupils should be challenged by 'Why?' questions. It may appear that junior pupils are not capable of explainer-level answers. However, Sutherland (1980) found this did not apply to the bright pupils: individual bright pupils gave explainer responses. Sutherland's research was conducted only in science, which has hitherto been little taught in primary schools. Now that science is a core subject, perhaps junior pupils will show quicker progress. In the other subjects traditionally taught in junior schools, it would seem reasonable to expect explainer responses from brighter and possibly even average pupils.

Many new skills and methods are being demanded of junior-school teachers. The most immediate are those needed to cope with national assessment. As Margaret Brown (1981) and others have argued, it is essential for primary teachers to have a sound grasp of developmental ideas if they are to implement the tests with any understanding of their diagnostic importance.

Sutherland (1989) found that junior teachers at five schools in London and Scotland were unaware of the constructivist message. This is to build on the strategies pupils bring from home to school rather than to impose strategies on the pupils without any regard for their present cognitive level. This is a challenge for a junior teacher. She needs to determine the existing strategies and level of each child in her class. Diagnostic national testing at 7 and 11 could help to achieve this. The teacher would need to prepare individual work to match each one of these needs.

Turning to metacognitive ideas, some teachers may be already implementing the metacognitive message without realizing it. Traditional teachers may be still teaching grammar. Under the influence of the metacognitive movement, such teachers might do even more to make their pupils consciously aware of the language they use. Even if this activity does not go as far as the old analysis of parts of speech, pupils will nevertheless be made aware of the different categories of words they use – such as 'doing', 'naming' and 'describing' words. Other teachers, who draw their ideas from both traditional and progressive sources, may focus their pupils' attention on language through a combination of structured work and creativity.

Information processors see the junior pupil as a human computer. The teacher needs to find ways of making this 'computer' function as efficiently as possible. Is the best way to do this for the pupil to work on an actual computer? This is a question that has yet to be researched properly.

The nursery and infant teacher

Nursery teachers have, to a large extent, been the best customers for the Piagetian message – after all, this wasn't so different from the Montessorian or Froebelian message, i.e. that 3–7-year-olds learn best from practical activity. Piaget's influence did add a new emphasis on conceptual development as an aim of learning activities.

However, Piaget put more stress than did Montessori and Froebel on the responsibility of teachers of young children for those pupils' later performance in junior and secondary schools. This applies particularly to the version of Piaget's stages Bruner used in his spiral curriculum, as described in Chapter 6 and illustrated in Figure 6.1. Here an activity, which the nursery/infant teacher organizes at a pre-operational level, lays the conceptual foundation for the upper primary teacher to come back to at a concrete operational level. The secondary teacher returns to the same concept at a formal operational level.

In terms of Piagetian stages, the nursery child is at the transition between the preconceptual and intuitive substages. In terms of my critique of these substages (see Chapter 2), teachers should be helping children to bring their concepts closer to a more mature level. Pupils will be striving for this. They will need help from their teachers to guide their verbal understanding along more advanced lines, e.g. rephrasing a pupil's articulations of understanding at a slightly more 'advanced' level. This would act as a model for the child to learn from and possibly imitate. This is the process already outlined for language growth in Chapter 3.

This is, of course, a labour-intensive activity, so classes should be as small as possible and there should be as many adults as possible to assist the teacher. Nursery teachers have a nursery nurse who supplements her role. Infant teachers are often helped by mothers on a voluntary basis. In areas of deprivation there may be a learning-support teacher as well.

The infant teacher has the responsibility of initiating the teaching of reading and writing. This will proceed more easily if a strong foundation of spoken language has been laid. The metacognitive movement is one of great relevance here. Pupils can be encouraged to be consciously aware of language. They may become aware of different types of words, such as 'name' words and 'do' words. Whether this should go as far as grammar lessons remains a major debating point. Vygotsky (1986) is one distinguished developmentalist to support the formal teaching of grammar. But if grammar is regarded as suitable only for pupils gifted in language, perhaps these pupils could be given extension lessons on these lines. However, it could be said that the lower achiever in language needs such structured help with grammar.

For nursery and infant teachers the constructivist message means to look out for and encourage any learning strategies pupils bring to school. Pupils may also evolve new ones at nursery school, which should be encouraged. For instance, Sutherland (1989) found second-year infants to have the ability to count on their fingers (at least on one hand). They had learnt this strategy before starting primary school. It was a very reassuring and self-motivating standby for them, as they struggled to cope with the strategies expected of them in the infant school. Children may also be learning strategies for disembedding letters and digits from pictures on TV screens in educational programmes, such as *Sesame Street*. In other words, they may be able to extract the letter 'A' from the programme and recognize it in other contexts. If the pupils go to gymnastics classes, they may have developed learning strategies primary teachers can build on in PE, for example, the toddler may have learnt a strategy for gripping onto the climbing frame that can be used in PE lessons.

Information processors see the young pupil as a rather inefficient learner. According to this school, teachers should be looking for ways of making them more efficient in the basic skills of information processing (IP). Perhaps exercises to improve memorizing can be devised. Sutherland found (*ibid.*) this was the most common deficiency of children with learning difficulties in maths.

The learning—support

In terms of cognitive development the task of the learning—support teacher may seem easier. She does not need to cater for the full range of stages or ability, but she may have to deal with a wide range and variety of difficulties. In Piagetian terms, many of her pupils (those whose difficulties lie in the cognitive domain alone) will be at either the sensorimotor or the pre-operational stage. Some might argue that the chances of these children reaching concrete operations or even formal operations should not be reduced by the very labels given to them and the consequent low expectations of them by teachers.

The post-Piagetian message for learning—support teachers would seem to be the same as that for the nursery and infant teachers only more so: to make pupils' experiences as vivid as possible. As many senses as possible (not neglecting touch) need to be utilized.

Vygotskyans might argue that the verbal mediation of experiences by the teacher needs to be more strongly articulated and repeated. This will, it is hoped, help pupils make the connection between their experience and the verbal coding of that experience. For younger pupils this connecting will happen more in the oral than in the written mode. However, the teacher has a duty to try to help any pupil who is capable of it to achieve basic literacy.

Constructivists emphasize the need for teachers to find out what learning strategies pupils have mastered and to build on these. This seems more important and perhaps easier to achieve in segregated schools catering for particular special needs than in any other type of school.

Behaviourists see the need for much structured experience and repetition. Computer-assisted learning can be useful for this — for example, it can give an amount of repetition in number tasks that all but the most patient teacher would find unbearably boring. At the same time this may help with IP skills, such as perception (or visual scanning).

The metacognition movement implies that even mentally handicapped children should be made aware of their learning and of the language they use. It would be useful to learning—support teachers if methods of doing so could be spelt out by supporters of metacognition. Then the teacher's time used to do this could be evaluated for 'cost-effectiveness'.

Since the Warnock Report (1978) and the subsequent Education Act 1981, special-needs teaching should, as far as possible, be carried out in the ordinary school. The teacher often operates in a learning-support role alongside the class teacher or subject teacher. This approach has largely replaced the previous one whereby pupils with special needs were withdrawn from the ordinary class and taught separately by the 'remedial teacher' (as she was then known).

What are the implications for the learning-support teacher operating in this way of the four theoretical orientations summarized above? In the case of the constructivist, the behaviourist and the metacognitivist approaches, it is probably easier for the learning-support teacher to operate in this way than for a teacher of a mixed-ability class. To diagnose the existing learning strategies (as the constructivists advocate) of the minority who are categorized as having special needs is probably easier to do if they are only a small number within a class. The structured work demanded by the behaviourists is also probably easier to organize for a small group than for a whole class. Likewise the metacognition movement's focus on language may well be easier to implement for a small number within a class. Post-Piagetians might argue that pupils who are still preconceptual might be more expeditiously coped with in a separate class.

Possibly the wisest course for teachers and psychologists concerned with special needs is to try to extract relevant findings and ideas from all the approaches (if they are appropriate) and to synthesize a new model suitable for these problems within education.

The primary science teacher

Since science is now a core subject of the National Curriculum, it is one of the three most important subjects taught at school. This is a challenge for primary teachers, many of whom have had a very scanty and largely biological science education themselves. It is also a problem for the education authorities who have to remedy the situation immediately.

The child should have opportunities to build up concepts based on his own experiences. This is the view of both constructivists as well as Piagetians. A prominent constructivist, Ros Driver (1983), has written about the importance of the development of *gut feeling* during the earlier years. This is a similar notion to Piaget's intuitive understanding.

Ideally gut feeling should give way to a proper scientific understanding further up the school, under the impact of science teaching, just as intuitive thinking gives way (via concrete operational thinking) to formal operational thinking. However, Driver realizes that for many children this will not happen. They will enter adult life with this gut understanding garnered from school science, experiences at home and TV programmes. In many cases this will be the basis of their scientific understanding for the rest of their lives.

Since primary teachers start the process of science education off, they have a big responsibility to establish a solid foundation. Perhaps many of them will themselves still be operating on a gut rather than on a scientific basis. If so, it is important for them to be aware of this and to be able to refer their children to scientific curriculum materials. An empirical study into the understanding shown of certain scientific topics by primary children was done by Sutherland (1980). The theoretical background to the study was a Piagetian—Peelian one. The understanding of two central topics in primary science was investigated on an age-developmental basis from infants to upper juniors.

One was breathing (particularly as it applies to humans). Infants were found to have a vague awareness that something happens to organs such as the chest. However, they had no idea what it was. By 7 and 8 children, on average, realized that breathing is essential for human life. But it was not until the upper primary years that they realized that air is involved in the process and that it is going in and out of the lungs. 'Clean' air goes in while 'dirty air' comes out. Only the brightest pupils were aware of oxygen. At the end of primary school the majority of these children still did not realize that the volume of air inhaled is (approximately) equal to the volume exhaled (a fundamental aspect of Piaget's concrete operational thinking).

A vital prerequisite for the understanding of breathing is an understanding of the concept of air. For infant children at the inner-city multiracial school visited, this meant blowing. Breathing was defined in terms of what happens rather than in terms of any underlying concepts. The invisibility of air was an insuperable problem until the upper primary years. Even then awareness that air is a mixture of gases was minimal until the secondary years.

The negative version (or negation) of air in the form of a vacuum proved even more difficult. It was only understood (on average) at a later age. These primary pupils had no conceptual grasp of a vacuum. They thought only in terms of a vacuum cleaner pulling air and dirt in — in other words, in describer terms.

The other topic was the water cycle. Here only the most able understood the reversible nature of the process. In other words, only a minority achieved concrete operations in this domain before the end of primary school. Pupils showed much greater understanding of melting and freezing than of evaporation and condensation. This was not surprising in view of the more visible nature and easier language of the former pair.

Evaporation in particular baffled most children. A few drops of nail-varnish remover (acetone) were put on their hands. They were sure the liquid disappeared *into* their hands. Without being able to conceive of an invisible gas called water vapour, a scientifically valid explanation was not available to them. In a similar way the condensation of drops of water on a cold window in winter mystified them. Other winter weather phenomena did not seem to be part of these London infants' cognitive concepts.

However, experienced infant teachers have cast Donaldsonian-type doubts on this finding: the children probably did not understand what the author was asking them. Nevertheless, they could deal with the melting of a block of ice in front of them − at a describer level. Likewise the freezing of water in a fridge was meaningful to them − at a describer level. They were not aware, however, that both transformations took place at a definite temperature, let alone that it is 0° C for both. Details of secondary pupils' understanding of these concepts and further details of this study are to be found in Chapter 16.

The messages of this research for primary teachers are, first, that pupils need lots of practical experiences of phenomena. Second, these experiences need to be mediated in scientific terms for them by their teachers. For these tasks teachers will need helpful schemes such as Children's Learning in Science Project (CLISP − for older pupils) or Science 5 to 13, in-service programmes and advisers.

Summary

Two major recent government initiatives for schools are the National Curriculum and national testing. These seem to be underpinned more by behaviourist theory than by post-Piagetian, constructivist or metacognitive ideas. At the same time the introduction of GCSE, egalitarian political pressure and falling numbers have led to classes in the secondary school consisting of mixed stages. Junior and infant teachers have long coped with the mixed stages by means of some form of stage grouping within their classes. Secondary teachers are advised to follow suit. There is a controversy as to whether children with special needs are best taught within such classes or in a segregated situation.

Primary teachers need to be aware of the worthwhile scientific experiences pupils bring to school. They need to provide more at school and mediate these in terms of scientific concepts.

Questions for discussion

1. Is the idea of a National Curriculum backed up by any theories of development?
2. Should we have national testing? If so at what ages? Will it benefit all children?
3. Should testing be diagnostic or norm referenced?
4. How can teachers cope with testing alongside their existing duties?
5. How should teachers use the results of the tests?

6. Is the strategy of subdividing a mixed-ability class in some way a realistic one in your teaching situation?
7. Should all teachers, including secondary subject teachers, be teachers of language — as the metacognitive movement implies?
8. Can individualized learning be achieved in a class of twenty-five?
9. Are the brighter children adequately challenged at present? If not, what can be done about it?
10. Are the less able best helped by being kept within a normal class, by being extracted for small-group teaching or by being taught in a separate school?
11. Is the constructivist goal for teachers an achievable one, i.e. that teachers should be aware of the learning strategies their pupils bring to the class and should build up on these?

Primary Science

1. How can primary teachers improve their pupils' conceptual understanding?
2. What help do non-specialist teachers of science in primary schools need by way of curriculum material and resources?
3. What should the role of the science co-ordinator be?
4. Has educational television a role to play or does this simply become an excuse for teachers to opt out of teaching?

Further reading

Kelly, A. V. (1990) *The National Curriculum: A Critical View*, Paul Chapman Publishing, London.
Sigel, I. E. and Cocking, R. R. (1977) *Cognitive Development from Childhood to Adolescence: A Constructivist Perspective*, Holt, Rinehart & Winston, New York, NY.

15
TEACHING MATHEMATICS

Since the introduction of the National Curriculum, maths has become a core subject. Testing pupils' attainment in maths is now a significant part of the teacher's job for those who teach maths to children of 7, 11, 14 and 16 years. The stated aim of national testing is to monitor standards and help to raise them. The individual teacher's results may be compared with those of colleagues in the same school to check a satisfactory standard of maths teaching is being maintained. All in all, the teaching of maths is a matter of considerable national importance within education.

A summary of pertinent recent, empirical, psychological research is given. The chief aim is to work out the implications for mathematics teaching of the various schools of cognitive development. In the first section we examine the considerable empirical contribution psychologists have made to the teaching and learning of maths.

Preschool studies

Much of this work has involved preschoolers, such as the famous study by Hughes (1981). He found that children developed many strategies of their own and these were genuine attempts to tackle the problems facing them. For example, children would often use their fingers to represent the objects they were counting. They evolved different strategies for adding smaller numbers than for adding larger numbers. They were more successful at adding and subtracting smaller numbers than larger numbers.

Preschoolers operate most successfully with familiar objects. As the psychologist put bricks into a box or took them out, the children were asked to do the adding or subtracting. Preschoolers could do this very well when the box was open, and fairly well when they were asked to imagine the situation. However, most of these youngsters could not operate at all without props. For instance, Hughes would say 'If I take one away from two, how many will I have?' If children are going to be able to apply the maths they learn to other contexts, it is vital they eventually acquire this sort of context-free language. But at the preschool phase, children find problems put to them in a general way difficult to cope with. Specific problems set in their own world are much easier to handle.

Hughes showed that preschoolers could see the need for symbols if they received appropriate cues from their teachers. He showed a child a match-box, then put three stones into it, closed it and then put another two stones in. When they were prompted by an adult, these 3-year-olds saw the need to write this operation down and to give it their own version of the plus sign. Under Hughes's guidance, 3- and 4-year-olds were able to carry out similar activities in subtraction.

A great deal of research has also been done in American universities' nurseries on preschoolers, in this case the children of the lecturers. This method of sampling, however, does not include the range of home background and ability range in the general population. Nevertheless, much of this research is fascinating. One piece of work that has rightly become famous is that of Gelman and Gallistel (1983), who investigated counting and analysed the criteria that have to be fulfilled before counting can be successfully carried out:

1. *The 1:1 principle* Each item is 'tagged' or named, e.g. 'one' or 'six', but only one tag is given to each item.
2. *The principle of abstraction* It does not matter what the objects look like, provided they belong in the set to be counted, e.g. four toy cars may vary in size, colour and design, but they still represent the number 'four'.
3. *The stable-order principle* We count the numbers in an unvarying order: one, two, three, etc.
4. *The principle of cardinality* The final tag denotes the actual number of the set of objects. In counting the cars, when the child gets to four, this gives him the number he is counting. This may be obvious to us but is a difficult concept for young children.
5. *The principle of order invariance* It does not matter in which order the child counts the four cars. Whether he starts with the red one or the blue one has no effect on the final number. The order in which the objects are counted is irrelevant.

In reality many preschoolers have a particular problem knowing where to start counting from. If they are counting a row of toy cows, they may start in the middle and not include each cow once only. They tend to put a great deal of emphasis on the last item they happen to count but they are not systematic in the actual process of counting.

Gelman and Gallistel indicated the important role played in preschoolers' mathematical development by gestures in general and pointing in particular. Gelman also called attention to an important process in preschoolers, which she called *subitizing*. This enables a child to obtain an approximate idea of the numerosity of a collection of objects from perceiving its apparent size. We all subitize on occasions. Roughly how many people were at the party? Well the room seemed full. Perhaps about thirty. Unlike preschoolers, however, we can use an efficient counting strategy to check the subitizing. Preschoolers are left with the apparent denseness as their guide. Nevertheless Gelman, unlike some other experts, sees subitizing as a high-level strategy that can also be used later in life.

Gelman makes an important distinction between the mathematical laws of number and the development of understanding of number and its representation. The understanding and representation of number is a matter of concern for psychologists. However, the laws of number are a matter for mathematicians and are beyond the scope of this book. Maths teachers should, however, be aware that often the two do not go hand in hand. Although Gelman agrees with the importance constructivists place on the child's own strategies, she has found that certain vital, but difficult, concepts do need teaching, such as zero and negative numbers.

According to Donaldson and Wales (1970), preschoolers have great difficulty in understanding concepts of more and less. Their work was done with 3-year-olds. It would seem advisable for teachers to wait at least until the end of nursery schooling or the reception class of the primary school before beginning to teach these concepts.

Frydman and Bryant (1988) hypothesized that the difficult concept of proportion would be more easily learnt if it was linked to the easier one of division or sharing. After all, the child's first understanding of proportion is of half. He can then understand 'more than' and 'less than', initially applying them both to a half, for example, 'My sweets are more than half'. Frydman and Bryant's team investigated sharing in 4-year-olds: most could share out physically in an effective way. A child could count a share but he could not infer that, therefore, all the other shares must be the same. For instance, if twelve sweets had to shared among three children, he could physically share out the twelve into three piles of four each. This was assumed to mean that 4-year-olds have an effective understanding of 1:1 correspondence (matching a sweet in each pile). He could count his own share as four, but could not deduce that each of the other children's shares must also be four.

The 4-year-olds found the task much more difficult when the objects being shared out were not all the same, such as a mixture of Smarties and apples. However, Frydman and Bryant found the 4-year-olds could be trained to solve this problem by using colour codes: the child was helped if the Smarties and the apples were both red.

American studies of primary children

The transition from preschool experiences to primary school is of course a very important one. In the USA this occurs at 6. Carpenter and Moser (1982) undertook a longitudinal study of the first three years of primary schooling, i.e. up to 9 years. They agree with Hughes (1981) that adding and subtraction are best introduced in pictoral or physical form. Then follows the important transition from the informal strategies children bring to school to the formal number facts taught at school. However, Carpenter and Moser fear the strategies preschoolers bring to school may be smothered by the number facts and algorithms primary teachers force them to learn.

Carpenter and Moser's particular interest lies in verbal problem-solving. They found that infant pupils can solve simple verbal problems, even if they have not yet mastered addition and subtraction. Their specialized contribution is to analyse the semantic structure of these verbal problems. Other psycholinguists have done the same in terms of syntax. This is all part of the language dimension of maths, with which maths education is starting to get to grips.

Herbert Ginsburg is another strong advocate of using children's own strategies. He studied (1977) slow learners, many of whom had effective mental strategies that were not utilized by teachers in school. When George (12 y.) was asked to add $4 + 2$ on paper, he erroneously transformed this to 4×2 because of his faulty formal knowledge. This is an example of how children often think of maths as an isolated game with peculiar sets of rules and no evident relation to reality. George could work the sum out informally with paper-clips.

Lauren Resnick (1977) argues it is no good investigating changing concepts of number in children without paying attention to actual number performance. She is also one of the few constructivists who has concentrated on primary-school children rather than on preschoolers. However, like many constructivists, she is a keen advocate of teachers appreciating and using the informal strategies preschoolers and young primary children bring to school: for instance, in order to add, many youngsters evolve a *counting-on* strategy. For example, a child starts with five sweets and counts four on to reach nine. For subtraction there is a similar *counting-*

on strategy whereby a child subtracting three from eight counts on five from three. There is an alternative *counting-back* strategy, whereby the child counts backwards from the eight.

Resnick faces up to reality and argues that, by the end of primary school, these informal strategies have to be replaced by formal ones. The task then for primary teachers and their curriculum planners and advisers is how best to manage the transition from informal to formal strategies. She also argues that understanding on its own is not enough: the child must gain procedural skill to underlie the understanding.

Ginsburg (1977) argues that perhaps we should learn from the Russians in these matters. Gal'perin and Georgiev (1969) believe teaching should start with measurement, rather than with number as such. This is because young children judge by visual comparison rather than by measured unit. Teachers could implement this recommendation using Unifix cubes.

From an information processing (IP) standpoint, Davis (1984) argued that the type of thinking involved in maths is the same as in many other activities in everyday life, such as chess and map reading. To teach arithmetic only is regarded as being too narrow and ambiguous a basis for teaching maths. It is the broad sweep of mathematical thinking that is of major interest. The precision and convergent nature of maths answers (only one right answer) makes maths a particularly suitable case for IP treatment. From a psychological point of view we need to have precise information on the maths learner: exactly what it is he can*not* do; exactly what obstacles there are to his progress; exactly what errors he makes; and why he makes them. To an information processor, a person's memory is one of his or her most important characteristics. What is stored in the memory is more important than the pupil's current activities. *Registers* are the equivalent of pigeon holes for the memory. One register stores one word. The vital aspect for successful performance is that the registers are active. We need to be able to retrieve our previous learning out of the passive memory into the active memory. These units are then combined in new ways, modified or extended in order for new learning to take place.

Like the constructivists, Piagetians and most other schools of psychology, the information processors are against learning that has no enduring character for the pupil. Davis refers to such learning as 'disaster studies', where students pass courses without developing a gut feeling for the subject-matter. They develop no problem-solving ability or ability to transfer learning to new situations.

Van Lehn's (1983) repair theory is an example of how maths teachers can actually use IP. For instance, children often master the operation of adding as long as it involves only two digits. As soon as three digits are used, their mastery breaks down and repairs are called for to teach them where they are going wrong, for example:

$$\begin{array}{r} 128 \\ + 71 \\ \hline \end{array}$$

Children get confused in the third column and either ignore it and get an answer of 99 or they muddle the tens and hundreds columns up and get an answer of 899.

IP implies strong, directive teaching. However, this does not mean passive learning. According to Davis, two vital elements are

1. hypothesis testing. Pupils must be continually asked to check their answers. Are they correct on the criteria given? This often follows the computer model: either A or B;
2. for a pupil to use his visual imagination and apply this as far as possible to real-life situations.

British studies of primary-school children

In contrast with Ginsburg and Gal'perin and Georgiev, Margaret Brown (1981) found that 12-year-olds failed to transfer their learning from measurement to calculation. They had measured circumferences and radii of circles but could not understand and use the mathematical symbol *pi*.

The constructivist influence dominates prestigious maths education circles in Britain, such as PRIME (Primary Initiatives in Maths Education) and King's College, London. Constructivists argue that the pupil's own learning strategies he has mastered (often before coming to school or else outside school when 5 or older) should be central to teaching. Teachers should be aware of the learning strategies each child has and build their teaching onto these, e.g. the pupil may have learnt to count on his fingers in order to add.

Denvir (1985) made the most extreme case for constructivist teaching. She found each pupil has his own pattern of learning, different from that of all the other pupils. If Denvir is correct, the implications for the teacher are forbidding. The teacher has to be aware of the initial learning strategies of all the children in her class and of the learning patterns they are following. This is of course immensely demanding on the teacher. Denvir did find an extremely gifted teacher who could do this, at least with a class of about 15.

If Piaget is wrong (i.e. there is no universal pattern of learning) and Denvir and the constructivists are correct (i.e. that each child has a unique learning pattern), this would pose enormous problems for education to solve. The obvious first answer is to have smaller classes. This would make it easier for the teacher to monitor each individual's progress. A second answer was provided by Denvir when she stressed the need for more teacher–class discussion and small-group work.

As mentioned earlier in this chapter, many primary teachers are still unaware of constructivist concepts. The Piagetian influence is still pervasive among teachers since most were exposed to it during their own teacher-education courses. This emphasizes young children learning by doing. Since young children cannot work at a formal operational level, teachers need to prepare lessons for them on an intuitive or concrete operational level. In order to learn the concept of *time*, the child plays with clocks and eventually learns to tell the time exactly. In order to understand *fractions*, the child starts by cutting up toy cakes into halves or quarters. Only when he reaches the top classes of the primary school will he be expected to be able to write

$$\frac{1}{4}$$

According to Sutherland (1982, 1983), Shayer, Kuchemann and Wylan (1976) and Shayer and Wylan (1978), by the upper years of the primary school or the first year of the secondary, children of average ability will be fully concrete operational in science. If we assume the domain-general position, this finding can be applied to the very similar subject of maths. One important aspect of concrete operational thinking is the understanding of reversibility, for example

$$\text{as} \quad 3 \times 11 = 33$$
$$\text{then } 33 \div 3 = 11$$

Once he is thinking operationally, a child's competency will no longer simply be in manipulating numbers but will also include awareness of various logical patterns.

It is only when a pupil reaches formal operational thought that he will be able to work in purely symbolic form: in other words, doing calculations (with understanding) with no reference to anything concrete. This will only occur for the average child during the secondary years, perhaps only at 16 or not at all. This leaves the secondary teacher with a challenging task: to help adolescents in the middle and lower sets across the transition from concrete to formal operations. One way of doing this might be for the teacher to set work that needs to be finished in an abstract (formal) way, but having concrete aids (such as computer programs) for those who need them.

Mental algorithms that teachers decide to encourage in pupils should, according to Plunkett (1979), have certain desirable qualities. They should be flexible, active, holistic, iconic, require understanding, work from one part of the question towards the answer and give an early approximation. Mary, when asked to subtract $98 - 29$, uses her own strategy for regrouping and subtracts first

$$98 - 10 = 88$$
$$\text{then } 88 - 10 = 78$$
$$\text{and then } 78 - 9$$

to arrive at the correct answer.

Bryant has made a major contribution to understanding cognitive development in children. His general ideas are outlined in Chapter 7. In maths he has focused both on pre-primary and primary children, with an emphasis on the four processes (addition, subtraction, multiplication and division). He advises teachers to start from a concept such as a half (which is mastered in the preschool years) and build more difficult concepts – such as quarter – on to this.

Bryant found (1985) that 6-year-olds did not know when to use a particular skill they had learnt. The children were taught a more sophisticated strategy for subtraction to replace their existing strategy of counting on from the lower number. The children could utilize this skill when cued to do so, but when they had to work out what they needed to do for themselves, they could not. Bryant and Bradley (1985) hypothesized that young children would make more progress in multiplication if they could link it conceptually with the easier process of addition, which they had already mastered, and this hypothesis was borne out by a controlled experiment.

Metacognition is an idea that could spread from language to maths teaching. This would mean encouraging pupils' awareness of their own learning of number and other mathematical concepts and of the thought processes accompanying this learning. This may be particularly difficult for primary teachers when maths is only part of their teaching programme. Perhaps it is up to the teacher with special responsibility for maths and the adviser to raise awareness.

Constructivists argue that the pupil's own learning strategies he has mastered (often before coming to school or else outside school when 5 or older) should be central to teaching. The pupil may have learnt to count on his fingers in order to add. Formal teachers insist on pupils rote learning the number bonds (e.g. $5 + 4 = 9$) and suppressing the learning the child brings to school. Although constructivists find all rote learning an anathema, there is a compromise case whereby absolutely essential rote learning should be retained. This consists of the addition and subtraction number bonds and the multiplication tables up to 10, but very little else. These are essential for using algorithms for calculating the four processes (addition, subtraction, multiplication and division). Failure to learn these leaves a pupil merely with a few simple strategies he has learnt for himself (plus the electronic calculator). Since the IP school focuses on discrete learning tasks, it is hoped that they will provide computer programs for effecting this basic rote learning.

Sutherland's studies of primary children with difficulties in maths

Most slow learners were found by Sutherland (1989) to have little idea of whether the answers they get using the calculator are approximately correct or not, so it does not seem to be a worthwhile technique to teach them. This was one of a number of themes investigated in this study, which involved case studies of children with learning difficulties in maths in four London schools (both inner city and suburban) and one Scottish school (small town, drawing on the surrounding farming community). The most important aim was to see whether such children could carry out the Donaldsonian operation of disembedding a simulated real-life shopping situation into a 'sum' on paper.

In general they could do this. They could usually work out the answers to the adding and subtraction 'sums', where these involved only single digits. However, where two digits were involved, many children had difficulties with subtraction, particularly if 'borrowing' was involved. The real problem lay in the failure of nearly all children to translate the correct answer back into the 'real-life' situation again. In many cases this did not even go as far as putting 'pence' or 'p' when the answer was a sum of money.

It may be that teachers have laid such stress on getting 'the right answer' that children do not think there is anything else to be done. But if maths is *not* seen as a means of solving problems in real life, then it is not being well taught. An associated aim was to investigate the physical props used by children with learning difficulties, such as their fingers, counters and Unifix cubes. Can such children be helped to acquire effective formal strategies so that they no longer need to use physical strategies? Can such children even be helped over the transition into concrete operational thinking?

Results showed that even some of the best-known curriculum aids did not seem to be helping. Place value is a major weakness as has been shown also by the APU (1978−82) and AAP (1983) national surveys (DES, 1978−82). Cuisenaire rods were designed to help children understand that, for instance, ten little white cubes equal one long orange rod. But these children showed no ability to transfer such knowledge to sums being attempted on paper. Nor did they turn to Cuisenaire as a strategy when they were struggling with a subtraction sum on paper. It was concluded that it remains difficult to help children with learning difficulties in maths to overcome their need for physical props. Perhaps information processors and designers of computer programs will succeed where designers of educational toys have failed.

Cieran was an especially interesting case study. He was a 14-year-old boy who lived in a run-down industrial town in Scotland. There was little money in the home for number activities. The boy was physically small and frail for his age, and his general academic and mathematical performance was poor. Yet he had established a reputation, of which he was very proud, for his great feats of long multiplication. Cieran could multiply any two−digit numbers mentally within a few seconds. When this was investigated by the author, the boy's strategy was revealed. For instance,

16×18:
Step 1 $16 \times 10 = 160$ (hold this in his short-term memory)
Step 2 $16 \times 8 = 128$ (hold this in his short-term memory)
Step 3 (add up the subtotals) $160 + 128 = 288$.

Had he evolved this very effective strategy for himself along constructivist lines? When probed, he revealed he'had had a dedicated primary maths teacher who had taught him the strategy.

Cieran also had another unorthodox strategy for adding two-digit numbers. He started with the *left*-hand side (LHS), for example,

$48 + 35$:
Step 1 add LHS $4 + 3 = 7$
Step 2 add second column from the left, $8 + 5 = 13$ (3 with 1 carried over to the LHS column, holding it meanwhile in the short-term memory)
Step 3 adjust LHS column $7 + 1 = 8$
Step 4 the answer is 83.

He had evolved this strategy for himself. It is a classic example of the constructivist case where the child has evolved a perfectly adequate strategy for himself. The teacher should be aware of this and not impose the orthodox right-hand side strategy on such pupils, particularly not on a child like Cieran who finds effective learning difficult. However, unlike most slow learners in maths, Cieran had an excellent short-term memory he could use for both strategies.

Are there, on the other hand, children who have learning problems only in maths and not in literacy as well? These are dyscalculics, the mathematical equivalent of dyslexics. One such was uncovered: Vivien, a 10-year-old boy of Jamaican descent, living in a London inner-city area. Vivien enjoyed reading; it was only in maths he had a block. Teachers at the school pointed out that one of his two sisters had had a similar block. Motivation was part of the problem. Not even simulated shopping for sweets could arouse enthusiasm for his lessons (perhaps real sweets might have done the trick). Poor short-term memory was also part of the problem. The use of his fingers was all he had by way of strategies. He used them for counting on in adding, and for counting back in subtraction. He had rote learnt very few number bonds nor could he use many algorithms efficiently. So he could not calculate two-digit adding or sub-traction sums consistently. Unfortunately, his teacher's strategy was one of class teaching. Vivien was at least two years behind the rest of the class, so maths lessons were practically meaningless to him. He received no learning support in maths.

There was a general pattern of impoverished strategies at Vivien's inner-city school among both West Indian and white children. This prob-ably stemmed from a lack of mathematical help in their homes. This was not because of a lack of willingness, but because the (usually) single mother was battling hard enough just to keep the family unit afloat. There was also very little money for expeditions to the corner shop. However, mothers somehow generally did find pocket money.

It would be most helpful to such children's mathematical development if health visitors (as well as teachers) were to try to educate such parents about the importance for their children of home number activities. This has been done for language, with some success. Such activities do *not* have to be expensive. Counting games can be played with stones, potatoes and other free or cheap objects around the home. Nearly every home has a TV set. Children could be encouraged to watch such numeracy-enriching programmes as *Sesame Street*.

Gender was not a vital factor in mathematical difficulties, although boys were referred to me twice as often as girls. This went against the general assumption that boys lead in mathematical skills. In this small-scale study of slow learners boys were more likely to have difficulties.

In a follow-up study, the focus was narrowed down to the subtraction of two-digit numbers. The school was in an area of considerable deprivation. The strategies each child brought to school were probed; many had none. The help children get at home in subtraction activities was investigated and this was found to be variable. As in the original study, a high proportion of children were from single-parent families or two-parent families where the father was unemployed and so there was very little money in the home. Where there was, some children did odd errands to the corner shop for their mothers. However, they apparently did not check their change. Most of the children did get pocket money (£1 a week was typical), so they could choose for themselves how to spend their money. A few would save towards an expensive item, thereby giving themselves valuable experience in adding. The others would buy sweets, ice creams, etc., but (by their own account) they did not systematically check their change in order to see how much they had left to spend.

A mock shop was a fundamental feature of the follow-up study. The researcher acted as a mediator in a 1:1 interaction with each pupil. Various items, such as a rubber ball, a child's book and a tin of sardines, were 'for sale'. The pupil was given token money, usually a 50p coin or £1, to buy as much as he could. Most pupils did realize the need for change, but they were very poor at getting it. They needed a great deal of help in breaking the coin of larger denomination into the correct number of smaller ones: for instance, exchanging a 50p coin for two 20ps and one 10p in order to buy a ball for 30p. They had not grasped the principle of exchange: in other words, that the new total should equal the initial one. (The understanding of equivalence is a criterion for Piaget's stage of concrete operational thinking.) These children found it particularly difficult to break a 10p down into 5ps and/or 2ps and 1ps in order to obtain 6p for a sweet. Subsequently they found getting the correct change problematic. Because it used token coins instead of real coins and had a mock shop instead of a real one (where pupils actually buy and keep their purchases), this study has been criticized as lacking in reality, meaningfulness and credibility to pupils. The effectiveness of real shopping on pupils' subtraction performance will be investigated in a future project.

The school taught the double decomposition method of subtracting (better known as 'borrowing'). Some pupils could use this accurately, but others were handicapped by not having rote learnt their subtraction number bonds. The infant teaching was highly informal and did not teach number bonds systematically. Pupils had to learn these on their own. Those who had difficulties in maths generally had failed to learn their number bonds. Most of them, however, did have a counting-back strategy, either mentally or on their fingers. They had evolved this for themselves and it worked reliably and efficiently.

The experimenter used both a practical and a formal approach. The practical one was based on a reconciled post-Piagetian–constructivist paradigm. This involved helping children in the shop situation and using such learning strategies the children had. The formal one provided remedial tuition in the use of the double decomposition algorithm. Teachers were neither aware of, nor saw any need for, the pupils to have their own strategies. The researcher was referred to as the 'decomposition man'. Pupils generally were not aware there are two alternative strategies for calculating the same thing. The formal paper-and-pencil approach was probably slightly more successful in terms of pupils getting the correct answer. A third strategy of using the calculator was also used occasionally with variable results. Very few of these pupils had sufficient 'feel' for numbers to be able to check whether their answers were approximately correct or not.

An abiding problem whichever strategy is used is the inability of pupils struggling with maths to hold numbers in their short-term memory. Psychologists of the IP school could do teachers a great service if they could discover a technique for helping children to overcome this deficiency.

The role of the learning-support teacher

What then should the role of the learning-support teacher be in maths? First and foremost it is to have a role. For the learning-support teacher to concentrate entirely on children's language problems is to ignore the vital role basic numeracy has in everyday life.

Should she work alongside the class teacher, giving 1:1 tuition to those children diagnosed as needing help with maths, or should she teach them separately, in the library, a spare room or a special learning-support room? The overwhelming post-Warnock (1978) ideological orthodoxy is in favour of the former. This argues that the integrated approach prevents the struggling child feeling inferior by being labelled and having to leave the classroom. If the learning-support teacher works in an unostentatious way, the rest of the class may not realize whom she is helping.

Accepting the argument at an emotional level, cognitive developmentalists nevertheless have a duty to find out whether in fact this is the most efficient way for such children to learn. An MEd student examined this. By means of a controlled experiment, she compared a small group, randomly divided into two small subgroups, taught in each way. Those slow learners taught separately made significantly more progress than

those taught alongside the class teacher over the three mont[...]
experiment. When she probed this further by means of case st[...]
children revealed that a situation in which they had to work wit[...]
class of about twenty-five was inhibiting to them. They felt shy an[...]ed
to show their ignorance in front of the whole class. However, in a 1:1 or a
small-group situation, the vital pupil−teacher verbal interaction flowed
more easily. The children were more open to being taught.

Summary

The post-Piagetian message is that children learn most effectively from
practical activity. Secondary teachers need to find ways of helping children
over the transition from concrete to formal operations. The IP message is
that teachers and psychologists need to try to specify exactly what they
want children to learn. If the exact conditions of learning can then be
controlled, it may be possible to help pupils to learn more effectively.
The metacognitive message is that teachers should help children be more
aware of numbers and the learning of mathematical skills.

The constructivist message is that teachers should be aware of the
learning strategies children bring to school. Teachers should start from
these and help children to use their strategies during lessons. A powerful
message emerges: that children have a number of modes of operating in
maths − the oral and the practical as well as the traditional written.
Teachers should appreciate that some children may be much better at the
oral or the practical than at the written. Ways must be found for using all
the mathematical abilities children bring to school.

Questions for discussion

1. To what extent should the electronic calculator be used in maths teaching?
2. How can the maths teacher treat each pupil as an individual?
3. To what extent does the maths teacher have to be a teacher of language?
4. How can the infant teacher use the informal strategies children bring to her class?
5. How can a secondary teacher help average pupils across the transition from concrete to formal operations?
6. How can a teacher stimulate both formal and concrete operational in the same mixed-stage class?
7. What should the role of the learning-support teacher be?

Further reading

Dickson, L., Brown, M. and Gibson, O. (1984) *Children Learning Mathematics: A Teacher's Guide to Recent Research*, Holt, Rinehart & Winston, Eastbourne.

Hart, K. M. (ed.) (1981) *Children's Understanding of Maths 11–16*, John Murray, London.

Hughes, M. (1986) *Children and Number*, Blackwell, Oxford.

Skemp, R. R. (1971) *The Psychology of Learning Mathematics*, Penguin Books, Harmondsworth.

16
THE SECONDARY TEACHER

If one teaching aid has dominated in most subjects, it is the worksheet. This is very similar to the research technique used by E. A. Peel and his students (1971) at Birmingham to study adolescent judgement. In most cases this involved presenting pupils with a written passage, then asking them questions based on it. The higher-level response that is sought involves bringing in other material in addition to the passage given, and the adolescent using his imagination on both.

The widespread adoption of individualized learning has given renewed relevance to the work of Peel and his school. This method helps teachers cope with a mixed-ability class, with each pupil working on material at his own level. There is criticism by ambitious parents that many of the worksheets are not sufficiently stimulating: they tend simply to ask the pupil to look for simple facts from the passage.

The synthesis of Peel's work presented in Chapter 10 should encourage teachers to ask more 'Why?' questions and to demand *explainer*- and not merely *describer*-level responses. In this chapter, Peel's system for categorizing adolescents' responses is applied to some of the subjects of the secondary curriculum. This system is an alternative to Piaget's stages and different subject specialists have applied Peel's ideas to their own subject.

Other cognitive developmental viewpoints relevant to secondary teaching include metacognition and information processing (IP). They will be applied to the subjects to which they are relevant.

English

Mason (1974) made a study of adolescent response to poetry, using sixteen poems from school anthologies. First-formers showed a lack of comprehension of poems — a surprising finding with poetry being part of the primary curriculum. These 11-year-olds merely repeated the content of the poem. Second-formers made emotional responses to the poems, but their cognitive responses were limited to a single strand. Only some fifth- and sixth-formers demonstrated the ability to fuse emotional and cognitive responses. By the fifth-form, pupils could generalize and explain in terms of hypotheses linking the poem to wider human parallels.

Ellis (1975) made a study of adolescent understanding of stability and change in literature. He focused on passages from novels that illustrated sudden traumatic changes in people's lives, for example, Tess's seduction by Alex in Hardy's *Tess of the D'Urbervilles*. In common with others working with Peel's theories, he found that slower pupils would focus on just one aspect of the situation while more advanced pupils could take several aspects of the circumstances into account and the most advanced made imaginative responses. A criterion of Peel's explainer stage was their ability to discuss the dynamics of crisis and its consequences.

Michell and Peel (1977) applied Peel's describer–explainer dichotomy to the teaching of English literature in the secondary school. They found that only the more mature, generally older, pupils understood literary material in an explainer way. In view of the oral discussion methods of teaching emphasized by GCSE, Michell and Peel's work on the intellectual quality of such oral discussions is now particularly relevant. Many pupils discussed only at a describer level, with much repetition and many sweeping generalizations. A minority of pupils operated at an explainer level. Their contributions were *open* in that they did not arise only from the presented text, but were introduced on the pupil's own initiative. Only the explainers could make statements that were tentative and hypothetical. Only the explainers seemed capable of discussion in any worthwhile sense.

In their written responses, Michell and Peel's pupils showed very similar categories to Sutherland's (1982), outlined in Chapter 10. Because Michell and Peel were investigating only secondary but not primary pupils, it was not surprising they found a much reduced system of describer categories:

1. In the more basic category, only a single item was picked out of a text.
2. In the slightly more advanced category, more than one item was picked out.

(In neither category could the pupil bring information or independent judgement apart from the material given.) Michell and Peel found three explainer categories:

3. The first a transition between describer and explainer thinking. The

pupil could comment on the situation and express tentativeness, but his arguments were not made explicit.

4. Arguments were only made explicit in the explainer category. Here, the pupil could also consider a number of possibilities.

5. Michell and Peel's superior category was not qualitatively different from ordinary explainer thinking, but quantitatively superior. The pupil's arguments are mature, explicit and well reasoned. His responses are full, sensitive and possibilities are considered at length. Issues are developed well beyond the scope offered by the text.

In her later (1979) work with Lambourne, Michell developed four alternative literary styles: a local newspaper version using simple language, a BBC oral documentary version, a tabloid version with much colourful language, and a statistical-factual account using 'objective' language. A report on a road accident was presented in the four styles to 216 16-year-old pupils. Each pupil made two responses, one without discussion and the other after lengthy discussion in friendship groups. (Discussion techniques had been used in their English class for some time.) Pupils' written responses were examined. Five different questions were asked, none of which could be answered directly from the text. For instance, those getting the tabloid version were asked 'Should newspapers report accidents in lurid detail?' Those who received the statistical version were asked 'Would accidents be prevented by the use of safety belts?'

No significant differences in the stage of the pupils' written responses were found between having had a discussion after the presentation and not having had one. This is disappointing evidence for those educators who believe in discussion.

The statistical technique of factor analysis revealed an interesting polarized factor. Those high on it would be concerned primarily with social relationships and therefore with monitoring the task of discussion. These pupils were interested primarily in people. On the other hand, those low on this factor were mainly interested in the ideas and issues arising from the text and not in social relationships. These pupils were interested primarily in the content.

Other developmental approaches that may be relevant to the teaching of English are Vygotsky's, IP and metacognition. Vygotsky's ideas (such as the need for instruction in grammar) are discussed in detail in Chapter 4. IP may have a role in the learning of facts and simple structures. This might apply especially to pupils with learning difficulties. Metacognition might involve making pupils aware of their own learning of such language concepts as verbs and plurals.

Science

Physics and chemistry are both subjects in which IP would seem to have a potentially very valuable role to play. Pupils can work problems out on screens, as is already being done by Tim O'Shea and his colleagues in the Educational Technology Department at the Open University. Besides this, the pupils' learning situations can be controlled in terms of the factors being quantified and put on the screen. It should be possible to assess learning outcomes fairly accurately. In biology the computer is already being used as an integral part of teaching. However, there is scope for far more use of the computer in pupils' actual learning.

The constructivists have had a major impact on science teaching. The work of Ros Driver (1983) has been very influential in making teachers aware of how pupils arrive in a secondary class with many rich scientific experiences. Even if they have been taught very little primary science, they will nevertheless have watched a great many TV programmes where scientific concepts are introduced, e.g. *Sesame Street*. In addition they will all have had some experiences of physical, chemical and biological phenomena in everyday life.

Much of this understanding will be at what Driver calls the *gut* level. This is similar to Piaget's *intuitive* understanding. Such gut understanding is not scientific, so science teachers will be trying to raise their pupils' level of understanding to the scientific. They will not, however, be successful with all pupils. Many will go out into adult life with gut-level understanding. Others will be superficially at a scientific level, sufficient to pass exams, but who really still think in a gut way, particularly when under pressure. Pupils also bring certain initial strategies for learning science into the classroom that teachers should know about. These can then either be used and built on or the teacher can attempt to supplant them with more suitable strategies for 'real' science.

From a post-Piagetian perspective, Sutherland (1980) applied his version of Peel's stages to the respiration cycle in biology and to the water cycle – a standard topic for integrated science in the first three years. He focused on the reversibility aspect, one of the crucial characteristics of concrete operational thought. When did pupils realize that the volume of air inhaled is (approximately) equal to the volume exhaled? When did pupils realize that, when water freezes and then thaws, the volume of water remains the same? As a pool of water evaporates and later condenses and falls as rain, when does a pupil realize the volume is the same? Both topics are examples of the conservation of volume. The results for primary pupils are discussed in Chapter 14. Both these and the results for secondary pupils brought out the fact that a child has to grasp many other more fundamental concepts before these can be understood. Breathing presupposes a concept of air. It was generally only in their second or third year that secondary pupils became aware that oxygen is one of the gases making up air.

First- and second-year pupils had a vague notion of a vacuum. It is impossible to demonstrate a vacuum positively, only to demonstrate its effect, e.g. the famous Magdeburg hemispheres at the Science Museum or an empty petrol-can filled with steam, which then collapses as the steam condenses to leave a vacuum. For this reason it is not surprising it was not grasped at the concrete operational level; the abstract nature of the concept led to it being understood only at the formal operational level.

On the topic of breathing, pupils in the first and second year did realize that oxygen reaches the blood. They were relating organs (heart and lungs) to their appropriate role in the respiration process. The secondary pupils were more scientific than primary pupils in their understanding and knew that oxygen is inhaled and carbon dioxide is exhaled. In Piagetian terms, they were fully concrete operational, since they understood that the volume inhaled is equal to the volume exhaled. Only by the middle years (at 13 and 14) did pupils show any awareness of the *chemistry* of the respiration process. The concept of energy was mentioned for the first time; pupils could also relate this to real life in terms of the need for more oxygen for exercise and less for sleep.

The bright fifth- and sixth-formers could give theoretical explainer-level responses on a true scientific basis. When the question was biological, these brighter older adolescents gave explanations in terms of cell theory. When questioned about the organs used for breathing, students talked of alveoli and capillaries. When the question was chemical, their explanations were in terms of molecular theory.

The reversible nature of the water cycle was grasped at about 12. This means it was only after a year at secondary school that most pupils became fully concrete operational. Even at the end of their secondary schooling very few pupils could label condensation correctly, and even then only the most scientifically minded could give an explanation in terms of saturation. Despite the popularity of the water cycle as a topic in both primary and secondary schools, few pupils at this particular comprehensive school could give an explainer account of it. These secondary pupils only realize the exact temperature at which ice changes to water $(0°C)$ at the end of formal schooling.

Perhaps the importance given to science as a core subject in the National

Curriculum will do a great deal to improve concept attainment. The new emphasis on science in the primary school, from the age of 4 or 5, should give pupils a more solid foundation of scientific concepts when they enter the secondary school.

Other developmental approaches relevant to teaching science are constructivism, IP and metacognition. Driver, a leading constructivist, has written (1983) vividly about the way children bring meaningful concepts to school. These might be built up from experimenting with home science kits, exploring the local environment or watching TV programmes. IP should help pupils in problem-solving situations, particularly those posed on the computer screen. Metacognition may help make pupils more aware of their own learning, particularly of such skills as microscope technique or glass-blowing.

Geography

How do children interpret the facts they are given by their geography teacher? Can they give genuine geographical responses? Rhys (1972), in his investigation, operated on the basic premise that the understanding of geographical material at the secondary stage compels the adolescent to place a person other than himself in an environment other than his own, and furthermore, he must take into account the complex interplay of a miscellany of factors within the foreign environment. The environment in this case means the Behavioural Environment – a particular field of human action – involving an application of human physical forces active within a particular setting.

He gave children maps, statistical data, etc., relevant to a number of localities: crofters in the Hebrides, a wandering Masai tribe in Kenya and prairie farmers in Canada.

In the case of the crofters, the poor quality of the land was emphasized. Charts were provided showing the proportion and nature of crops as against pasture and the number of sheep and cattle. Charts of rainfall and temperature were also given. The children were asked: 'Are the crofters making the best use of their land by growing crops only over such a small area?'

The child has to use deductive reasoning to resolve the conflict between the quantity and quality of the land available and the grazing habits of the animals. Rhys's sample consisted of the top two years of a junior school and all five years of a secondary-modern boys school. There were no grammar-school boys or secondary girls. Grammar-school pupils might have given explainer-level answers at an earlier age.

The responses followed the usual Peelian pattern. Younger children tended to give personal, tautological replies, such as 'Yes, because they've got the beauty of the deer in the forest'. However, a 16-year-old answered (Peel (1971) p. 91):

I think they are using their land to full extent because what they can't grow, they can get by selling the fish that they catch, to other places far inland who cannot fish for their own fish. Also on the rough ground they can graze their cattle and sheep from which they can obtain milk and also meat. From the milk they can make their own butter and cheese. What cereals and vegetables cannot be grown, can be imported from nearby Scotland.

In Rhys's study of the Masai, the children were given data about the two grazing areas, one with an annual rainfall of over 50 in per year and the other of under 20 in per year. Children were asked to deduce that the Masai would need to migrate with their cattle to the high rainfall area after the three months of highest rainfall. Younger children allowed their judgement to be swayed by the visual dominance of the high rainfall on the chart. They also found the abstract nature of the isohyets[1] meaningless to them. But a 16-year-old could put forward a hypothesis and use the data provided to substantiate it (*ibid.* p. 191):

The Masai migrate twice a year ... to get the best seasonal rainfall they can. The reason why they keep moving is that the waterholes in the valley are non-permanent, but the waterholes in the highlands are. Another reason for their task is that when they are in the valley using the grass and water, the grass in the highlands is building up. This means that when they return to the highlands, the water and food is there for them.

For his exercise on the prairie farmers, Rhys showed children aerial photographs of a small town built about the intersection of a road and railway in the Canadian wheat belt. Another picture showed the harvesting of wheat. Pupils were then asked: 'Why has this small town grown up just here, where the main road and railway cross each other?' They were also asked a second question: 'Is it wise for a farmer to grow only one crop over such a very large area?' Resolution of the second question requires the understanding of the marketing of the single crop thousands of miles away. This cannot be worked out from the immediate data of pictures, but has to be deduced. For instance, a 12-year-old grasps (*ibid.* p. 193) that 'because you can get the wheat here by road and rail, and seeing how the railway goes straight through it can pick up all the wheat from the farms'.

Summarizing all the studies, Peel concluded (1971) that the understanding of the dynamics of the balance established by man with his geographical environment are not clearly perceived until an average age of 14 and upwards.

Other approaches that seem relevant to geography teaching are IP and constructivism. IP might give insight into how pupils learn the quantitative, factual aspects of geography. Constructivism would utilize the geographical concepts pupils gain outside school: on their summer holidays, watching TV documentaries and reading books.

History

History is one subject area where the Peelians have lost the argument in recent years, coinciding with a radical change in the nature of history teaching. Initially Hallam (1967), testing across the secondary-school range, found that on average concrete operations was only achieved at 12 years and formal operations at over 16. This finding was replicated by Da Silva (1972), who came to the conclusion that history, in any meaningful sense, can only be started from the age of about 16. Prior to this the subject has to be taught in a descriptive way. The vast majority of pupils will be transitional between describer and explainer thinking and will need help in reaching full explainer thought. However, there will be a minority of bright pupils who will have achieved formal operations, perhaps as young as 11.

If Da Silva's conclusions are accepted, there are immense and difficult consequences for history teaching now that the same course is being taught to the whole range of ability and being assessed by a unified GCSE exam. One way of overcoming this problem (as discussed in Chapter 14) is to have a core syllabus that caters for the average and below-average pupils, with challenging extensions at an abstract level for those capable of thinking historically.

One of the main problems in any subject is terminology. Da Silva found that this is certainly true for history. If pupils have not mastered the terms, they tend to rely on context. He investigated this using the artificial word, 'malmir', meaning slump or depression. Pupils had to learn the concept from the following passage (*ibid.* p. 175):

> The years that followed the victory of Waterloo were some of the worst that Britain had ever passed through. The 'false and bloated prosperity' of the war, as Cobbett called it, gave way to a terrible malmir. The government no longer needed to buy huge quantities of munitions and clothing for the army and the Allies; the people of Europe after more than twenty years of war, were too poor to buy the goods that British manufacturers would have liked to sell; instead the foreign governments often used their discharged soldiers to make their own goods.

Results followed the classical Peelian pattern. The average 13-year-old was logically restricted. He would pick on just one word, for example, 'terrible', and reply that 'it meant a terrible disaster to the people of Britain, it gave way to a terrible disaster as it would say'. The circumstantial thinker picked on one aspect, for instance, 'I think it is a famine because all the money had been spent on guns and ammunitions. Therefore there was no money left to pay for the goods'. Pupils who were operating at a comprehensive circumstantial level combined two or more strands of the extract, for instance, 'Redundancy, I think so because it is said that Europe was too poor to buy things Britain made because of twenty years of war. Also it is said that European people used to make their own clothes.' The imaginative adolescent could go beyond the passage given. He is also capable of deductive conceptualization. This is probably a better term than 'imaginative' to describe this example from a 16-year-old: 'Slump, after the war Britain found it could not sell the stuff as it could before the war as other countries took over the market in Europe. This made industry poor. The word "slump" fits in place of "Malmir" as it happens to most countries after the war.'

Naturally in a real teaching situation, as opposed to research to determine pupils' understanding, the use of the artificial word is a distraction and the correct word would be used from the outset.

Within history education there has been a much more hostile reaction to the Peel—Da Silva findings than in other subjects. A leading critic is Booth (1980), who found that pupils are capable of a far higher level of understanding than did Peel. In a seventeen-month longitudinal study, Booth discovered that where there was sound teaching and a stimulating syllabus, considerable progress was made in the development of concepts. When tested orally, most pupils could draw meaning, inferred from evidence, into a convincing synthesis. Booth argued that history is not ultimately about hypothesis testing and deduction. The pupil's performance does not depend on his IQ, socioeconomic status or his degree of cognitive maturation but on the syllabus content and on the quality of the teaching. The quality of teaching implies pupils learning from copies of original documents, like junior historians (as required by the GCSE). This involves induction by the pupils of what happened from the written material. Dickinson and Lee (1978) argued that historical situations cannot be set up in a laboratory in the Piagetian manner.

There has also been a radical change in the nature of history teaching. This has moved away from chronological sweeps of time to the use of source material. The new orientation means that it is not so important whether or not pupils have a concept of historic time. What is important is their ability to use written documentary evidence. Despite these criticisms, it is argued here that Peel's approach is not irrelevant, since he and his workers studied pupils' ability to answer questions from passages, as in the Da Silva (1972) example quoted above.

Metacognition is also an approach relevant to current ideas on history teaching. These are dominated by resource-based learning, as discussed by Booth (1980). In order to handle this, the pupil first needs to learn how to obtain factual material from these documents. Then he needs to learn how to use this factual knowledge to tackle a project for GCSE. According to metacognitive ideas, all this learning needs to be *conscious* on the part of the pupil. The teacher should try to help him towards this goal. The point about facts also applies to skills. The teacher should try to help the pupil's awareness of his own skills, whether these be of interpretation, analysis, referencing or reading.

IP would seem to be the essence of learning history. Prima facie there would appear to be the potential for an ideal marriage between this school of developmental psychology and history education. The application of developmental psychology should be able to maximize pupils' ability to store and retrieve historical facts.

Religious studies

Peel's PhD student Ronald Goldman (1965) pointed to the very abstract concepts of the Christian religion. This implies that it would not be easy to teach such concepts to non-formal operational pupils. Goldman advised teachers to make concepts as visual as possible: for instance, the Holy Trinity could be taught in terms of three drops of water being merged together. When teaching primary pupils concepts should be presented even more strongly in terms of seeing and doing. This advice to teachers was based on his Peelian–Piagetian stages. The first three are pre-operational.

Pre-Religious Thought (up to 7 Years)

God is seen in purely physical terms. Religion is merged with fairy tales: God and Father Christmas are perceived as conceptually equivalent. Prayer is magical and any religious language used shows no understanding.

When asked why Moses was afraid to look at God, a pupil replied it was because God had a funny face.

Sub-Religious Thought I (7—9 Years)

God is beginning to move out of fairyland, but he is still seen as a large man with long white robes and a beard. Jesus is seen as a 'magic' man. Prayer is egocentric and materialistic. However, the 'religious' and 'real' worlds are seen as separate.

Sub-Religious Thought II (9—11 Years)

There is still a conflict between the ideas of the 'religious' and those of the 'real' world. For instance, miracles are now queried. Simultaneously there is confusion over God. He is thought to be everywhere, a pantheistic viewpoint.

The last three stages are operational.

Personal Religious Thought I (11—13 Years)

This is the concrete operational stage. The first signs of questioning and doubts emerge. At the same time there is the start of altruism in prayer, although magical ideas still persist. The youngster's view of Jesus is more down to earth.

Personal Religious Thought II (13—14 Years)

Children are now capable of understanding religion in the abstract way in which it is presented to adults. Symbols of an even more abstract nature can now be understood. God is now conceived as unseeable. There is interest in Jesus in terms of his meaning and mission. Prayer is no longer automatically seen as being answered. Parables can now be understood, e.g. the parting of the Red Sea.

Advanced Formal Operational (15 Years Upwards)

An even greater degree of abstract symbolism is evident. Hypotheses are much more ingenious but realistic. Implications are clearly stated and not just implied.

When asked why Moses was afraid to look at God, a pupil might reply that Moses like most people of his time showed a sense of awe in the presence of the holy.

Besides using the well-tried Peel technique of getting pupils to respond to passages (in this case from the Bible), Goldman also tested the pupils' interpretation of a number of religious experiences (such as going to church, praying and reading the Bible) by showing pictures, e.g. of the Bible being torn up by one pupil's brother.

The overall message for teachers is that pupils build up their concepts through experiences. These will come from a number of different modes: verbal, intellectual, emotional, moral and aesthetic. The complexity of religion makes it a difficult subject to teach and to some extent it is up to the teacher to provide appropriate experiences. But how do the pupils internalize these experiences? Goldman argued that it is how internalization occurs that determines whether the experiences are going to be valuable to the pupils or not. Discussion is valuable, particularly in building up abstract ideas.

There has been an anti-Goldman reaction since the 1970s, when his ideas dominated the teaching of religious studies in Britain. Critics have pointed out that he examined neither the child's ability to communicate his own experiences nor his ability to discern a religious dimension within these experiences. Goldman's assumptions have been criticized by Slee (1990), in particular the way Goldman presupposes the validity of the Piagetian account of cognitive development. Details of Goldman's methodology have also been criticized by Slee: the selection of the three Bible stories, the questions asked in the interview and the use of content and scalogram analysis to analyse the data. Her theological critique noted the liberal Protestant model underlying Goldman's definitions of religious thinking.

However, other workers have found evidence for stage development and merely modified Goldman's findings. Peatling (1977) found the transition between concrete and abstract religious thinking is much more complex and much slower than Goldman had indicated. This would imply religious-studies teachers putting even more emphasis on helping pupils across the transition by using pictures, videos and other visual props.

On the other hand, some workers have not found evidence for stage development. These include Tamminen (1976) in Finland and Kay (1981) in England. Their evidence pointed to an even progress in development. Other workers did find evidence for stages. However, in contrast to Goldman, they found that abstract ideas can be taught in the primary school as well as in the first year of secondary school. Murphy (1977) found that such children could understand the allegorical meaning conveyed by parables, even though they were not yet at the formal operational stage.

Interestingly for teachers of all subjects, Goldman found some pupils had poor concepts but were able to verbalize impressively from them, and some pupils with strong concepts were unable to verbalize them. Richmond (1972) found greater maturity in religious judgement with age — a not surprising finding. But he also found that younger pupils did better when they received more cueing or helping from teachers in the form of coding of the passages.

Despite her criticisms outlined above, Slee (1990) has admitted that there has been a swing back towards the ideas of Goldman in religious-studies circles during the past five years. In some ways Goldman is putting a constructivist argument: that children build up vivid concepts for themselves, e.g. the sun. Teachers need to be aware of these and build religious concepts on them, e.g. God.

Metacognition seems relevant to teaching religious studies. This assumes that making pupils aware of both their own learning and their own evolving skills of interpretation and analysis leads to more efficient overall learning. In a subject where the learning and memorization of facts is no longer seen as a goal, IP can presumably make little contribution.

Summary

English Mason found that only some fifth- and all sixth-formers could respond to both the cognitive and emotional elements of poems. In his study of pupils' responses to novels, Mason found that the less able could only respond to one aspect, whereas the most able could handle the various strands bearing on the narrative. Michell and Peel found that only older, generally more mature, pupils could handle material in an explainer way.

Science Sutherland's study showed that children needed some hier-archically simpler concepts (such as air) before they could grasp the concept of breathing. This only happened on average in the early years of secondary schooling. Once the concept of oxygen was grasped, that of breathing became more scientific. A minority could relate respiration to the concept of energy by 16. The reversible nature of the water cycle was also only grasped at about 12. Evaporation and condensation were ex-plained only by a minority, even at school-leaving age.

Geography Rhys's study indicated that the responses of pupils from 9 to 16 followed the classic Peelian pattern. High-level responses can be evoked by giving pupils charts and statistical data and challenging them with questions that go beyond what is immediately visible.

History Da Silva argued that teachers need to wait until pupils are about 16 before proper history can be taught. However, in this case, the Peel school would seem to have lost the argument. Booth's work argues that history can be taught at all ages, provided the teaching is lively and appropriate.

Religious studies   When he investigated pupils' religious concepts across the school age-range, Goldman found a progressive set of stages of development. This started with pre-religious, magical, pre-operational thinking among younger primary pupils to advanced formal operational thinking among intelligent 16-year-olds. From these findings, he deduced a need for teachers to use visual methods with younger and less able pupils.

Note

1. Isohyets — lines connecting points with the same precipitation over a given time.

Questions for discussion

General

How can we get more pupils to the theoretical explainer stage in as many subjects as possible by the time they leave school?

English

1. How can English teachers get more pupils to make imaginative responses to literature?
2. Should the English teacher be a general teacher as well as a guide to good literature? (For instance, pointing out health-education issues that arise in the text?)

Science

1. What can be done to improve the failure of pupils to grasp the lower-level concepts necessary to cover secondary topics (e.g. air) as a necessary prerequisite for the understanding of respiration?
2. Would integrated teaching of the sciences during the first three years help overcome the failure to link biological, chemical and physical concepts revealed by Sutherland's study?
3. Is this also an argument for covering all three sciences for GCSE, while counting this as two, instead of three?

4. How can we get more pupils to the theoretical explainer stage by the time they leave school (and so provide students to fill the vacancies on science degree courses)?

Geography

1. How can pupils be helped to give genuinely geographical answers and to operate at an explainer level?
2. How could a teacher make use of concepts pupils learn out of school?

History

1. Do you agree with Booth that with appropriate teaching, history can be taught to all ages?
2. What is appropriate teaching?
3. To what extent is the history pupil an information processor?
4. Would it be productive to concentrate on making pupils aware of their own learning, as the metacognitive movement implies?

Religious Studies

1. What is the best method of teaching academically less able pupils?
2. How can this be done in the normal mixed-ability teaching situation?
3. What is the best way for religious-studies teachers to get discussion going?
4. Do you agree with Goldman that religious-studies teachers should take Piaget's stages into account when planning their teaching?

Further reading

Science

Driver, R. (1983) *The Pupil as Scientist?*, Open University Press, Milton Keynes.

History

Dickinson, A. K. and Lee, P. (eds.) (1978) *History Teaching and Historical Understanding*, Heinemann, London.
Dickinson, A. K. and Lee, P. (1984) *Learning History*, Heinemann, London.
Shemilt, D. (1980) *History 13–16: Evaluation Study*, Holmes McDougall, Edinburgh.

17
MORAL DEVELOPMENT

Piaget's original ideas

A dimension of Piaget's work that evolved into a field of its own is his early study of moral thinking (1932). What stages do children go through in their understanding of moral behaviour? Piaget's empirical work was based on a study of the rules of a game as played by primary-age children. The game he chose was marbles, part of childhood folklore passed down from generation to generation by word of mouth. He derived a stage theory to explain his findings, as he had done in the general field of cognitive development (outlined in Chapter 2). These corresponded in the two key stages.

A particular question Piaget also asked was: 'Johnny by accident trips and breaks three cups; Billy on purpose smashes one cup − who has done the greater wrong?' The children's responses were classified hierarchically into four stages using terms derived from the Greek word *nomos*, meaning law.

1. *Anomy* − the absence of morality. The child simply does what he wants to do. Basic instincts are gratified at will. Teachers may sometimes think some of the children they are given to teach are still at this phase, if the parent(s) have not socialized them at all. Punishment has to take the form of physically preventing the child from indulging in the undesirable activity.
2. *Heteronomy* − the imposition of rules by others. Children accept the rules applied imposed on them by adults. Lying is wrong because Daddy says so. Stealing is wrong because Mummy says so. Cheating is wrong because Teacher says so. Rules are absolute. Those for marbles have the quality of the Ten Commandments: it is not for children to question them in any way. This has been called the stage of moral realism: issues are understood by children in black-and-

white terms. This stage corresponds roughly with pre-operational thinking. Piaget alleged that egotism is an inherent part of this mode. In other words the child is not able to co-operate genuinely with others. In answer to the question about the cups, the heteronomous child says that Johnny has done the greater wrong since he has broken more cups than Billy. Neither circumstances nor intentions are taken into account. Hence the punishment derives from the 'crime' committed and should follow automatically.

3. *Socionomy* – the imposition of rules by society. At this stage a child starts to internalize the rules he has learnt from adults. He is no longer totally egotistical. He can accept that other people's perceptions may be different from his own. Hence discussion is possible. There is an awareness of other people, their needs and his responsibilities towards them. Punishment now takes the form of social disapproval. He is now sensitive to the censure of others. However, this is a major limitation to this stage since, if no one is present and there is no chance of being found out, the controls do not work. This corresponds to the general stage of concrete operations.

4. Autonomy – imposing rules oneself. As the term suggests, the adolescent is becoming independent in his judgements. He no longer accepts the values he has internalized from his parents and other significant adults. This stage corresponds to the general stage of formal operations. The adolescent starts to reason about moral problems at a more abstract level. He now realizes the relativity of rules. The rules of marbles are changeable and were constructed by the players themselves as human beings. So youngsters can argue about the rules but have to agree in the end on what the rules are, in order to play a game. Punishment should fit the crime and take account of circumstances. When they answer the question about the cups, adolescents now say that Billy was more in the wrong since he broke his cup on purpose. Johnny could not really be blamed since it was not his fault he tripped over a block someone else had put there and he couldn't see.

The interest of these findings for teachers and psychologists lies not in the particular context of marbles but in the general findings. It should be remembered that Piaget's study was carried out in a democratic society (French-speaking Switzerland) where relative thinking is more highly valued than absolute thinking. Perhaps in an authoritarian society the results would have been different.

Within Western societies the growth of relative (autonomous) thinking in older children (Piaget indicated 11–13 years) is seen as desirable. It creates problems, however, in a democratic society, in that every rule can be negotiated, whether this be among children playing marbles, between teacher and pupil or between parent and child. This may prove arduous for teachers, not to mention parents.

Kohlberg's development of Piaget's ideas

The initial seed of Piaget's theory was germinated into a colourful plant by Lawrence Kohlberg (1987). His six-substage theory of the development of moral thought has been described by some commentators as more Piagetian than Piaget. Both Piaget and Kohlberg derived the notion of pre- and post-conventional morality from Kant. Kohlberg's contribution was to test actual adolescents and young people to see whether stages do in fact exist in the population in general.

He carried out similar 1:1 interviews to Piaget, posing moral dilemmas to children, adolescents and adults. He asked young children if it is right to steal if you are hungry. He asked adolescents if one should kill in time of war. He asked adolescents and adults whether mercy killing should be allowed. One of his famous dilemmas involves a wife who is very ill and who requires medicine, yet the chemist's shop is shut for the night. Is it right for the husband to break into the shop?

Overall, he was testing young people for their answer to the question, 'What is justice?' On the basis of the responses to these dilemmas, Kohlberg drew up his well-known stage system, outlined in Table 17.1. This falls neatly into three stages (some prefer to call them levels), each of which divides into a pair of substages. As can be deduced from Table 17.1, Kohlberg's concept of moral development is strictly hierarchical and culminates in the final stage of abstract thought, equivalent to Piaget's formal operational thought. From a philosophical point of view, he is valuing justice as the highest virtue. This is achieved by attaining a state of moral autonomy. This is a goal admired by several of the philosophers (such as John Wilson) who have responded to these findings, as discussed below.

Kohlberg and subsequent workers throughout the world have collected a great deal of empirical evidence for the existence of these stages. This established that, in his system, the whole is greater than the parts. No substage can be skipped; youngsters have to work through them systematically. The substage a person reaches at about the age of 25 is that in which he will think in moral terms, most of the time, for the rest of his life. However, as with Piaget's stages, regression to a more primitive

Table 17.1   Kohlberg's stages of moral development

Level 1   The stage of preconventional thought

Stage (a)   Avoiding pain   Pre-moral thought where behaviour is simply the response to stimuli. Doing the 'right' thing is decided purely in terms of obedience to an absolute external authority (moral literalism). This is more or less the same as Piaget's first stage. There is no consideration of other people in their own right: only as authority figures. For example, a toddler stops shouting in order to avoid a smack

Stage (b)   Reciprocal hedonism   The person can do something for another, but only in exchange for a favour. You scratch my back and I'll scratch yours. The person is now aware of others (and their points of view) and can co-operate with them, but only on a basis of bargaining with them. The overall focus is on desirable possessions. If co-operating with others helps one obtain them, one does so. For example, an infant pupil lends his steam train to another boy in exchange for a tractor

Level 2   Conventional thought

Stage (c)   The good boy   Behaviour is aimed at conforming to the group. An action is 'good' if it meets with the acceptance of the peer group. A person's norms and values are those of his peer group. The stress is on group solidarity. The person is now aware of other people in his peer group and is concerned with their opinion of him. For example, an adolescent starts smoking because it is the 'done thing' in his peer group

Stage (d)   Law and order   Behaviour aims at conforming to the law, whether that be the law of the land or the rules of the school. This implies an identification with the structure of society that creates the order. The person is now aware of his own moral behaviour in society's terms and needs to justify it. For example, an older adolescent caught stealing admits he has offended against society's code

Level 3   Post-conventional thought

Stage (e)   Contract   Moral thinking centres around the negotiation between the individual and those in authority over him; for instance, between a pupil and his teacher. This involves the person realizing the relativity of moral codes. He rises above the particular code of the society and negotiates his own code with a significant other person. He accepts this contract as being binding on himself. For example, a sixth-former negotiates better recreation facilities in exchange for taking on the moral duties of being a prefect

Stage (f)   Altruism   Moral thinking is independent of the above influences and is determined by the individual alone, based on a universal code of principles that supersedes those of any particular society. The person does what he believes to be right, even if this costs him dear. In fact the person may decide to act against the conventions of his society and/or the pressures of his peer group. This may involve altruistic behaviour. For example, an intelligent adolescent rejects the moral codes of his parents and peers. He then works for a cause that does not benefit him in any way but that he believes to be just, such as for the starving children of Ethiopia substage is always possible. Kohlberg's methods have been tested in many different cultures and societies all over the world. Unlike so much university-generated psychology, he was not just describing the behaviour of upper-middle-class youth at élite colleges. On the contrary, teenagers in many non-Western cultures have been tested.

As would be expected, most young children were found to be at (a) or (b). So were many adolescents and adults who had not made moral progress, such as criminals. It has been a sobering thought for moral educators to discover that the vast majority of adults stick at (c) or (d). Only a minority have been found to reach any form of post-conventional thought: even (e), let alone (f). Kohlberg's stages apply most strongly to adolescent boys and young men up to the age of 25. Kohlberg claimed to be able to accelerate development during these years, but not afterwards. Even prisoners could be accelerated across the vital stage-(b)-to-stage-(d) gap. This means they are able to act in recognition of their obligations to society, and not just to themselves.

Kohlberg's ideas have been criticized from a feminist perspective by Carol Gilligan (1982), a fellow Harvard psychology professor of Kohlberg's. Gilligan denied that the intellectual ability to make independent decisions (linked strongly to Piaget's formal operational thought) is necessarily the pinnacle of moral thought. She also denies that moral thought that arises from the influence of a peer group is of the low substage (c) Kohlberg ascribes to it. If independent moral thought is the desirable pinnacle Kohlberg describes, this would mean a mother (or a father) might have to think morally in a way that was independent of that family's influence and needs.

A person may, for instance, be simultaneously a parent of a hostage in a foreign country threatening war and a minister of defence who may have to send troops into that country – an act that might lead to her child being executed. Which should she put first: the needs of her child or the demands of her political post? Another example is a mother who believes in working at home for Oxfam's campaign against hunger in Africa. However, her children want her to take them to the cinema instead. Does ignoring the 'needs' of her children mean she is working at Kohlberg's altruistic level?

Alternatively, Gilligan argues that moral thought linked to caring for people in a direct (rather than an abstract way) should be considered the peak of moral thought. In her highly influential book, *In a Different Voice* (*ibid.*), she puts her case than there are separate moral systems for the two genders. That described by Kohlberg applies only to males. He asked: 'What is the highest level of abstract moral thought a person is capable of?' She asks: 'To whom are we responsible and for what purpose?' Her female moral ethic is based fundamentally on caring for others and therefore on relationships. Gilligan's alternative levels of development are outlined in Table 17.2.

As Kohlberg posed his moral dilemmas, so Gilligan sets out hers. A major empirical study examined women's responses to a hypothetical situation in which they were pregnant and had to decide whether to have an abortion or to have the baby. This was perceived by the women not in abstract terms but in terms of the quality of relationship the woman had with the father. If this was good she was more likely to choose to have the baby.

The female dimension has been further explored by Gilligan, Ward and Taylor in their more recent book, *Mapping the Moral Domain* (1988). Like Kohlberg, she has focused particularly on adolescence. She calls for a reconsideration of adolescent development in our society. In particular, what is taught in schools needs to be reviewed. Her phraseology is almost Piagetian: 'Adolescence is a time of epistemological crisis.' She compares the position of the adolescent in the life cycle to that of the fool in a Renaissance play: 'exposing hypocrisy and revealing truths about human relationships'. So, along this line of reasoning, she argues for history and the humanities to be restored to an important role in the secondary-school curriculum. In a piece of empirical research, Gilligan *et al.* (1988) found that adolescents fare better in schools (and other institutions) when adults listen, rather than merely instruct. They see adolescent identity formation proceeding by a process of dialogue with others rather than by a process of mirroring or imitation.

As Schaffer (1989) has criticized Piaget for his failure to take the social dimension into account, so Gilligan has criticized Kohlberg. Gilligan

Table 17.2   Gilligan's levels of moral development

Level 1   To do what is expected of one by significant others such as one's mother or partner

Transition   To do the right thing by society's standards

Level 2   To sacrifice oneself in order to care for others

Transition   Moving from goodness to truth

Level 3   To behave in accord with one's answer to the question: 'which of the choices is the least evil?'

(1982) argues that women see themselves in terms of their relationships: to their children, husband, boss and work colleagues. For a woman today there are often clashes between them — for instance, between her role as a mother and as a worker. It has to be borne in mind when assessing her work, however, that Gilligan's work was done on an upper-middle-class professional sample and has not been shown empirically to be relevant to the whole range of society.

Kohlberg's system is in many ways a critique of the traditional teaching of moral education in secondary schools, which emphasizes conformity to majority values. Instead the emphasis should be on the individual deciding his own values and reaching substage (f). Schools should encourage values determined by the individual himself rather than values determined by society.

Wright (1971) argues that Kohlberg's work makes a strong case for the explicit teaching of moral issues in the secondary school. They should be made a focus in such subjects as history (is war ever defensible?) and science (should chemical effluent be poured into the North Sea?). In other words, moral education should be taught across the curriculum. Wright's view has been contested by Mary Warnock (1977). Warnock strongly emphasizes that morality is caught not taught. There are universal values that can be supported in a multicultural society: kindness, honesty, fairness, loyalty, understanding others and avoiding bullying. These apply particularly during the primary and lower secondary years.

Since morality is taught by example, teachers have to be a model for their pupils. In other words, moral education is fundamentally about the development of moral character in pupils, instilled by teachers with such moral character. Warnock is defending the British public-school ethos, as described a century earlier in *Tom Brown's Schooldays*. Secondary teachers cannot avoid this role by claiming they are solely subject specialists. It is in any case essential for them (and for primary teachers) to know their pupils as individuals if they are to be effective moral educators. Teacher educators need to lay the foundations for the teacher acting as a moral educator during pre-service courses — by being sound examples themselves.

On the other hand, the Oxford University moral educator, John Wilson (1973), believes moral education should be taught explicitly in school. Unlike Warnock he is concerned mainly with the secondary school. He proposes principles that should be taught, as outlined in Table 17.3.

There does not necessarily have to be a subject called 'Moral Education' on the timetable. Moral dilemmas can be taught through literature. *Hamlet* might be an Elizabethan example; *To Kill a Mockingbird* a modern one. In our environmentally conscious age, science should be a moral subject.

Table 17.3   Wilson's criteria for the morally developed person

1. Concern for other people
2. Ability to identify with the feelings of others
3. Knowledge to discern the rules necessary for decision-making
4. Ability to apply universal social concepts, such as fairness and justice, to the pupil's own society
5. Ability to construct rules for one's own behaviour
6. Ability to put all this into practice

Teaching chemistry should not be detached from the problem of the unwanted products of reactions: the greenhouse gases and industrial effluents. Human reproduction should be taught in the context of the population explosion.

R. S. Peters (1981) has been an enormous influence in the field of moral education throughout the English-speaking world. His critiques of Piaget and Kohlberg enabled us to see the limitations of their claims. He pointed also to their failure to consider the emotional element in moral development. At the same time, he put forward his own positive ideas. Young children should be trained in desirable moral behaviour without their necessarily being able to reason about it. Older pupils should be given reasons for punishments: 'One must enter the palace of reason through the courtyard of habit and tradition' (*ibid.* p. 53).

The ultimate aim of moral education and the greatest good is to be able to reason for oneself. Like Warnock and Wilson, Peters regards moral autonomy as the goal of the exercise. This requires personal insight and the acceptance of responsibility. Teachers should try to help as many pupils as possible to do this. By then the person should be able to argue the case rationally: 'What ought I to do?' This he would decide in terms of higher-order principles, such as impartiality, truth and liberty.

Peters analysed three levels of rules: the procedural, the relative and the fundamental. The procedural are specific to occasions and situations. The relative depend on circumstances. At the fundamental level, rules are justified under any conditions. At this level Peters argued that teachers should stress the rules. Less time should be spent on the procedural and the relative.

Alternative criticism of Kohlberg's work has focused on the over-intellectualism of his approach. It was not adolescents' real-life behaviour Kohlberg measured but their ability to give a cognitively high, intellectual-level answer to a hypothetical question asked in a laboratory.

Values education

Another route to moral education is to focus on values. Evidence about someone's values provides an indication of how that person is likely to behave, since behaviour results from the values held. If actual behaviour can be studied, this provides evidence that does not depend on inference, unlike most attitude and value studies. However, such studies are not easy to set up.

Sutherland (1988) studied sexual–moral values within a Roman Catholic context. Student teachers were asked about their values on issues such as birth control, abortion and other areas on which explicit Roman Catholic views have been articulated. These semi-structured interviews were conducted on clinical, Piagetian lines. The results revealed that retrospectively the girls regarded the crucial age for value formation to be at about 16 plus. Case studies revealed that these teenage girls appreciated the opportunity to discuss vital issues with other girls, with a teacher acting as a neutral chairperson. They then came to a peer-group consensus on important values to them at that age. One of the vital issues for which they need to establish firm values is whether sex before marriage is acceptable and, if so, whether this should be within a relationship or not. Another is whether to use contraceptives or to stick to 'natural' methods. A third is whether abortion should be allowed or not.

Some of the girls did not get the opportunity to work out their values in this way and were instead given by their teachers an authoritarian outline of values to be obeyed. They tended to delay the formation of their own values until they came to a largely residential college of education. By means of coffee-party discussions among their peers, they then worked out a similar set of liberal values in the same manner as the fifth- and sixth-form discussion groups.

With comprehensive schools generally being co-educational, there is a slight problem for secondary teachers in applying this finding. Girls really need the chance to discuss sexual values in a group of their own gender only. However, if value formation is seen as part of separate-gender sex education, the matter can be easily dealt with.

The power of the peer group over value formation in girls emerges strongly from this study. (It was not possible to draw any conclusions about the boys, as too few of them agreed to take part in this research.) Kohlberg would have classified the girls' moral thinking as substage (c). The girls did not look elsewhere for guidance. Authoritarian teachers were not acceptable to them. Only one young man worked out his own values by means of reflection in a Kohlbergian post-conventional substage (f) manner.

Values have also been studied empirically by Allport, Vernon and Lindzey (1960) and Rokeach (1973). Both studies developed tests to measure values. Allport, Vernon and Lindzey used the classification: religious, political, social, economic, theoretical and aesthetic. Items were derived to elicit these categories. This meant that, by the end of testing, the psychologist had a profile of the relative emphasis the young person put on these six categories. The modern-day 'yuppy' would be expected to be highest on the economic category; a priest to be highest in the religious category; and a university intellectual to be highest on the theoretical category. However, Allport, Vernon and Lindzey's categories have been criticized as being too narrowly male and intellectual to be of use outside higher education. They are therefore unsuitable for those teaching the whole range of youngsters in a comprehensive school. Neither caring values (which many teachers and psychologists uphold) nor doing something useful with one's hands are included.

Rokeach (like Allport, Vernon and Lindzey) studied values both theoretically and practically. He derived a rating scale to test for his categories. In terms of definition, he sees (1973) a value as 'having an enduring belief that a specific mode of conduct or end-state of existence is personally and socially preferable to alternative modes of conduct or end-states of existences'. He regards values as relative, but the importance of values lies in their being an imperative to action.

Like several other authors, he sees certain values as being *core* and others being *peripheral* to any one person's make-up. His own interest lies in political values. He has developed a bipolar system with freedom on the one hand and equality on the other. As shown in Figure 17.1, this leads to a fourway category system: low freedom and low equality equate with fascism; low freedom and high equality with communism; high freedom and high equality with social democracy; and high freedom and low equality with capitalism. Rokeach is an American. What he chooses as the two highs represents what he values as the best in American political values. An Afrikaner fascist might not be so happy to accept being categorized by Rokeach as the combination of the two lows.

In terms of moral education, however, Rokeach provides a helpful definition of values and a method of measuring the political dimension. Some educationists argue this should be an important aspect of the school curriculum, as it has been in the Soviet Union until recently.

Conclusions

Piaget provided the initial ideas on stage development nearly sixty years ago. These were taken up by Kohlberg who developed Piaget's stages.

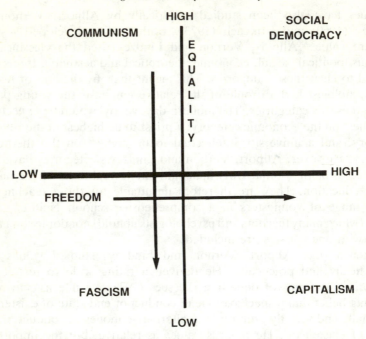

Figure 17.1 Rokeach's bipolar model of political values

Between Piaget and Kohlberg, this cognitive-developmental approach stimulated fruitful responses from many distinguished British philosophers of education. However, both perspectives have lost momentum. Since Kohlberg's death, the moral dimension no longer seems to interest cognitive developmentalists. Neither are philosophers of education coming up with anything original at present. This is a pity, at a time when AIDS has been added to drugs, smoking and inadequate parenting as moral problems for teachers and psychologists to help youngsters cope with. This is an area ripe for revival.

Summary

The understanding of rules and authority in absolute terms by pre-operational children was distinguished by Piaget from the realization of the relative nature of rules by formal operational adolescents. Kohlberg developed this into a six substage scale, which falls neatly into three levels: young children are preconventional, older children and the majority of the adult population are conventional, leaving only a small élite who achieve the post-conventional level. His ideas have been criticized from a number of standpoints, most notably from a feminist one by Gilligan. She regards caring for others as the highest virtue. A number of philosophers of education have started from these two cognitive developmentalists' stages and gone on to make distinguished contributions to moral education. Peters was critical yet, like Kohlberg, valued moral autonomy as the supreme virtue. Wilson has adopted a practical approach, claiming to be able to accelerate adolescents to autonomy by means of discussion.

An alternative approach to moral education is through the study of values. The pioneer work on values was done by Allport, Vernon and Lindzey and Rokeach. Both derived scales for measuring values, useful for determining the relative values pupils have after any programme of moral education. Sutherland found that discussion, with a teacher acting as a neutral chairperson, was appreciated by teenage girls in their own value formation.

Questions for discussion

1. How should children be socialized at school?
2. Is altruism, caring for others, moral autonomy or some other quality the highest virtue?
3. Should moral education be taught, caught or ignored?
4. If taught, what issues should the school focus on? Drugs? sex? AIDS? concern for others?
5. What is the role of the individual teacher in moral education?
6. What is the role in moral education of the school in general and the headteacher and senior management team in particular?
7. Is moral education possible in a multivalue society?
8. What (if any) values should be encouraged at school?

Further reading

Bull, N. (1969) *Moral Judgement from Childhood to Adolescence*, Routledge & Kegan Paul, London.

Carr, D. (1990) *Educating the Virtues: An Essay in the Philosophical Psychology of Moral Development and Education*, Routledge, London.

Straughan, R. (1982) *Can We Teach Children to be Good?*, Allen & Unwin, London.

Wright, D. (1971) *The Psychology of Moral Behaviour*, Penguin Books, Harmondsworth.

GLOSSARY

All terms are Piagetian, unless otherwise specified.

Accommodation A mechanism by which a child adjusts to the environment in some way.

Assimilation A mechanism by which a child alters the environment to fit in with his concepts, e.g. a brush 'becomes' a witch's broom.

Circular reaction An action repeated by a baby for the pleasure it gives.

Class A group of similar objects.

Class inclusion The ability to include the correct and exclude the incorrect members of a class, e.g. the class (or set) of cows includes the subset of white cows but excludes horses; the class (or set) of fruit includes both apples and oranges.

Concrete operational thought The ability to understand that processes are reversible, etc., provided the objects are visible.

Conservation This is reached when a child realizes the unalterability of a quality, despite apparent changes in appearance, e.g. a child achieves conservation of number when he realizes that four sweets are the same as four toys.

Decentre To be able to focus on one's whole visual range and not just part of it.

Disembedding (Donaldson) Abstracting an idea from its natural context so that it can be used more generally, e.g. the letter 'a'.

Equilibrium The process by which, as a result of alternating accommodation and assimilation, a child's thinking reaches a stable state for that stage.

Formal operational thought The ability to think in an abstract way.

Horizontal décalage (or **lag**) A child attains different aspects of the same stage at different ages.

Invariance A number is the same, whatever different form it is presented in, e.g. 4 is still 4, whether represented by 4 houses or 4 sweets.

1:1 correspondence Matching one set of objects with another on a 1:1 basis, e.g. pairing each child in a class with a toy.

Operational thought When a child realizes conservation of a number of qualities.

Relations The relationship of one concept to another.

Schema (plural **schemata**) A child's conception of an object, etc.

Scheme A set of schemata covering a particular area, e.g. the schemata of ice, water and heat necessary for the scheme of melting.

Sensorimotor activity That involving the five senses, but not language.

Seriation Arranging objects of different length in ascending order.

Transductive logic Falsely generalizing a connection on one occasion to all occasions, e.g. a man is dressed up as Father Christmas, so all men are Father Christmas.

Transitivity To be able to deduce logically that, for instance, if A > B and B > C, then A > C.

Vertical décalage (or **lag**) A child, responding cognitively to the same physical experience, does so at a 'lower' stage when younger and then at a 'higher' stage after maturation.

BIBLIOGRAPHY AND REFERENCES

Adey, P., Shayer, M. and Yates, C. (1989) Cognitive acceleration: the effects of two years of intervention in science classes, in P. Adey (ed.) *Adolescent Development and School Science*, Falmer Press, Lewes.

Allport, G. W., Vernon, P. E. and Lindzey, G. (1960) *Study of Values* (3rd edn), Houghton Mifflin, Boston, Mass.

Asch, S. E. (1956) Studies of independence and conformity. A minority of one against a unanimous majority, *Psychological Monographs*, Vol. 70, no. 9.

Ausubel, D. P. (1968) *Educational Psychology: A Cognitive View*, Holt, Rinehart & Winston, New York, NY.

Baldwin, J. M. (1925) *Mental Development in the Child and in the Race*, Macmillan, London.

Beard, R. M. (1957) An investigation of concept formation among infant school children (unpublished PhD dissertation), University of London.

Beard, R. (1969) *An Outline of Piaget's Developmental Psychology*, Routledge & Kegan Paul, London.

Beilin, H. (1987) Current trends in cognitive development research: towards a new synthesis, in Inhelder, de Caprona and Cornu-Wells (eds.) op. cit.

Bernstein, B. (1959) A public language; some sociological determinants of linguistic form, *British Journal of Sociology*, Vol. 10, pp. 311–26.

Boden, M. (1979) *Piaget*, Fontana, Glasgow.

Boden, M. (1989) *The Philosophy of Artificial Intelligence*, Oxford University Press.

Booth, M. (1980) A modern world history course and the thinking of adolescent pupils, *Educational Review*, Vol. 32, no. 3, pp. 245–57.

Bourdieu, P. (1980) *Le Sens Pratique*, Editions de Minuit, Paris.

Bovet, M. (1974) Cross-cultural study of conservation concepts: continuous quantities and length, in Inhelder, Sinclair and Bovet (eds.) op. cit.

Bower, T. G. R. (1977) *The Perceptual World of the Child*, Fontana, London.

Bowlby, J. (1953) *Child Care and the Growth of Love*, Penguin Books, Harmondsworth.

Boyle, D. G. (1969) *A Student's Guide to Piaget*, Pergamon Press, Oxford.

Brown, A., Campione, J. and Barclay, C. R. (1979) Training self-checking routines for estimating text-readiness: generalizations from list learning to prose recall, *Child Development*, Vol. 50, pp. 501–12.

Brown, A. L. and DeLoache, J. (1983) Metacognitive skills, in Donaldson, Grieve and Pratt (eds.) op. cit.

Brown, A. L. and Smiley, S. S. (1977) Rating the importance of structural units of prose passages: a problem of metacognitive development, *Child Development*, Vol. 48, pp. 1–8.

Brown, G. and Desforges, C. (1979) *Piaget's Theory: A Psychological Critique*, Routledge & Kegan Paul, London.

Brown, M. (1981) Number operations, in K. M. Hart (ed.) *Children's Understanding of Mathematics 11–16*, John Murray, London.

Brown, M. and Denvir, B. (1985) *Received Wisdom: Popular Beliefs about Children's Learning of Mathematics Considered in the Light of Recent Research*, Chelsea College, University of London.

Bruner, J. (1986) Child's talk: learning to use language, in J. Coupe and J. Porter (eds.) *The Education of Children with Severe Learning Difficulties*, Croom Helm, London.

Bryant, P. E. (1972) The understanding of invariance in very young children, *Canadian Journal of Psychology*, Vol. 26, pp. 78–96.

Bryant, P. E. (1974) *Perception and Understanding in Young Children*, Methuen, London.

Bryant, P. E. (1982) The role of conflict and agreement between intellectual strategies in children's ideas about measurement, *British Journal of Psychology*, Vol. 73, pp. 243–52.

Bryant, P. E. (1985) The distinction between knowing when to do a sum and knowing how to do it, *Educational Psychology*, Vol. 5, nos. 3 & 4, pp. 207–15.

Bryant, P. E. and Bradley, L. (1985) *Children's Reading Problems: Psychology and Education*, Blackwell, Oxford.

Bryant, P. E. and Goswani, U. (1990) Comparisons between backward and normal readers: a risky business, *Education Section Review of the British Psychological Society*, Vol. 14, no. 2, pp. 3–9.

Bryant, P. E. and Trabasso, T. (1971) Transitive inferences and memory in young children, *Nature*, Vol. 260, p. 773.

Burden, R. (1990) Feuerstein's instrumental enrichment programme: important issues in research and evaluation (unpublished paper).

Butterworth, G. (1981) *Infancy and Epistemology: An Evaluation of Piaget's Theory*, Harvester, Brighton.

Campbell, R. and Olsen, D. (1990) The study of language, in R. Grieve and M. Hughes (eds.) *Understanding Children*, Blackwell, Oxford.

Campione, J., Brown, A. L., Ferrara, R. A. and Campione, J. C. (1982) Mental retardation and intelligence, in R. J. Sternberg (ed.) *Handbook of Human Intelligence*, Cambridge University Press.

Carey, S. (1985) *Conceptual Change in Childhood*, MIT Press, Cambridge, Mass.

Carey, S. (1988) Are children fundamentally different kinds of thinkers and learners than adults?, in K. Richardson and S. Sheldon (eds.) *Cognitive Development to Adolescence*, Open University Press, Milton Keynes.

Carpenter, T. P. and Moser, J. M. (1982) The development of addition and subtraction problem-solving skills, in T. P. Carpenter, J. M. Moser and T. A. Romberg (eds.) *Addition and Subtraction: A Cognitive Perspective*, Lawrence

Erlbaum Associates, Hillsdale, NJ.

Carraher, T., Carraher, D. and Schliemann, A. (1985) Mathematics in the streets and in the schools, *British Journal of Developmental Psychology*, Vol. 3, pp. 22–9.

Case, R. (1985) *Intellectual Development*, Methuen, London.

Chi, M. T. H. (1978) Knowledge structures and memory development, in Siegler (ed.) op. cit.

Chomsky, N. (1959) Review of *Verbal Behaviour* by B. F. Skinner, *Language*, Vol. 35, pp. 26–58.

Cohen, D. (1983) *Piaget: Critique and Reassessment*, Croom Helm, Beckenham.

Cowan, R. (1979a) A reappraisal of the relation between performances of quantitative identity and quantitative equivalence conservation tasks, *Journal of Experimental Child Psychology*, Vol. 28, pp. 68–80.

Cowan, R. (1979b) Performance in number conservation tasks as a function of the number of items, *British Journal of Psychology*, Vol. 70, pp. 77–82.

Cowan, R. (1982) Children's perception of length, *Educational Psychology*, Vol. 2, pp. 73–7.

Cowan, R. and Daniels, H. (1989) Children's use of counting and guidelines in judging relative number, *British Journal of Educational Psychology*, Vol. 59, pp. 200–10.

Da Silva, W. A. (1972) The formation of historical concepts through contextual cues, *Educational Review*, Vol. 24, no. 3, pp. 174–82.

Davis, R. B. (1984) *Learning Mathematics: The Cognitive Science Approach to Maths Education*, Croom Helm, London.

Denvir, B. (1985) *GRAN. Group Assessment of Number*, Centre for Science and Maths Education, King's College, London.

DES, Assessment of Performance Unit (1978–82) *Mathematical Development, Primary Survey Reports, Nos. 1–5*, HMSO, London.

Dickinson, A. K. and Lee, P. (eds.) (1978) *History Teaching and Historical Understanding*, Heinemann, London.

Doise, W., Dionnet, S. and Mugny, G. (1978) Conflit sociocognitif, marquage social et developpement cognitif, *Cahiers de Psychologie*, Vol. 21, pp. 231–43.

Doise, W. and Palmonari, A. (eds.) (1984) *Social Interaction in Individual Development*, Cambridge University Press.

Doise, W. and Palmonari, A. (1984) The sociopsychological study of individual development, in W. Doise and A. Palmonari (eds.) *Social Interaction in Individual Development*, Cambridge University Press.

Donaldson, M. (1978) *Children's Minds*, Fontana, Glasgow.

Donaldson, M. (1986) *Children's Explanations*, Cambridge University Press.

Donaldson, M., Grieve, R. and Pratt, C. (1983) (eds.) *Early Childhood Development and Education*, Blackwell, Oxford.

Donaldson, M. and Lloyd, P. (1974) Sentences and situations: children's judgments of match and mismatch, in F. Bresson (ed.) *Problèmes Actuels en Psycholinguistique*, Centre National de la Recherche Scientifique, Paris.

Donaldson, M. and McGarrigle, J. (1975) Some clues to the nature of semantic development, *Journal of Child Language*, Vol. 1, pp. 185–94.

Donaldson, M. and Wales, R. (1970) On the acquisition of some relational terms, in Hayes J. R. (ed.) *Cognition and the Development of Language*, Wiley, New York, NY.

Driver, R. (1983) *Pupil as Scientist?*, Open University Press, Milton Keynes.

Ellis, J. I. (1975) Adolescent understanding of stability and change in literature (unpublished PhD thesis), University of Birmingham.

Entwistle, N. E. (ed.) (1985) *New Directions in Educational Psychology: 1 — Learning and Teaching*, Falmer Press, Lewes.

Feldman, D. H. (1986) How development works, in Levin (ed.) op. cit.

Feuerstein, R. (1979) *Dynamic Assessment of Retarded Performers*, University Park Press, Baltimore, Md.

Feuerstein, R. (1980) *Instrumental Enrichment: Intervention Program for Cognitive Modifiability*, University Park Press, Baltimore, Md.

Fischer, K. W. and Canfield, R. L. (1986) The ambiguity of stage structure in behavior; person and environment in the development of psychological structures, in Levin (ed.) op. cit.

Fischer, K. W. and Knight, C. C. (in press) Cognitive development in real children: levels and variations, in B. Presseisen (ed.) *The At-Risk Student and Thinking: Perspectives from Research*, National Educational Association, Washington.

Flavell, J. H. (1963) *The Developmental Psychology of Jean Piaget*, Van Nostrand Reinhold, New York, NY.

Fodor, J. (1983) *The Modularity of the Mind*, MIT Press, Cambridge, Mass.

Frazier, N. and Sadker, M. (1973) *Sexism in School and Society*, Harper & Row, New York, NY.

Frydman, O. and Bryant, P. E. (1988) Sharing and the understanding of number equivalence by young children, *Cognitive Development*, Vol. 3, pp. 323–39.

Furth, H. G. (1966) *Thinking without Language: Psychological Implications of Deafness*, Free Press, New York, NY.

Gal'perin, P. Ya. and Georgiev, L. S. (1969) The formation of elementary mathematical notions, in J. Kilpatrick and I. Wirszup (eds.) *Soviet Studies in the Psychology of Learning and Teaching of Mathematics*, University of Chicago Press, Chicago, Ill., Vol. 1.

Gardner, H. (1983) *Frames of Mind*, Basic Books, New York, NY.

Gelman, R. and Gallistel, C. R. (1983) The child's understanding of number, in Donaldson, Grieve and Pratt (eds.) op. cit.

Gilligan, C. (1982) *In a Different Voice: Psychological Theory and Women's Development*, Harvard University Press, Cambridge, Mass.

Gilligan, C., Ward, J. V. and Taylor, J. M. (1988) *Mapping the Moral Domain: A Contribution of Women's Thinking to Psychological Theory and Education*, Harvard University Press, Cambridge, Mass.

Ginsburg, H. P. (1977) *Children's Arithmetic: The Learning Process*, Van Nostrand Reinhold, New York, NY.

Ginsburg, H. and Opper, S. (1969) *Piaget's Theory of Intellectual Development*, Prentice-Hall, Englewood Cliffs, NJ.

Gold, R. (1987) *The Description of Cognitive Development: Three Piagetian Themes*, Clarendon Press, Oxford.

Goldman, R. (1965) *Readiness for Religion: A Basis for Developmental Religious Education*, Routledge & Kegan Paul, London.

Goodman, K. S. and Goodman, Y. M. (1979) Learning to read is natural, in L. B. Resnick and P. A. Weaver (eds.) *Theory and Practice of Early Reading*, *Vol. 1*, Lawrence Erlbaum Associates, Hillsdale, NJ.

Grieve, R., Hoogenraad, R. and Murray, D. (1977) On the young child's use of lexis and syntax in understanding locative instructions, *Cognition*, Vol. 5, pp. 235–50.

Grieve, R. and Hughes, M. (eds.) (1990) *Understanding Children: Essays in Honour of Margaret Donaldson*, Blackwell, Oxford.

Halford, G. S. (1978) An approach to the definition of cognitive developmental stages in school maths, *British Journal of Educational Psychology*, Vol. 48, pp. 298–314.

Hallam, R. N. (1967) Logical thinking in history, *Educational Review*, Vol. 19, no. 3, pp. 183–202.

Hamlyn, D. W. (1978) *Experience and the Growth of Understanding*, Routledge & Kegan Paul, London.

Haroutounian, S. (1983) *Equilibrium in the Balance*, Springer-Verlag, New York, NY.

Hartley, L. P. (1958) *The Go-Between*, Penguin Books, London.

Hickman, M. E. (1985) The implications of discourse skills in Vygotsky's development theory, in J. V. Wertsch (ed.) *Vygotsky and the Social Formation of Mind*, Harvard University Press, Cambridge, Mass.

Hughes, M. (1978) Selecting pictures of another person's view, *British Journal of Educational Psychology*, Vol. 48, pp. 210–19.

Hughes, M. (1981) Can pre-school children add and subtract?, *Educational Psychology*, Vol. 1, pp. 207–19.

Inhelder, B., de Caprona, D. and Cornu-Wells, A. (eds.) (1987) *Piaget Today*, Lawrence Erlbaum Associates, Hove.

Inhelder, B. and Piaget, J. (1958) *The Growth of Logical Thinking from Childhood to Adolescence*, Routledge & Kegan Paul, London.

Inhelder, B. and Piaget, J. (1966) *The Psychology of the Child*, Routledge & Kegan Paul, London.

Inhelder, B., Sinclair, H. and Bovet, M. (1974) *Learning and the Development of Cognition*, Routledge & Kegan Paul, London.

Johnson-Laird, P. N. (1983) *Mental Models: Towards a Cognitive Science of Language, Inference, and Consciousness*, Cambridge University Press.

Karmiloff-Smith, A. (1986) Stage/structure versus phase/process in modeling linguistic and cognitive development, in Levin (ed.) op. cit.

Kay, W. M. (1981) Religious thinking, attitudes and personality amongst secondary pupils in England and Ireland (unpublished PhD dissertation), University of Reading.

Keil, F. K. (1986) On the structure dependent nature of stages of cognitive development, in Levin (ed.) op. cit.

Kelly, G. A. (1963) *A Theory of Personality: The Psychology of Personal Constructs*, Norton, New York, NY.

Kendler, H. H. and Kendler, T. S. (1962) Vertical and horizontal processes in problem solving, *Psychological Review*, Vol. 69, pp. 1–16.

Kingman, J. (Chairman) (1986) *Report of the Committee of Inquiry into the Teaching of English Language*, HMSO, London.

Kirkman, S. (1986) It helps you to think better, *The Times Educational Supplement*, p. 18.

Kohlberg, L. (1987) *Child Psychology and Childhood Education: A Cognitive-Developmental View*, Longman, New York, NY.

Lerner, R. M., Hultsch, D. F. and Dixon, R. A. (1983) Contextualism and the character of developmental psychology in the 1970s, *Annals of the New York Academy of Science History and Philosophy of Science: Selected Papers*, Vol. 412, pp. 102–28.

Levin, I. (ed.) (1986) *Stage and Structure, Reopening the Debate*, Ablex, Norwood, NJ.

Levin, I. and Simons, H. (1986) The nature of children's and adults' conception of time, speed and distance, and their sequence in development: analysis via circular motion, in Levin (ed.) op. cit.

Lovell, K. (1964) *The Growth of Basic Mathematical and Scientific Concepts in Children*, University of London Press.

Lunzer, E. A. (1960) Some points of Piagetian theory in the light of experimental criticism, *Journal of Child Psychology and Psychiatry*, Vol. 1, pp. 191–202.

Luria, A. R. and Yudovich, F. A. (1971) *Speech and the Development of Mental Processes in the Child*, Penguin Books, Harmondsworth.

Mackworth, E. M. and Bruner, J. S. (1970) How adults and children search and recognize pictures, *Human Development*, Vol. 13, pp. 149–77.

Macnab, D., Page, J. and Kennedy, M. (1989) *Report of the Assessment of Achievement Programme, Second Round Mathematics Survey (1988)*, Northern College, Aberdeen.

Mason, J. S. (1974) Adolescent judgement as evidenced in response to poetry, *Educational Review*, Vol. 26, no. 2, pp. 124–39.

McGarrigle, J. and Donaldson, M. (1974) Conservation accidents, *Cognition*, Vol. 3, pp. 341–50.

McGarrigle, J., Grieve, R. and Hughes, M. (1978) Interpreting inclusion: a contribution to the study of the child's cognitive and linguistic development, *Journal of Experimental Child Psychology*, Vol. 26, pp. 528–50.

McNally, D. W. (1970) The incidence of Piaget's stages of thinking as assessed by tests of verbal reasoning in several Sydney schools, *Forum of Education*, Vol. 29, pp. 124–34.

Michell, L. and Lambourne, R. (1979) An association between high intellectual ability and an imaginative and analytic approach to the discussion of open questions, *British Journal of Educational Psychology*, Vol. 49, pp. 60–72.

Michell, L. and Peel, E. A. (1977) A cognitive dimension in the analysis of classroom discourse, *Educational Review*, Vol. 29, no. 4, pp. 255–66.

Mounod, P. and Vintner, A. (1985) A theoretical model: self-image in children, in V. Shulman, L. Restaino-Baumann and L. Butler (eds.) *The Future of Piagetian Theory: The Neo-Piagetians*, Plenum Press, New York, NY.

Mugny, G., De Paolis, P. and Carugati, F. (1984) Social regulations in cognitive development, in Doise and Palmonari (eds.) op. cit.

Murphy, R. J. L. (1977) Does children's understanding of parables develop in stages?, *Learning for Living*, Vol. 16, pp. 168–72.

Oakhill, J. V. (1984) Why children have difficulty reasoning with three-term series problems, *British Journal of Developmental Psychology*, Vol. 2, pp. 223–30.

Oakhill, J. (1988) The development of children's reasoning ability: Information processing approaches, in K. Richardson and S. Sheldon (eds.) *Cognitive Development to Adolescence*, LEA/OU.

Papandropolou, I. and Sinclair, H. (1974) What is a word?, *Human Development*,

Vol. 17, pp. 241–58.

Papert, S. (1980) *Mindstorms: Children, Computers and Powerful Ideas*, Harvester, Brighton.

Pascual-Leone, J. (1976) Metasubjective problems of constructive cognition: forms of knowing and their psychological mechanisms, *Canadian Psychological Review*, Vol. 17, pp. 110–25.

Pears, R. and Bryant, P. (1990) Transitive inferences by young children about spatial position, *British Journal of Psychology*, Vol. 81, pp. 497–510.

Peatling, J. H. (1977) On beyond Goldman: religious thinking and the 1970s, *Learning for Living*, Vol. 16, pp. 99–108.

Peel, E. A. (1971) *The Nature of Adolescent Judgement*, Staples, London.

Peters, R. S. (1981) *Moral Development and Moral Education*, Allen & Unwin, London.

Phillips, J. L. (1981) *Piaget's Theory: A Primer*, W. H. Freeman, San Francisco, Calif.

Piaget, J. (1926) *The Language and Thought of the Child*, Harcourt Brace Jovanovich, New York, NY.

Piaget, J. (1930) *The Child's Conception of Physical Causality*, Routledge & Kegan Paul, London.

Piaget, J. (1932) *The Moral Judgement of the Child*, Routledge & Kegan Paul, London.

Piaget, J. (1951) Autobiography, in E. G. Boring (ed.) *History of Psychology in Autobiography*, *Vol. 4*, Russell & Russell, New York, NY.

Piaget, J. (1952) *The Child's Concept of Number*, Routledge & Kegan Paul, London.

Piaget, J. (1953) *The Origins of Intelligence in Children*, Routledge & Kegan Paul, London.

Piaget, J. (1954) *The Child's Construction of Reality*, Basic Books, New York.

Piaget, J. (1955) *The Construction of Reality in the Child*, Routledge & Kegan Paul, London.

Piaget, J. and Inhelder, B. (1956) *The Child's Conception of Space*, Routledge & Kegan Paul, London.

Piaget, J. (1970) *Science of Education and the Psychology of the Child*, Viking Press, New York, NY.

Plunkett, S. (1979) Decomposition and all that rot, *Mathematics in School*, Vol. 8, no. 3, pp. 2–5.

Resnick, L. (1977) A developmental theory of number understanding, in H. P. Ginsburg (ed.) *Children's Arithmetic: How They Learn it and How You Teach it*, PRO-ED, Austin, Tex.

Rhys, W. T. (1972) Geography and the adolescent, *Educational Review*, Vol. 24, no. 3, pp. 183–97.

Richmond, R. C. (1972) Religious judgement between the ages of 13 and 16, *Educational Review*, Vol. 24, no. 3, pp. 225–37.

Rokeach, M. (1973) *The Nature of Human Values*, Free Press, New York, NY.

Schaffer, R. (1971) *The Growth of Sociability*, Penguin Books, Harmondsworth.

Schaffer, H. R. (1989) Joint involvement episodes as context for cognitive development, in McGurk, H. (ed.) *Contemporary Issues in Childhood Social Development*, Routledge, London.

Scottish Council for Research in Education (1983) *Assessment of Achievement*

Programme of Scottish School Children in Mathematics, Performance of Pupils at Primary Four and Seven, SED, Edinburgh.

Shayer, M. and Adey, P. (1981) *Towards a Science of Science Teaching*, Heinemann, London.

Shayer, M. and Beasley, F. (1987) Does instrumental enrichment work?, *British Journal of Educational Research*, Vol. 13, no. 2, pp. 101–20.

Shayer, M., Kuchemann, D. E. and Wylan, H. (1976) The distribution of Piagetian stages of thinking in British middle and secondary school children, *British Journal of Educational Psychology*, Vol. 46, pp. 164–73.

Shayer, M. and Wylan, H. (1978) The distribution of Piagetian stages of thinking in British middle and secondary children 11–14 to 16 year olds and sex differentials, *British Journal of Educational Psychology*, Vol. 48, pp. 62–70.

Siegler, R. S. (1978) The origins of scientific reasoning, in R. S. Siegler (ed.) *Children's Thinking: What develops?*, Lawrence Erlbaum Associates, Hillsdale, NJ.

Skemp, R. (1976) Relational understanding and instrumental understanding, *Mathematics Teaching*, Vol. 77, pp. 20–6.

Skinner, B. F. (1957) *Verbal Behavior*, Appleton Century Crofts, New York, NY.

Skinner, B. F. (1969) *Contingencies of Reinforcement. A Theoretical Analysis*, Appleton Century Crofts, New York, NY.

Skinner, B. F. (1976) *Walden II*, Macmillan, London.

Slee, N. (1990) Getting away from Goldman: changing perspectives on the development of religious thinking, *The Modern Churchman*, Vol. 32, no. 1, pp. 1–9.

Smedslund, J. (1961) The acquisition of conservation of substance and weight in children, IV: an attempt at extinction of the visual components of the weight concept, *Scandinavian Journal of Psychology*, Vol. 2, pp. 153–5.

Smedslund, J. (1966a) Les origines sociales de la decentration, in *Psychologie et Epistemologie Genetique, Thèmes Piagetiens*, Dunod, Paris.

Smedslund, J. (1966b) Performance on measurement and pseudo-measurement tasks by 5–7 year old children, *Scandinavian Journal of Psychology*, Vol. 7, pp. 81–92.

Smedslund, J. (1977) Piaget's psychology in practice, *British Journal of Educational Psychology*, Vol. 47, pp. 1–6.

Smedslund, J. (1980) Analyzing the primary code: from empiricism to apriorism, in D. Olsen (ed.) *The social Foundations of Language and Thought*, Norton, New York, NY.

Smith, F. (1978) *Reading*, Plenum Press, New York, NY.

Smith, L. (1982) Class inclusion and conclusions about Piaget's theory, *British Journal of Psychology*, Vol. 73, pp. 267–76.

Smith, L. (1986) General transferable ability: an interpretation of formal operational thinking, *British Journal of Psychology*, Vol. 4, pp. 377–87.

Sternberg, R. J. (1977) *Intelligence, Information Processing and Analogical Reasoning*, Lawrence Erlbaum Associates, Hove.

Sternberg, R. J. (ed.) (1984) *Mechanisms of Cognitive Development*, W. H. Freeman, New York, NY.

Sternberg, R. J. (1986) Cognition and instruction: why the marriage sometimes ends in divorce, in R. F. Dillon and R. J. Sternberg (eds.) *Cognition and Instruction*, Academic Press, London.

Sugarman, S. (1987) *Piaget's Construction of the Child's Reality*, Cambridge University Press.

Sutherland, P. A. A. (1980) An investigation into the attainment of physical and biological science concepts across the school age range and an outline of the stages of thinking involved therein (unpublished PhD thesis), University of Birmingham.

Sutherland, P. A. A. (1982) An expansion of Peel's describer-explainer stage theory, *Educational Review*, Vol. 34, pp. 69–76.

Sutherland, P. A. A. (1983) Indications of a possible acceleration in intellectual development at early latency and mid-adolescence, *Educational Studies*, Vol. 9, pp. 115–21.

Sutherland, P. A. A. (1988) A longitudinal study of religious-moral values in late adolescence, *British Educational Research Journal*, Vol. 14, no. 1, pp. 73–87.

Sutherland, P. A. A. (1989) Some case studies on learning difficulties in maths in the primary school, *Research in Education*, Vol. 42, pp. 1–16.

Tamminen, K. (1976) Research concerning the development of religious thinking in Finnish students, *Character Potential*, Vol. 7, pp. 206–19.

Thorpe, K. (1991) Metacognition and attribution for learning outcome among children in primary school, *Educational Review*, Vol. 15, no. 1, pp. 6–8.

Trevarthen, C. (1982) The primary motives for cooperative understanding, in G. Butterworth and P. Light (eds.) *Social Cognition*, University of Chicago Press, Chicago, Ill.

Uzgiris, I. C. and Hunt, J. McV. (1970) Attentional preference and experience: II – an exploratory longitudinal study of the effects of visual familiarity and responsiveness, *Journal of Genetic Psychology*, Vol. 117, pp. 109–21.

Van Lehn, K. (1983) On the representation of procedures in repair theory, in H. P. Ginsburg (ed.) *The Development of Mathematical Thinking*, Academic Press, London.

Vuyk, R. (1981) *Overview and Critique of Piaget's Genetic Epistemology 1965–1980, Volumes 1 and 2*, Academic Press, London.

Vygotsky, L. (1983) School instruction and mental development, in Donaldson, Grieve and Pratt (eds.) op. cit.

Vygotsky, L. (1986) *Thought and Language* (translated and edited by A. Kozulin), MIT Press, Cambridge, Mass.

Warnock, M. (1977) *Schools of Thought*, Faber & Faber, London.

Warnock Report (1978) *Special Educational Needs: Report of the Committee of Inquiry into the Education of Handicapped Children and Young People*, HMSO, London.

Wason, P. C. and Johnson-Laird, P. N. (1972) *Psychology of Reasoning: Structure and Content*, Harvard University Press, Cambridge, Mass.

Webster, A. and Wood, D. (1989) *Children with Hearing Difficulties*, Cassell, London.

Wells, G. (1987) *The Meaning Makers: Children Learning Language and Using Language to Learn*, Hodder & Stoughton, Sevenoaks.

White, R. (1988) *Learning Science*, Blackwell, Oxford.

Whorf, B. (1956) *Language, Thought and Reality*, Technology Press, Cambridge.

Wilson, J. (1973) *A Teacher's Guide to Moral Education*, Geoffrey Chapman, London.

Wittgenstein, L. (1961) *Tractatus Logico-Philosophicus*, Routledge & Kegan Paul, London.

Wright, D. (1971) *The Psychology of Moral Behaviour*, Penguin Books, Harmondsworth.

SUBJECT INDEX

NAME INDEX

Page numbers in italics refers to bibliographic details

Rhys, W. T. 164, 171, *194*
Richmond, R. C. 171, *194*
Richardson, K. and Sheldon, S. (eds) *100*, *124*
Rokeach, M. 183, 184, 185, *194*

Schaffer, R. 36, 48, 50, 77, 179, *195*
Sharron, H. 129
Shayer, M. 4, 76, 110, 112, 113, 116, 117, 118, 126−7, *195*
Shemilt, D. 173
Shuard, H. 83
Siegler, R. S. 88, *195*
Sigel, I. E. and Cocking, R. R. 143
Skemp, R. 45, *195*
Skinner, B. F. 35, 37, 52−6, *57*, 90, 98, *195*
Slee, N. 170, *195*
Smedslund, J. 4, 6, 102−4, 112, 113, 116, *195*
Smith, F. 39, *41*, *195*
Smith, L. 23, 101, 116, 117, *195*, *196*
Sternberg, R. J. 86−7, 92, *196*
Straughan, R. *185*
Sugarman, S. *196*
Sutherland, P. 4, 28, 76, 81, 107, 109,
112, 113, 116, 121, 133, 136, 138, 140−2, 152−6, 160, 162−4, 172, 182, 185, *196*

Tamminen, K. 170, *196*
Thorpe, K. 97−8, *196*
Trevarthen, C. 49, *196*

Uzgiris, I. C. and Hunt, J. McV. 9, *196*

Van Lehn 148−9, *196*
Vargas, J. *57*
Vuyk, R. *196*

Warnock, M., 180, *196*
Wason, P. C. and Johnson-Laird, P. 116, *196*
Webster, A. Wood, D. 34, *197*
Wells, G. 38, *197*
White, R. 80, *197*
Whorff, B. 30, 31, *197*
Wheldall, K. 56, *57*
Wilson, J. 176, 180, 185, *197*
Wittgenstein, L. 31, *197*
Wright, D. 180, *185*, *197*